ROCKEFELLER POWER

by Myer Kutz

PINNACLE BOOKS · NEW YORK CITY

The author gratefully acknowledges permission to reprint material from the following:

Harold B. Burton and the *New York Times* for Letter to the Editor, August 9, 1967, copyright © 1967 by The New York Times Company.

Foreign Affairs for the article "What Private Enterprise Means to Latin America" by David Rockefeller from *Foreign Affairs*, April 1966. Copyright © 1966 by Council on Foreign Relations, Inc.

Raymond B. Fosdick, *John D. Rockefeller, Jr. A Portrait*, 1956, Harper & Row, Publishers.

Lithgow Osborne and the *New York Times* for Letter to the Editor, September 10, 1967, copyright © 1967 by The New York Times Company.

Vital Speeches for "The U.S. Business Image in Latin America" by David Rockefeller from *Vital Speeches*, Vol. XXXI, No. 1, October 15, 1964.

Bertram D. Wolfe, *The Fabulous Life of Diego Rivera*, 1963, Stein and Day, Publishers.

ROCKEFELLER POWER

A Pinnacle Books edition, published by special arrangement with Simon and Schuster, New York.

ISBN: 0-523-00665-9

First printing, March 1975

Printed in the United States of America

PINNACLE BOOKS, INC.
275 Madison Avenue
New York, N.Y. 10016

I would like to thank Bob Boyle, Rod Vandivert, Nancy Mathews, Bill Werner and the Scenic Hudson Preservation Conference for their kind assistance in research on the Rockefellers and conservation. I would also like to thank my friend Dick Balser, and Peter Carey, Joseph Goldberg, Rick Nagen and Wardell B. Pomeroy for their kind assistance. I would also like to thank the Foundation Center for the use of its research facilities.

I am especially grateful to five people for their encouragement, patience and invaluable advice: Theron Raines, my agent; Dan Green, my editor; my friends Bill and Em Smith; and my wife, Cynthia.

WELCOME TO THE WHITE HOUSE . . .

Most of us are brought up to believe in the homely and virtuous idea that our leaders are above the temptations of material wealth, and that our nation's highest offices are beyond the reach of men who would use them for personal gain.

Watergate shattered that fairy tale.

But Watergate had one positive effect. The press—and the public now want to know more about the men and women who seek public office, what they've done, what they believe, *and* what they own and who their friends are.

But do the President and Congress really want to know?

This book should have been read by President Gerald Ford, who nominated Nelson Rockefeller for Vice President, and by every Senator and Representative who voted to confirm him. It shows how the Rockefeller family use the vast, indeed excessive, power concentrated in their hands—not always to serve the public interest, as they so often claim, but too often to promote their own interests.

Wealth alone did not make Rockefeller power. Philanthropy on a grand scale was a major factor. But for all its good works, Rockefeller philanthropy has a dark side. This book shows that dark side in a cold light.

To Cynthia, Bill and Em

Contents

I have always felt, as my father did, that one of the greatest satisfactions in life comes from doing worthwhile things. While favorable comment is gratifying, our family has so often through the years been subjected to unfavorable comment that if we had allowed ourselves to be swayed one way or the other by other people's characterizations of our acts, favorable or unfavorable, we would have found it difficult to adhere to the line of action which the voice from within impelled us to follow.

—JOHN D. ROCKEFELLER, JR.,
writing to the dean of the
Harvard Business School in 1951

Foreword

The Rockefeller\family wields enormous power. It controls one of the largest private fortunes in the United States and the nation's third largest bank, the Chase Manhattan. It has penetrated deep into many important public and private areas of American life, including relations with the Middle East, Latin America, particularly oil-rich Venezuela, the Soviet Union and China; into monumental publicly and privately financed construction projects, not only in New York, but also, with new-cities construction, across the country; and into development of our natural resources, from the Hudson River Valley to San Francisco Bay.

If a Rockefeller were to become President of the United States, he would, with the administrative power of the Federal government under his command, be in a position to expand Rockefeller power to even greater proportions than it now enjoys. No American family with comparable clout has seen one of its members achieve the Presidency, so we have no experience with such a situation. But we should realize that it is inherently dangerous.

(Our wealthiest President, at least in this century, was

1

John F. Kennedy. But the Kennedys' financial clout has never matched the Rockefellers'. The Kennedys, of course, have never controlled a bank the size of Chase Manhattan.)

Although Nelson Rockefeller had been elected Governor of New York four times and had been a candidate for the Republican Presidential nomination several times, his wealth and his family's vast financial interests had never been political issues. He had never even made public the size of his personal fortune. But when he was nominated by President Ford to be Vice President, Rockefeller power and wealth did become political issues.

There are several interrelated reasons for this. The nomination came at the height of Watergate, less than two weeks, in fact, after Richard Nixon, his Presidency in ruins because of the scandals, had resigned, and Ford had been sworn in as President. Integrity of high government officials had been a leading political issue for months. Many people now felt that the potential for conflict of interest in a Rockefeller Vice Presidency—and possible Presidency—had to be thoroughly explored. The issue was underlined by the source of the Rockefeller fortune: it had once been entirely in oil stocks, reliably estimated to have been worth about a billion dollars shortly before World War I. Although the stockholdings of the Rockefeller family's members were not known publicly at the time of the nomination, it could safely be assumed that the members still held, outright or in trust, large blocks of shares in major oil companies. In view of the energy crunch, which in large part is an oil crunch, a Rockefeller Vice Presidency—and possible Presidency—would inevitably raise conflict-of-interest problems.

The question was this: Should a member of a family controlling vast financial interests be confirmed for high public office? The Senate Rules Committee and the House Judiciary Committee would hold hearings on Rockefeller's nomination. Based on the hearings, the committees would then vote on whether to submit the nomination to the full senate and house, which would then debate the nomination and vote on it. The confirmation proceedings would provide a forum for examining the question.

The Senate Rules Committee began its hearings on September 23rd. The sessions, held in the Senate Caucus Room, the scene of the 1973 Watergate hearings, were only moderately well-attended. There was no live network television coverage. The Public Broadcasting Service televised the sessions on a delayed basis. The only live coverage was on radio.

Nelson Rockefeller testified for two and a half days. At the outset, he summarized a 72-page autobiographical statement in which he stressed his family's philanthropic works. He reported that he himself had given $33 million to various philanthropic and charitable institutions and undertakings and had pledged an additional $20.5 million in art and real estate.

Interest centered on Rockefeller's financial statement and his characterization of his family's financial empire and its influence. Rockefeller provided data showing that his own wealth and that of his wife, Happy, and his children, total $218 million (later revised upward to $229 million). The data show Rockefeller and his wife owning $62 million (later revised upward to $73 million) outright, most of it in stocks, works of art and real estate. He is the life beneficiary of trusts totaling $116.5 million; his wife is the beneficiary of securities and trusts worth $3.8 million; and his six children hold assets totaling $35.6 million in trust or outright. The data show his income for the ten years 1964 through 1973 as totaling $46.8 million. During the ten-year period, he had paid $21.7 million in Federal, state, and local taxes of all kinds and had listed $14.6 million as charitable contributions.

Rockefeller said that he hoped the "myth or misconception" about the Rockefeller family financial empire and its influence would be "exposed and dissipated." He attempted to minimize the extent of his family's financial interest in the oil industry by saying that no member of the family was on the board of any Standard Oil Company, "nor do we have any control over the management of these companies." He said that he himself owns no more than two-tenths of one percent of the outstanding shares in any oil company and that the total holdings of the family do not amount to more than 2.06 percent of the shares of any of the oil companies.

The committee's most persistent questioner, Senator Robert C. Byrd, Democrat of West Virginia, hammered away at the issue of the family's economic power. On the first day of the hearings, he said that this power gave the family a "stranglehold" on many areas of the national economy and would give Rockefeller greater power than any previous Vice President. Byrd returned to the issue on the second day. Noting that Rockefeller's wealth is "far greater" than that of previous occupants of high offices such as Franklin D. Roosevelt, Byrd said that the combination of wealth and political power of a Rockefeller Vice Presidency might "be greater than the component parts." When Rockefeller countered that he still believed that the concept of a vast Rockefeller empire was a myth, Byrd interrupted to say: "But can't we even agree the influence is tremendous—tremendous, colossal influence?" "Can't I add the word 'potential'?" Rockefeller asked. "Very well," Byrd said.

The issue remained unresolved. All of the committee members, including Byrd, said after the sessions that nothing in Rockefeller's testimony would bar his confirmation by the committee or the full Senate.

The committee put off a final vote on the nomination pending final outcome of audits of Rockefeller's tax returns. But those returns were to throw the nomination into doubt.

Criticism was leveled at the fact that in 1970 Rockefeller had paid no Federal income tax on a taxable income of $2,433,703. He had deducted a million and a quarter for charitable contributions, another half-million for payments of non-income taxes and another three-quarters of a million for "office expenses." Michael C. Jensen reported in *The New York Times* in mid-October that some tax experts who had scrutinized the financial information Rockefeller had provided to Congress and subsequently released to the public said they believed the deductions for business and office expenses were exceptionally large. As it turned out, the Internal Revenue Service had been auditing Rockefeller's returns—a standard annual practice for individuals in his income bracket—at the time of his nomination. In order to expedite the audit, the revenue service had beefed up the auditing team—to about thirty employees—and had received help from the Joint Congressional Committee on Internal Revenue Taxation. On the night of October 18, Rockefeller disclosed that an audit for the past five years had found that he had underpaid his Federal taxes by $903,718, and that together with an interest penalty of $122,875 he owed a total of $1,026,593. The revenue service had disallowed $824,598 in deductions claimed over the five years by Rockefeller for running offices and managing investments. These items amounted to almost one-fifth of the total deductions of $4,215,601 claimed for such office and investment expenses. Rockefeller also disclosed that he would have to pay $83,000 more in gift taxes.

On the following day, the *New York Post* ran two

Rockefeller stories on its front page. One concerned the medical prognosis for Happy Rockefeller, who had undergone a mastectomy two days before. The second story concerned Nelson Rockefeller's taxes. Its lead contained a quote from New York Republican Senator Javits on the tax issue: "I would not think it was a fatal blow, but this is a cumulative thing," the Javits quote went. "It might be that the taxes plus other things could sink him."

Those "other things" were far more serious than the tax delinquency. The tax returns showed that in addition to giving to philanthropic institutions and undertakings, Rockefeller had given princely sums to individuals who had held—and in some cases hold—influential positions in public life.

The gifts were disclosed over a period of six days.

On October 5 Rockefeller disclosed that he had made gifts of $50,000 to Henry Kissinger; $86,000 to L. Judson Morhouse; and an unspecified sum to William Ronan.

Kissinger's gift had been made in January, 1969, after Kissinger had left Rockefeller's employ and before he joined the White House as President Nixon's national security adviser. Kissinger had worked for Rockefeller for fifteen years.

The Morhouse gift had been made in 1973 in the form of a cancellation of the bulk of an outstanding loan of $100,000 made in September 1959, some nine months after Rockefeller had taken office as Governor of New York. At the time of the loan, Morhouse was chairman of the state Republican Party. The position was unsalaried then. Rockefeller's testimony would be that the loan had been made so that Morhouse could get into the real-estate business— specifically by acquiring control of a commercial property on Long Island—so that he would have some income and be, in Rockefeller's words, "independent of temptation." According to a headline in the *New York Post* on December 2—MORHOUSE RAN ROCKY $$ UP TO $600G—the loan did make Morhouse rich. And as if to make sure of that, Laurance Rockefeller, again in 1959, made Morhouse an additional loan of $49,000 in order to enable him to buy stock in two technological companies that Laurance was bankrolling.

The whole story was neck deep in a sea of inferences and facts. The date of the loan was troublesome, since at the time it was made Morhouse was state GOP chairman and recently had been instrumental in Rockefeller's securing the Republican gubernatorial nomination. Morhouse resigned as state chairman in 1962. He later became a member of the State Thruway Authority. But in 1966 he was convicted of, among other things, participating in the bribery of the chairman of the State Liquor Authority to obtain a license for the Playboy Club in Manhattan. Morhouse was sentenced to two concurrent two-to-three-year terms in prison. So Rockefeller's 1973 gift went to a convicted felon.

A resolution of some of the questions brought up by the loan and subsequent gift was unlikely, since Morhouse was reportedly confined to his home because of illness. Rockefeller had commuted Morhouse's sentence in 1970 on advice that Morhouse, suffering from Parkinson's disease and cancer of the colon, would not survive in prison. Perhaps it had been good advice: Morhouse, after all, was still alive.

Disclosures on the night of October 7 revealed that Rockefeller had made a gift of $550,000 (later it was disclosed that over $600,000 was involved) to William Ronan by cancelling a series of loans he had given Ronan during their association of more than seventeen years. Ronan had first been associated with Rockefeller as staff director of a state Temporary Commission on Constitutional Revision, which Rockefeller chaired shortly before he made his successful race for Governor. In 1958 Ronan headed the research staff for that race, then was named Rockefeller's personal secretary after the election. Eventually, Rockefeller made Ronan chairman of the Metropolitan Transportation Authority, which controls mass transit in the greater New York region. In May 1974 Ronan stepped down from that chairmanship and became a "senior adviser to the Rockefeller family," at an annual salary of $100,000. Two weeks after leaving the MTA, Ronan became the unsalaried chairman of the Port Authority of New York and New Jersey, and a $12,500-a-year trustee of the New York State Power Authority. Rockefeller had turned the loans into a gift during that two-week period.

On October 10 Edward J. Logue, the $65,000-a-year head of the New York State Urban Development Corporation, one of the nation's largest and most powerful state agencies, became the disclosed beneficiary of more Rockefeller largesse—in the form of $176,300 in loans and gifts.

The following day, Rockefeller let most of it hang out—not all of it, as it turned out—by making public the text of a letter sent to the chairman of the Senate Rules Committee in which he acknowledged having made gifts since 1957 to eighteen current or former state officials and members of his staff totaling $1,778,878, on which he had paid Federal and state taxes amounting to about $840,000.

In his letter, Rockefeller defended his gifts as an outgrowth of his family's habit of philanthropy. He said: "Throughout my life I have made loans to friends and associates to assist them in meeting the kind of pressing human needs which all people have from time to time . . . I have been especially fortunate in being able to share in the meeting of those needs. That sharing has always been part of my upbringing, and we have always lived our lives that way."

Rockefeller's press spokesman, Hugh Morrow, the recipient of a gift himself, attempted to put a good face on the disclosures. Morrow explained that the gift to Ronan "could be related to the year-end bonus given corporation executives." The remark put the gifts into an interesting perspective.

A number of them went to men who at one time or another held major positions in state agencies dealing with construction, natural-resources management, and finance: in addition to Ronan and Logue, the list included Henry Diamond, state environmental conservation commissioner; James Gaynor, state commissioner of housing and community renewal; G. Russell Clark, state superintendent of banks; and Richard S. Aldrich, a Rockefeller first cousin and chairman of the State Housing Finance Agency.

During Rockefeller's nearly four terms as Governor, the state had embarked on perhaps $10 billion worth of construction projects and had become embroiled in controversial large-scale projects for developing natural resources. Had Morrow meant to say that Rockefeller had run New York State for fifteen years as if it were a private corporation in business to make the visions powered by Rockefeller's famous "edifice complex" into reality? If so, it would have been perfectly natural for Rockefeller to have treated state officials as officers of his personal corporation and reward them accordingly.

Morrow's remark brought up legal questions. Two New York State laws regarding "tipping" of public employees might be involved. For example, statute 200.35 of the penal code says: "A person is guilty of giving unlawful gratuities when he knowingly confers or agrees to confer any benefit upon a public servant for having engaged in official conduct which he would be required or authorized to perform, and for which he was not entitled to any special or additional compensation." Giving such a gratuity is a Class A misdemeanor, punishable by up to one year in jail or a $1,000 fine.

The dates of the gifts were important. Rockefeller's disclosure made clear that each gift was given at a time when its recipient had either left public service for good or was a private citizen between government jobs.

Were the gifts disqualification for holding high office? The situation was deteriorating. And the gifts were not the only controversy in which the nomination was embroiled.

At the same time the nearly $2 million in gifts were disclosed, it was also disclosed that Rockefeller money had financed the publication and distribution of a derogatory biography of Arthur J. Goldberg during his unsuccessful campaign against Nelson Rockefeller for the New York Governorship in 1970. The book, entitled *Arthur J. Goldberg, the Old and the New,* written in several weeks by Victor Lasky for a sum of $10,000, had been paid for by Nelson Rockefeller's brother Laurance; $65,000 of his money had been channeled by Rockefeller family advisers through a dummy corporation, called Literary Properties, Inc., to the publisher, Arlington House. The book had been distributed free by the New York State Republican organization during the campaign. Nowhere in the book did it say that Rockefeller money had financed it.

Contending that his nomination was "being tried in the press . . . without my having the opportunity to present all the facts," Rockefeller in mid-October asked the chairmen of the Senate Rules Committee and the House Judiciary Committee to convene "immediate" hearings.

As if to reinforce his reputation as a philanthropist, Rockefeller soon released a long list of the charitable gifts he had made from January 1, 1959 to June 30, 1974. During those years he had given $24.7 million to 193 organizations. For the most part, the largest gifts had gone to Rockefeller institutions: $6,592,179 to the Museum of Primitive Art, which Rockefeller had founded himself; $2,563,420 to the Museum of Modern Art, whose board of trustees Rockefellers have usually headed; and to such Rockefeller philanthropic foundations as the American International Association for Economic and Social Development ($1,626,751), the Government Affairs Foundation ($1,026,180), the Rockefeller Brothers Fund ($880,510), Jackson Hole Preserve ($959,721), and the Third Century Corporation (the fundraising arm of Nelson Rockefeller's Commission on Critical Choices, $1,034,047).

Suspicious minds went to work on the list, and three weeks after its publication, Martin Tolchin reported in the *Times* that the Academy of Political Science, the recipient of a gift of $89,952, had published a book, *Governing New York State: The Rockefeller Years*, lauding Rockefeller's governorship. The book, circulated to members of the Congressional committees considering the Rockefeller nomination, contained such passages as: "although he came to understand and value the use of patronage, Rockefeller insisted that his appointments secretary and the Republican state chairman realize that high professional competence was the underlying consideration in making appointments." Rockefeller said later that the gift had been solicited in order to help finance a study of which the book is a summary.

Late in October Rockefeller published a new list of loans. During the past seventeen years he had made $507,656 in loans to friends, associates and family members—in addition to the loans and gifts previously disclosed. $147,773 of the loans had not been repaid yet.

The Senate Rules Committee did hold a second set of hearings, but not until November 13, some seven weeks after the first set had been concluded. In September there had been no live television coverage and the atmosphere had been relaxed, except perhaps for the questioning by Senator Byrd. The $2 million in gifts and the Goldberg book changed all that. Now, in November, the national commercial networks were rotating coverage on a daily basis, and in the glare of the television lights there were sharp exchanges between committee members. Furthermore, President Ford was prodding Congress to "fish or cut bait" in confirming the nomination, then some three months old. At a news conference at the annual convention of the Society of Professional Journalists in Pheonix, Ford declared his continuing support of the Rockefeller nomination in no uncertain terms, saying there were "no conditions that I can imagine or know of under which I would withdraw Governor Rockefeller's name."

At the outset it appeared that the committee might be entering into a discussion of Rockefeller power and questions of potential conflict of interest should Nelson Rockefeller be confirmed as Vice President. In his opening remarks, the committee chairman, Howard W. Cannon, Democrat of Nevada said: "Never before in our history has a member of a great American family—a family possessing greater wealth and broader business interests than any in this country—been this close to achieving the second, or the first, highest office in this land. And Governor Rockefeller is to be congratulated. But the potential wedding of this economic and political power requires a comparable scrutiny by those of us charged with such scrutiny." Rockefeller himself seemed to sense the necessity for addressing the issue by means other than calling Rockefeller power a myth, as he had done in September. "The abstract questions about private wealth and the power of the Presidency come down finally to a direct personal question about my being in the line of succession," Rockefeller said in *his* opening statement. "Am I the kind of man who would use his wealth improperly in public office? Or, more generally and more importantly, would my family background somehow limit and blind me, so that I would not be able to see and serve the general good of all Americans? I think the answer is no."

Rockefeller addressed the issue more concretely by publishing an account of his political campaign contributions since 1957. In summary, he listed contributions of $3,265,374 for the eighteen-year period. About $1 million of that total was for his own Presidential campaigns. (In response to a question put by Senator James Allen, an Alabama Democrat, Rockefeller agreed that two-thirds of the $3.2 million total had gone for his own campaigns. In addition, he agreed, his brothers and sister had contributed some $2,850,000 to his campaigns. Also, his step-mother, Martha Baird Rockefeller, had contributed some $11 million to his campaigns, Rockefeller said. He and Senator Allen finally agreed on a figure of "somewhat over $20 million" for all Rockefeller family campaign contributions, both to his own campaigns and to those of other politicians. Actually, the reported total is $27 million.)

Senator Cannon returned to the issue at the beginning of the questioning: "I sincerely feel ... that the real basic concern of the citizens of this country regarding your nomination is the fear of the wedding of great economic and great political power and its potential abuse. Especially important in this context, I feel, are specific examples of situations where you and your family have utilized your economic resources to advance your political interests.

"You have previously stated before the committee that your economic power is largely a myth. This power becomes much less mythical when concrete examples of large gifts and loans to persons serving in official positions is made public, and also when information is made public concerning questionable campaign activities by your family."

But the committee merely touched on the issue of whether

Rockefeller's great wealth disqualified him from holding high office. Instead, the committee concentrated on the legal and moral aspects of the Goldberg book and the gifts and loans to public officials. Was the Goldberg book comparable to the "dirty tricks" associated with the Watergate scandals? Had Nelson Rockefeller violated the New York State statutes which prohibit gifts or "benefits" to state employees?

With regard to the book, the committee examined ten witnesses, including Rockefeller himself who told the committee, "in regard to the financing of the book on Mr. Justice Goldberg, let's face it—I made a mistake;" Goldberg *himself*, who refused to accept an apology by Rockefeller on the grounds that he found Rockefeller's explanation of the circumstances of the book's financing "inherently not credible"; Laurance Rockefeller, who said that he had invested about $65,000 in the book as a business venture on the basis of a five-minute conversation (with a woman now dead, incidentally) and had forgotten all about the matter until it had come under investigation with regard to his brother Nelson's nomination; seven lawyers and Rockefeller family financial advisers, who held to a description of the undertaking as a commercial venture which would coincidentally be helpful in the gubernatorial campaign; and Victor Lasky, the author of the book, who, joking, smiling, and continually relighting an enormous cigar, identified himself as a writer, columnist, and commentator, and added that he was "available for bar mitzvahs and funeral orations."

It was a farce that went nowhere. While Senator Byrd characterized the book as "an out-and-out effort to influence the campaign . . . a misguided political adventure . . . a very serious factor," he allowed that "it in itself will not cause me to vote against the nominee."

With regard to the gifts and loans issue, Rockefeller said he would make no gifts or loans to Federal employees, except for "gifts in nominal amounts" for such festive occasions as weddings, birthdays, and Christmas, and except for assistance "in the event of medical hardships of a compelling human character." The committee examined several recipients of loans and gifts, including Ronan, who denied any "sinister purpose" in loans and gifts made to him by Nelson Rockefeller, and said the gifts had been "motivated solely by friendship and a lifelong practice of sharing."

This, too, went nowhere. After discussing the possibility that Rockefeller might have violated New York State statutes that prohibit gifts or "benefits" to state employees, Senator Byrd said that the nominee ought to be given the benefit of the doubt.

The House Judiciary Committee hearings, which began on Thursday, November 21, were expected to be more critical in tone than the senate hearings—which, after all, had recessed back in September without a whisper about either Nelson Rockefeller's cash gifts to public officials or Laurance Rockefeller's financing of the derogatory biography of Arthur J. Goldberg. More importantly, the house hearings were expected to focus on the question of Rockefeller economic power to a far greater extent than in the senate.

The opening remarks of committee chairman Peter W. Rodino, a New Jersey Democrat, heightened the latter expectation. "We must attempt to measure the network of Rockefeller family wealth," he said, "and place it into the perspective of both the American economy and the American political system." This expectation was further heightened when Democratic Representative Robert W. Kastenmeier of Wisconsin suggested to Nelson Rockefeller that the committee might want to ask questions not only about *his* wealth, but also about that of his three living brothers and one sister.

Rockefeller took the suggestion as a personal matter. "My brothers and sister have been very tolerant about my political activities," he said. "I can't say all of them approve." His politicking, he went on, was "a source of, particularly to the next generation, some embarrassment. I would like to minimize the disruption of the family's lives . . . I would like to avoid involving them in what they think is my thing . . . They're not very enthusiastic." Was he serious?

Representative Don Edwards, a California Democrat, pressed Rockefeller on the idea that the size of his and his family's wealth made conflict of interest inevitable. Rockefeller disputed this idea by contrasting his family's wealth unfavorably with that of the unpopular Arab oil sheiks saying "the Arabs are accumulating capital at the rate of $200 billion a week." He contended that this "dwarfs to the point of absurdity" the Rockefeller holdings. "The Arabs in a week accumulate more money than my family has after three generations of work," he said.

Eleven days later the committee heard testimony from two University of California professors proposing a line of inquiry into the extent of Rockefeller economic power. G. William Domhoff, a psychology professor at the University of California, Santa Cruz, and Charles L. Schwartz, a physics professor at the University of California, Berkeley, presented a thirty-seven-page study called *Probing the Rockefeller Fortune*. In a statement, the professors said: "Fifteen employees of the Rockefellers, working out of the family's central office, have been identified on the boards of directors of nearly 100 corporations over a number of years, and the combined assets of these corporations currently is some $70 billion." They continued: "We would suggest that the question of conflict of interest can be addressed only after you have succeeded in gaining a full and clear picture of what the Rockefeller family's interests really are." The professors identified a dozen major corporations on whose boards Rockefeller family advisers sat—including the Chrysler Corporation, International Business Machines, Eastern Air Lines, American Motors, Howard Johnson, Bendix, and the S. S. Kresge Corporation. "We have established that the family's management staff is actively involved in directing the business affairs of these corporations," the professors said.

As if in rebuttal, on the following day the committee heard testimony from J. Richardson Dilworth, for sixteen years the Rockefeller family's senior financial adviser. Dilworth heads the office at 30 Rockefeller Plaza—known as Rockefeller Family & Associates—which handles the investments of the eighty-four members of the family and of some of the Rockefeller philanthropic institutions, including the Rockefeller University and Colonial Williamsburg, but excluding the two largest foundations—the Rockefeller Foundation and the Rockefeller Brothers Fund. In addition, Dilworth is a director of such large companies as Chrysler and R.H. Macy.

Dilworth's detailed presentation showed the eighty-four members of the Rockefeller family to be worth more than $1 billion in assets owned outright and in trust. This figure does not include the considerable Rockefeller assets in such things as personal real estate (including residences) and art (including at least five major collections).

He provided only aggregates of the largest holdings. The five largest blocks of shares owned outright by the family members included holdings in three oil companies—Exxon, Standard Oil of California, and Mobil—in IBM and in the Chase Manhattan Bank. The five largest blocks of shares held in trusts created by John D. Rockefeller, Jr. (Nelson Rockefeller's father) included holdings in the same three oil companies, in IBM, and in Rockefeller Center.

Thus the Rockefellers own, outright and in trust,

2,288,171 shares in Exxon (1.02 per cent of total shares outstanding), worth $157,700,000 at December, 1974 market value; 3,410,148 shares in Standard Oil of California (2.01 per cent of total shares outstanding), worth $85,300,000; 1,762,206 shares in Mobil (1.74 per cent of total shares outstanding), worth $63,600,000. The Rockefellers own all the shares in Rockefeller Center—valued at $98,300,000, although the buildings themselves are undoubtedly worth much more—and 1.34 percent of the shares in the Chase Manhattan Bank.

Throughout his testimony, Dilworth contended that each family member's investments were handled individually. He said that providing the aggregate figures should not be taken to indicate "that this family acts in concert when in fact this has never been the case."

Furthermore, Dilworth denied that the Rockefellers were even interested in controlling corporations. "It should be stressed," he said, "that both the family members and their investment advisers in the family office are totally uninterested in controlling anything. The family investors are simply investors."

During the question period, Dilworth described the investment operation at the family office as being interested not in short-term profits but in long-term appreciation. "The quick turn," he said, "we're not interested in that."

Dilworth said that some family members were so uninterested in their investments that it was difficult to get them to meet with an investment counselor from the office even once a year. In particular, he described Nelson Rockefeller as tending to leave mangement of his investments entirely to Dilworth and his staff. "He doesn't call me up and suggest I ought to do this thing or the other thing," Dilworth said of Nelson. He "is always concerned about the conflict-of-interest question arising from any of his investments," Dilworth added.

Again and again in his testimony, Dilworth denied that the holdings of Rockefeller family members gave them control over any corporation.

But the next day the committee got another glimpse of what it means to be as rich as Rockefeller—and to be Rockefeller—when it was disclosed on September 1, 1961 Laurance Rockefeller, at Nelson's request, lent New York Republican Congressman William Miller $30,000. The loan, at an annual interest rate of five percent and payable in three years from the date of issue, was to enable Miller to buy stock in two companies from Laurance Rockefeller, who was, in effect, providing Miller with investment funds and giving him a tip in the stock market. Eventually, Miller paid back all but $1,900—which Rockefeller told him to forget.

The disclosure stirred up a squall—in the first place, because at the time of the loan Miller was Republican national chairman; in the second place, because Laurance Rockefeller had made no mention of the loan in his previous testimony before the Senate Rules Committee several weeks earlier; in the third place, because Laurance had made a loan in 1959 to GOP state chairman L. Judson Morhouse; and in the fourth place, because Laurance had financed the publication of the derogatory biography of Arthur J. Goldberg during the 1970 campaign.

When the House Judiciary Committee's hearings ended, the Rockefeller nomination, which had been in deep trouble, looked like a sure thing. Rockefeller himself knew this, judging by his comments to chairman Rodino, reported by Linda Charlton in the *Times*. Rockefeller told Rodino he was "a great chairman" and added "I feel as though this was the most thorough examination that has ever been made of any citizen in this country."

But I was a lot less than satisfied with the hearings in both the senate and house, especially the latter, which at the

outset had promised so much. Sure, the committee had heard
Domhoff and Schwartz, and Dilworth had presented detailed
information on the Rockefeller fortune. But it had all gone
by in a rush. There had not even been time, for example, to
add together the holdings in any corporation, such as Exxon,
of the family (both outright and in trust), the Rockefeller
philanthropic institutions, the Chase Manhattan, and Rockefeller Center. Did the Rockefellers and their financial advisors
control a significant sector of the economy? The committee
hearings, to say the least, were inconclusive on this point. It
seemed to me that the committee had missed a glorious
opportunity.

A few days after the hearings were over, I stopped in at the
office of one of the Judiciary Committee's members,
Democratic Congressman Edward Mezvinsky of Iowa. Mezvinsky had achieved national prominence during the impeachment hearings when he introduced an impeachment resolution involving possible tax fraud on Nixon's part. I spoke
both with Mezvinsky's legislative assistant, Doris Freedman,
and with the Congressman himself.

What they said, in summary, was this: The committee was
divided on philosophical grounds. While some members
thought that everything about the nominee—Rockefeller—
should have been brought out, others felt that Ford had a
right to his choice and their role was to rubber stamp that
choice—unless the nominee was a crook.

The committee had been unable to get to its normal work
for more than a year. First there had been the hearings on
Nixon's nomination of Ford; then the impeachment hearings;
then the Rockefeller hearings.

The committee was tired, furthermore. And the Rockefeller question was not black and white. It was awesomely
complex. Mezvinsky said: "Once you enter the Rockefellers'

world and learn something about it, you realize there must be so much more you don't know."

There was a feeling in the air of wanting the confirmation process over and done with. The press did not push for a full inquiry into Rockefeller power. (*The Washington Post* published editorials objecting to requests by Judiciary Committee members that the financial interests of all members of the Rockefeller family be made public. The *Post* called this a gross invasion of privacy.) Congress was being pressured—to stop wasting time on the nomination and start dealing with stagflation. And if the Rockefeller nomination was turned down, whom would Ford put up next?

Perhaps everyone knew that the nomination was a foregone conclusion. The Judiciary Committee hearings were not a big public attraction. At the outset, chairs in the committee chambers had been jammed together to seat as many people as possible, but they were only half filled when the opening session began. There was no television coverage. Only the Pacifica Foundation's radio stations—with correspondent Robert Krulwich doing a first-rate job—broadcast the hearings.

The Senate Rules Committee voted nine to nothing to recommend approval of Nelson Rockefeller's nomination for Vice President. In its 200-page report (transcripts of the hearings run on for 1,400 pages), the committee congratulated itself on having conducted a "consideration [that] ... probably represents the greatest in-depth confirmation inquiry ever carried out by a committee of the United States"; noted that it "accepted Governor Rockefeller's candor and straightforward responses that he would be guided by public interest considerations vis-a-vis his family's business interests;" and concluded that it had "found no bar or impediment which would disqualify him [Rockefeller] for the office to which he had been nominated."

The full Senate was for Rockefeller by a vote of ninety to seven. Among the dissenters were Barry Goldwater, whom Rockefeller had opposed in a bitter struggle for the Republican Presidential nomination in 1964, and Democrats Birch Bayh, the author of the Constitutional Amendment that prescribes the method for filling a vacancy in the Vice Presidency, and Gaylord Nelson. Before the vote, Senator Goldwater wrote to President Ford that he believed Rockefeller "did in effect use his own personal money to accomplish the purchase of political power." While not suggesting any "improper" use of the "political leverage" available to "the [sixty-six-year-old Rockefeller] as a result of his gifts and loans to his political associates," Goldwater said he believed that the nation "will be better served by the selection of a younger man—one who would not carry the burden of suspicion which is clearly in the public mind regarding the power of the Rockefeller fortune." During the debate preceding the vote, Bayh said he believed Rockefeller "does not command and would not command the confidence of large numbers of the American people." Nelson objected to the nomination on the basis of the concentration of economic power he said Rockefeller represented. "Giantism in all its forms," Senator Nelson said, "threatens freedom in all of its forms."

Mezvinsky and eleven other Democrats on the House Judiciary Committee voted against Rockefeller's confirmation. Their votes were based on what Mezvinsky called the "confidence-shattering conflict of interest" inherent in Nelson Rockefeller's occupying the office of Vice President while he and his family enjoy massive wealth and economic power. John F. Seiberling, an Ohio Democrat and a member of the wealthy family that manufactures Seiberling tires, called the "central issue" in the vote the "undue concentration of power in one man's hands." Merging political power with Rockefeller power would eliminate the basic checks and balances concept that underlies the American system of government, Seiberling said, according to Linda Charlton's dispatch in the *Times*. And Jerome Waldie, Democrat of California, who had said that he gave Rockefeller no credit for his philanthropic activities, charged that Rockefeller "has used his private wealth and his family's wealth in concert to enhance Nelson Rockefeller's political career," and spending $20 million on Nelson Rockefeller's political career was "not within the public interest or acceptable."

On the day the Senate voted to confirm Nelson Rockefeller as Vice President, there was a hint that the relationship between Rockefeller and Gerald Ford might not be quite the same as the relationships that traditionally have prevailed between Presidents and Vice Presidents. Ford spent seven hours that day—December 10—at the Waldorf Astoria Hotel in New York. In the evening he attended the Football Foundation's dinner and reception. But before that he attended a meeting of members of the Commission on Critical Choices.

The Commission was a project that Rockefeller had formed in 1973, when he was still Governor of New York State. He resigned as Governor in December of that year, and began to devote himself to heading the commission and to stomping the country giving speeches in an apparent attempt to convince the Republican Party faithful that he was worthy of their trust and would be their best hope for 1976 should Ford falter in his abbreviated term in the White House.

The commission had started out as a state study, but before Rockefeller resigned from office he expanded it into a national study with Presidential and Congressional backing. (Nixon was still President.) The commission was working toward publishing reports on such topics as world stability and peace; food, health, population, and the quality of life; and the developing and sharing of raw materials.

The commission was given the trappings of philanthropy. Its fund-raising arm, the Third Century Corporation, is a non-profit establishment. The commission, like a philanthropic foundation, is supported by tax-deductible contributions.

According to estimates Rockefeller provided early in the life of the commission, it was to cost $6.5 million. (Initial estimates ran as high as $20 million, however.) Before Rockefeller resigned as Governor, he and his brother Laurance each gave the commission $1 million. Additional funds were requested from Congress. But in December 1973 the Senate Appropriations Committee quietly killed the commission's request for a $1 million appropriation for an energy study.

The official reasons for the rejection were that the study would duplicate others already underway and that the request had been submitted without enough advance preparation. (As Governor, Rockefeller had successfully rammed emergency legislation through the New York State Legislature, but Congress was somewhat less awed by his power.) The unofficial reason involved speculation that the commission was being used as a Rockefeller vehicle for a 1976 Presidential campaign. The commission had been dubbed "Rocky's vehicle."

The following April Rockefeller announced that the commission had decided not to pursue requests for funding from either the Executive or Congress. Instead, the commission was to be financed by contributions from foundations and individuals. There was to be a low key fund-raising effort. Some half-dozen foundations soon signed up.

When Rockefeller was nominated for Vice President, Henry Diamond, the commission's executive director, and other Rockefeller aides predicted that the commission would fade away. It was suggested to some of the commission's forty-five staff members that they look for new jobs.

The December 10 meeting of the seven key members of the commission with President Ford was billed as a briefing session, but also served as a bid for Presidential support for the commission, according to the report of the meeting in *The New York Times*. White House press Secretary Ron Nessen said after the meeting that "in some form, it is going to continue," although he also said that there was no specific talk of the commission's future at the meeting. Instead, Ford heard a series of proposals to meet national and world-wide shortages of energy, raw materials, and food. It was reported that one proposal called for hiring a private contractor to manage the nation's energy program, this role to be similar to the role of private industry in developing ballistic-missile and space programs.

This proposal was made by John Foster, vice president for energy research and development for TRW, Inc. Other participants at the meeting were Carroll L. Wilson, a professor at the Massachusetts Institute of Technology; Hans Mark, director of Ames Laboratories; Oscar M. Reubhausen, a New York lawyer; Dr. Edward Teller, known as the father of the hydrogen bomb, and a Rockefeller associate for at least fifteen years; George D. Woods, a banker and long-time Rockefeller associate; and William J. Ronan. Nelson Rockefeller moderated the meeting.

It was, at the *Times* report put it, an "unusual" session, "in that the President came to the experts rather than the reverse."

Was the session a precursor of things to come? Will Gerald Ford be President in title only—and will Nelson Rockefeller be President-in-Effect? Night after night, it seems, Ford attends ceremonial banquets. Will the Presidency be split into two offices—a ceremonial one and a ministerial one—during Ford's incumbency? And will Ford hold the former and Rockefeller the latter?

Several hours before Ford nominated Rockefeller, Bill Toohey, New York Bureau Chief of National Public Radio called me. "It's Rockefeller," he said. "How do you know?" I asked. "Three planeloads of aides just took off from the Westchester airport" (which is near the Rockefeller estates), Toohey said.

Rockefeller may very well overwhelm Ford with his fleets of experts, particularly in the area of foreign policy; after all, the quintessential Rockefeller expert—Henry Kissinger—is Secretary of State.

Whatever the relationship between Rockefeller and Ford, one thing is certain: Nelson Rockefeller will be unlike any other Vice President in the nation's history. He may be the most energetic. Author William Manchester once wrote that Rockefeller was "the greatest advocate of the strenuous life" since Theodore Roosevelt. He may be, despite his age (sixty-six at this writing), the most ambitious. He is still a candidate for President, apparently. Shortly after his nomination for Vice President, he made a reference to Konrad Adenauer and Golda Meir, both of whom were national leaders of their countries when in their seventies. He may be the most controversial. His mammoth construction projects, his backing of natural resources development, and his activities as a quintessential cold warrior—all covered in his book—have been detested by many people, although supported by others. Finally, he will be the most powerful. But because two hallmarks of Rockefeller power have been self-interest and arrogance—as this book shows—Nelson Rockefeller's vice presidency could be unpopular.

As I write this a week before Christmas, the nation's

economic problems become more and more confusing and desperate. Every trip to a supermarket promises yet another shock. On Manhattan's West Side, where I live, the number of men loitering in the streets in the December cold, without jobs to go to, grows week by week. President Ford seems hopelessly incompetent. Nelson Rockefeller will be able to assert himself. Let us hope that he proposes and does not only what is good for the Rockefellers, but what is good for all of us.

New York City
December, 1974

The Rockefellers'
Philanthropic Responsibility:
The Making of
Rockefeller Power

Early in this century, John D. Rockefeller, perhaps the richest and most powerful industrialist and the most widely hated and feared man in America, established a series of important philanthropic institutions to promote medical research, education and public health. In the period between the two World Wars, John D. Rockefeller, Jr., an important philanthropist in his own right, established more philanthropic institutions and made major contributions to conservation and historical restoration in the United States. His signal enterprise was a commercial one: Rockefeller Center, the greatest private construction project in American history. His wife, Abby Aldrich Rockefeller, founded the Museum of Modern Art, which set out to influence American art, architecture and design and had remarkable success. Since about 1940, the Rockefeller brothers—the third generation—have been prominent in private and public affairs, as philanthropists (having established a whole new series of philanthropic institutions), elected public officials, heads of Presidential commissions, businessmen and bankers. Using both private and public funds, the brothers have undertaken and sponsored huge construction projects in New York, and are working on more projects, including entirely new cities and towns, throughout the nation. They have undertaken and sponsored both the conservation and the development of natural resources. They have exerted significant influence on U.S. military and foreign policy.

The Rockefeller brothers have wielded this power with the announced intention of promoting the public interest. The intent of this book is to show how, in the face of the hatred of the Rockefeller name, the work of the first and second generations generated the power of the third, and then to show how, in light of the brothers' announced intention, the power is used, and to examine the brothers' competence for exercising it. To do so, the book studies Rockefeller power in four areas: the Rockefellers' construction program; their involvement with art; their natural resources policy; and their influence on U.S. military and foreign policy.

The Rockefellers do not consider themselves ordinary men. In the Union Church, close by the vast Rockefeller estates (which are spread over several thousand acres at Pocantico Hills, a high ridge between the Hudson and Saw Mill River Valleys in Westchester County, about thirty miles north of Manhattan), the Rockefellers have shown that their ambitions and activities are inspired by a profound vision of a role in the world.

The church has ten beautiful stained-glass windows. The rose window on the east wall, a memorial to Abby Aldrich Rockefeller designed by Henri Matisse in 1954 on commission by Nelson Rockefeller, avoids "employing any kind of symbol," in the words of the artist. A decade later, however, when

David Rockefeller commissioned Marc Chagall to create a companion window on the west wall as a memorial to John D. Rockefeller, Jr., the Rockefellers began to embellish the church with familial symbolism. The theme of Chagall's painting (if you look closely, you can see his scratches in the glass; the work is irreplaceable) is the Biblical story of the Good Samaritan. Chagall then was commissioned to illustrate eight carefully chosen Biblical texts on eight more windows, these for the north and south walls. One of these windows, depicting the Crucifixion, is a memorial to Nelson Rockefeller's son Michael, who died at the age of twenty-three, while he was on an anthropological expedition in New Guinea. Visitors may obtain a small, buff-colored sheet which gives a brief history of the church and the eight Biblical verses represented on the north and south walls. The verses are:

THE CRUCIFIXION (In memory of Michael Clark Rockefeller)
Matthew 7:7
"Ask, and it will be given you; seek, and you will find; knock, and it will be opened to you."
JOEL Joel 2:28–31

"And it shall come to pass afterward, that I will pour out my spirit on all flesh; your sons and your daughters shall prophesy, your old men shall dream dreams, and your young men shall see visions. Even upon the menservants and maidservants in those days, I will pour out my spirit. And I will give portents in the heavens and on the earth, blood and fire and columns of smoke. The sun shall be turned to darkness, and the moon to blood, before the great and terrible day of the Lord comes."

ELIJAH II Kings 2:9–12
"When they had crossed, Elijah said to Elisha, 'Ask what

I shall do for you, before I am taken from you.' And Elisha said, 'I pray you, let me inherit a double share of your spirit.' And he said, 'You have asked a hard thing; yet, if you see me as I am being taken from you, it shall be so for you; but if you do not see me, it shall not be so.' And as they still went on and talked, behold, a chariot of fire and horses of fire separated the two of them. And Elijah went up by a whirlwind into heaven. And Elisha saw it and he cried, 'My father, my father! the chariots of Israel and its horsemen!' And he saw him no more."

DANIEL Daniel 8:15–18

"When I, Daniel, had seen the vision, I sought to understand it; and behold, there stood before me one having the appearance of a man. And I heard a man's voice between the banks of the Ulai, and it called, 'Gabriel, make this man understand the vision.' So he came near where I stood; and when he came, I was frightened and fell upon my face. But he said to me, 'Understand, O son of man, that the vision is for the time of the end.' As he was speaking to me, I fell into a deep sleep with my face to the ground; but he touched me and set me on my feet."

CHERUBIM Genesis 3:24

"He drove out the man; and at the east of the garden of Eden he placed the cherubim, and a flaming sword which turned every way, to guard the way to the tree of life."

EZEKIEL Ezekiel 2:8–3:3

"But you, son of man, hear what I say to you; be not rebellious like that rebellious house; open your mouth and eat what I give you." And when I looked, behold a hand was stretched out to me, and, lo, a written scroll was in it; and he spread it before me; and it had writing on the front and on the back, and there was written on it words of lamentation and mourning and woe. And he said to me, 'Son of man, eat what is offered to you; eat this scroll, and go, speak to the house of Israel.' So I opened my mouth, and he gave me the scroll to eat. And he said to me, 'Son of man, eat this scroll that I give you and fill your stomach with it.' Then I ate it; and it was in my mouth as sweet as honey."

JEREMIAH Lamentations 3:1–9
"I am the man who has seen affliction under the rod of his wrath; he has driven and brought me into darkness without any light; surely against me he turns his hand again and again the whole day long. He has made my flesh and my skin waste away and broken my bones; he has besieged and enveloped me with bitterness and tribulation; he has made me dwell in darkness like the dead of long ago. He has walled me about so that I cannot escape; he has put heavy chains on me; though I call and cry for help, he shuts out my prayer; he has blocked my ways with hewn stones, he has made my paths crooked."

ISAIAH 59:21
"And as for me, this is my covenant with them, says the Lord: my spirit which is upon you, and my words which I have put in your mouth, shall not depart out of your mouth, or out of the mouth of your children, or out of the mouth of your children's children, says the Lord, from this time forth and forevermore."

We read in these verses that the Rockefellers believe they have been called to undertake a journey to learn what work they must undertake. This calling comes to them at an important moment in history, for the current epoch, which had a disastrous beginning, when man was driven out of the garden of Eden, is coming to an end. They know that in order to carry out their work they must not succumb to a similar defeat; they must not devote themselves to pleasure, but must rise above the trivial life. Their calling gives them a vision of a new day; it shows them the way to creating a new garden of Eden. They know their work is difficult and perilous, that they will suffer hardships and deprivations, but they have been charged by God Himself. They must take on missionary work, offer themselves for leadership, build the new garden of Eden. Once they plunge into their work, they find joy in it, and the results render any adversities worthwhile.

The great responsibility the Rockefellers have accepted so joyfully is philanthropic: to promote the well-being of mankind throughout the world. They have been driven to discharging it for more than a century, dating all the way back to the years when they did not have the wealth for which they are so celebrated. A few glances at Allan Nevins' biography, *Study in Power: John D. Rockefeller, Industrialist and Philanthropist*, demonstrate how deeply the first Rockefeller was devoted to philanthropy; it was a lifelong habit, preceding even his accumulation of great wealth. Between December 1855 and April 1856, when he was but sixteen years old, he gave away almost 10 percent of his earnings of $95. In 1857 he gave $28.37 to several churches and the YMCA; in 1858, $43; and in 1859, $72.22, the latter amount being fully one tenth of his income. The amounts increased as steadily as his wealth. In 1860 he gave away $107.35; in 1864, $671.85. Five years later, as he was nearing the end of his first decade in the oil business, the business that made him rich, his contributions totaled $5,489.62. Their level remained somewhat stationary for about a decade, but in 1878 they rose to $23,485.65. By 1881 he more than doubled them, and by 1884 more than doubled them again, giving away $119,109.48. In 1887 they exceeded a quarter of a million dollars. In 1890 they topped the million-dollar mark.

Rockefeller's great wealth came from the operations of Standard Oil, the great monopoly he had created in the 1870s to tie together the oil industry's three elements—pumping crude oil, refining it, and transporting the products to consumers throughout the world. Standard Oil had brought order to an unstable industry cursed with overproduction and subject to wild economic fluctuations and controlled it with steady growth and guaranteed profits. Rockefeller summarized his organizational innovations with this comment: "The combination is here to stay. Individualism is gone, never to return."

Profit and philanthropy were Rockefeller's highest duties. His philosophy was: "A man should make all he can and give away all he can." By the turn of the century, however, while Rockefeller was sought after for his philanthropy, he was not honored for it. Instead, public esteem for him was low, brought to that estate by Henry Demarest Lloyd, Ida M. Tarbell and other muckrakers,* who published accounts of his business operations in such mass-circulation magazines as the *Atlantic Monthly* and *McClure's*. His name stood for neither philanthropy nor oil, but for blood money. Allan Nevins would explain later that Rockefeller had been an organiza-

---

* In the late 1800s and early 1900s, a wholly unfavorable portrait of Rockefeller was imprinted on the public mind, mainly by Lloyd's article, "The Story of a Great Monopoly," in the March 1881 *Atlantic Monthly;* his book, *Wealth and Commonwealth,* published in 1894; Tarbell's serial, "Methods of the Standard Oil Company," beginning in the December 1902 *McClure's;* her book, *The History of the Standard Oil Company,* published in 1904.

tional genius and the founder of the modern corporation, who had done what he did because he had to. Nevins would demonstrate that the Rockefeller forces had been better organizers, administrators and technicians than their rivals. Rockefeller's large, well-planned facilities, combined with his attention to detail, provided maximum economy and efficiency. His extensive capital had funded research leading to technological breakthroughs and had been of terrific advantage in a series of industrial wars. But in the early 1900s he was despised throughout the United States. Attention focused on the muckrakers' charges that tactics he had employed to subjugate and ruin rivals had been immoral. These had included secretly obtaining from the railroads not only rebates on Standard Oil's shipping fees but also large percentages of competitors' fees, forcing shippers to deny competitors access to markets, choking off supplies of crude oil from competitors, buying competitors in secret, price-cutting, bribery and industrial espionage. To be sure, these tactics were typical of the Robber Baron era. "It is well for us to remember," David Rockefeller would write many years later, echoing the judgment of Allan Nevins, "that the evolution of business ethics in the United States was a relatively slow process. Corporations did things in the 1870s and 1880s which advancing standards made clearly improper."

Rockefeller's rivals in the oil fields had been predatory and greedy petty capitalists who had been swallowed up by Standard Oil because of their lack of discipline in battle. "The growth of a large business is merely a survival of the fittest," Rockefeller told a Sunday School class. "The American Beauty rose can be produced only by sacrificing the buds that grew up around it. This is not an evil tendency in business. It is merely the working out of a law of nature and a law of

God." But there was more to Rockefeller's defense than social Darwinism. He had been trusted to honor his agreements with banks and railroads, and "Standard Oil," he said, "has no water in its stock, has never issued bonds or stocks through bankers, no underwriting syndicates of selling schemes, keeps 60,000 men employed, pays well, cares for them when sick, pensions them when old, brought a million dollars a week into the country." Finally, Rockefeller refused to attend the debate. "God gave me my money," became his answer to his critics.

The public was not easily appeased by Rockefeller's devotion to philanthropy. Amid general distrust of his motives, his gifts provoked controversy. The most famous brouhaha occurred when Dr. Washington Gladden, moderator of the National Council of Congregationalist Churches, objected strenuously to Rockefeller's contribution of $100,000 in 1905 for grounds, buildings and equipment for Congregationalist foreign missions. Dr. Gladden did not know that this first gift from Rockefeller to a denomination outside his own Baptists had been solicited originally by the Congregational Board of Foreign Missions through Rockefeller's wife, who had been a Congregationalist in her girlhood. The Congregational secretaries had forgotten their appeal and received Rockefeller's check "with surprise." "Tainted money" had been thrust upon the Congregationalists, Dr. Gladden cried, on the grounds that the source of Rockefeller's profit overshadowed the good his philanthropy could do.

Others would solicit Rockefeller's philanthropy, but none would dare express gratitude for it in public. Public esteem for Rockefeller did not rise high enough to mask his sinister reputation and render his philanthropy wholly acceptable until after he had demonstrated for many years that having made all he could he indeed gave away all he could, until the public became satisfied that the scale of his good works matched that of his wealth, and his philanthropy was judged not to be self-interested. This long, halting process involved establishing large philanthropic institutions with conduct of their operations detached from Rockefeller personally and delegated instead to staffs of experts.

The architect of these institutions was Frederick T. Gates, a Baptist minister and fund raiser. Gates was not a simple churchman; he was a capitalist and philanthropist on a grand scale. He could think big—as big as Rockefeller himself—and he saw the philanthropic power inherent in the Rockefeller fortune. Gates gave structure and meaning to Rockefeller's philanthropy. Gates was to the Rockefeller philanthropic institutions what Rockefeller had been to the oil industry: a visionary and an organizational genius. Rockefeller said of him: "Mr. Gates has been the guiding genius in all our giving. . . . He combines business skill and philanthropic aptitude to a higher degree than any other man I have ever known."

Gates and Rockefeller met in the late 1880s, when Gates was head of the American Baptist Education Society and Rockefeller was first considering the location of the great Baptist university he intended to establish. He decided to found the school in Chicago, and Gates was one of the men assigned the task of raising funds and making plans for what was to be the University of Chicago. After a lunch in New York, when the proposed university was discussed, Rockefeller subjected Gates to an aptitude test of sorts: he interviewed Gates on a train ride out to Cleveland and then asked him to inspect an iron mill when he would be in the South and some other Rockefeller property when he would be out

West. Rockefeller wrote about Gates' inspection tour and subsequent report in his memoirs: "I gave him the name and address of property in that region in which I held a minority interest. I felt quite sure that this property was doing well, and it was something of a shock to me to learn through his clear and definite account that it was only a question of time before this enterprise too, which had been represented as rolling in money, would get into trouble." Gates was impressed with his new mentor. Rockefeller was "the greatest man I have met," he told his parents, "the broadest, clearest-headed, most universal in his sympathies, most calmly self-poised, most devoted to what he regards as duty, least influenced by considerations of position, or the authority of advocates of special causes."

Rockefeller eventually launched Gates on his second career —guardian of Rockefeller's investments outside Standard Oil. Gates became president of thirteen of these corporations. He straightened out a mess in the Pacific Northwest, where Rockefeller money was tied up in a land company, a mining company (which Gates proved was almost worthless), a ship-building yard, a paper mill and other enterprises. He developed a timber company and managed to recoup all Rockefeller losses in the region and even make a small profit of several million dollars. According to Rockefeller, Gates "did all the work" on iron-ore interests in Minnesota and on the parallel development of mines, railroads and an ore-bearing fleet. The entire business was later turned over to United States Steel for an estimated $88.5 million.

In March 1891, soon after his philanthropic disbursements had surged over the $1-million mark, Rockefeller launched Gates on his third, and major, career. Rockefeller's reputation for giving away money was a heavy burden. He was hounded by petitioners at his office, his home, his church, on his walks and on the elevated trains he took daily. He was "hunted like a wild animal," according to Gates, by both scoundrels and representatives of legitimate causes. In a typical thirty-day period he received over 50,000 letters of appeal. "I am in trouble, Mr. Gates," Rockefeller said. "The pressure of appeal for gifts has become too great for endurance. I haven't the time or strength, with all my heavy business responsibilities. I am so constituted to be unable to give away money with any satisfaction until I have made the most careful inquiry as to the worthiness of the cause. These investigations are now taking more of my time and energy than the Standard Oil itself." Rockefeller made Gates an offer that he accepted immediately: "I want you to come to New York and open an office here," Rockefeller said. "You can aid me in my benefactions by taking interviews and inquiries and reporting the results for action."

"And so," Gates recalled, "nearly all comers, near or remote, friend or guest, high or low, were blandly sent to my office at Temple Court. I did my best to soothe ruffled feelings, to listen fully to every plea, to weigh fairly the merits of every case." Rockefeller, who ruined his health running Standard Oil (in 1893 he lost his hair as a result of a nervous disease—generalized alopecia), was forced to give up active control of his business before he reached the age of sixty. He turned over direction of his philanthropy to Gates, as well. Rockefeller Junior became the emissary between Gates and Rockefeller Senior. "Gates did the heavy thinking," Rockefeller Junior said of his early years in philanthropy, "and my part was to sell his ideas to Father." "I gradually developed and introduced into all his charities the principle of scientific giving," Gates said of his work for Rockefeller, "and he found himself in no time laying aside retail giving almost wholly, and entering safely and pleasurably into the field of whole-sale philanthropy." Gates scorned "retail business" as giving petty sums; by "wholesale philanthropy" he meant single gifts in the millions.

Based on the combined ideas of Rockefeller Junior and Gates, strict rules for this scientific philanthropy were developed. They provided that money should be given to proven organizations, which should be able to continue their work after gifts have been exhausted or cut off; gifts should be "seed money"—they should stimulate support from other sources and also develop independence in their beneficiaries; money should be given neither to individuals nor to purely local institutions or enterprises, except those that are established as models to other localities; research institutions, which go to the roots of problems, are preferred beneficiaries over those that treat individuals' problems.

In a letter to Rockefeller on June 3, 1905, Gates prescribed how the Rockefeller fortune could provide philanthropy under these rules in perpetuity: "You and your children while living should make final disposition of this great fortune in the form of permanent corporate philanthropies for the good of mankind," Gates wrote, ". . . or at the close of a few lives now in being it must simply pass into the unknown, like some other great fortunes, with unmeasured and perhaps sinister possibilities.

"Any other course than this is morally indefensible," he went on. "If you and Mr. John, Jr., are to discharge this trust while you live there is only one thing possible to be done, and that is to provide legally incorporated endowment funds under competent management . . . which shall be specifically devoted to the promotion of human well-being."

Gates then provided a list of funds to accomplish this purpose: "A great fund for the promotion of higher education in the United States . . . a fund for the promotion of medical research throughout the world . . . a fund for the promotion of the fine arts and the refinement of taste in the United States . . . a fund for the promotion of scientific agriculture and the enrichment of rural life . . . a fund for the promotion of Christian ethics and Christian civilization throughout the world . . . a fund for the promotion of intelligent citizenship and civic virtue in the United States."

In the letter's most important passage Gates spoke about the nature of the funds: "These funds should be so large that to become a trustee of one of them would make a man at once a public character. They should be so large that their administration would be as much a matter of public concern and public inquiry and public criticism as any of the functions of government are now. They should be so large as to attract the attention of the entire world, and to their administration should be addressed both directly and indirectly the highest talent in those particular spheres of every generation through which the funds would go. . . ."

In the early 1900s John D. Rockefeller embarked on just such a program. He established several large philanthropies, beginning with the Rockefeller Institute for Medical Research, whose principal task was to wage war on disease, "the supreme ill of mankind," as Gates put it, "the main source of almost all other ills—poverty, crime, ignorance, vice, inefficiency, hereditary taint, and many other evils." The Institute became an example of "the best philanthropy," which, according to Rockefeller, "involves a search for a cure, an attempt to cure evil at its source." This was followed quickly by the founding of the General Education Board, whose initial purpose was to promote education in the South.

The General Education Board's charter was shepherded through the United States Congress by Senator Winthrop Aldrich of Rhode Island, who was John D. Rockefeller, Jr.'s father-in-law. But continuing with an ambitious program like the one described in Gates' letter, and giving Rockefeller philanthropies "a public character," were not simple matters, for in the years following the muckrakers' attacks on Standard Oil, it became involved in still more controversy. In 1906, Theodore Roosevelt, a constant Rockefeller antagonist, made public a report of the Bureau of Corporations announcing that Standard Oil "has benefited enormously almost up to the present moment by secret rates" obtained from the railroads. More important, a suit was begun in the Federal Circuit Court in Eastern Missouri to dissolve the Standard Oil combination as a conspiracy in restraint of trade. In 1907, seven Federal and six state actions were pending against Standard Oil and its subsidiaries. In deciding one action, Judge Kenisaw Mountain Landis of the Federal Circuit Court in Illinois fined Standard Oil $29,240,000 on 1,462 instances of fixing shipping rates. His ruling was set aside by the Circuit Court of Appeals in Illinois in 1908, but in September of that year William Randolph Hearst made public letters from Standard Oil vice-president John D. Archbold (who ascended to the presidency despite the scandal) to Senator Foraker of Ohio and Mark Hanna, Republican boss of Ohio, directing them to work for antimonopoly legislation. The letters revealed that in the first four months of 1900 Foraker had received $30,000 from

Standard Oil. Several notes referred to the enclosure of $15,-000 certificates of deposit to the Senator. Another letter mentioned that Archbold had sent Foraker $50,000 "in accordance with our understanding." Hearst read from the letters in speeches from coast to coast. He used the material during the next few years to boost circulation in his newspapers. Senators from New York, Pennsylvania, Ohio and Texas were burned and several were driven from office, as were the Governor of Oklahoma and Republican Representative Sibley of Pennsylvania, who had written to Archbold: "Anything you may desire here in my power please advise."

All through this climactic period of attack on Standard Oil, the scope of Rockefeller philanthropy was increasing. In 1905 the General Education Board's original capitalization of $1 million had been raised by $10 million in order that the Board's work be expanded to include support of institutions of higher education, including technical and professional schools, throughout the United States. The first building of the Rockefeller Institute for Medical Research, which had commenced work in the fields of pathology, physiology, pharmacology and biological chemistry in a loft building on Lexington Avenue, had been opened on Manhattan's East Side in 1906. In 1909 the Rockefeller Sanitary Commission had been established and provided with $1 million to undertake the eradication of the Southern hookworm disease as a demonstration project to improve general health in the Southern United States. Around this time, Rockefeller contributions to the University of Chicago totaled more than $30 million.

In 1909 the Federal government scored a success in its legal battles against Standard Oil. The government had asserted that Standard Oil of New Jersey, a holding company controlling sixty-five corporations, operated in violation of the

Sherman Anti-Trust Act by indulging in "rebates, preferences, and other discriminatory practices," thus restraining its
competitors from their right to trade and maintaining a virtual
monopoly over the oil industry. Rockefeller himself had been
summoned to testify; he had claimed in Standard Oil's defense
that the system of rebates had been forced on the combination
by the railroads. On November 20, the Federal Circuit Court
in Eastern Missouri ruled against Standard Oil, finding it a
"combination in restraint of trade." Standard Oil, naturally,
appealed the verdict.

Rockefeller philanthropic disbursements continued to increase. In 1910 the General Education Board, for example,
received a $32-million contribution. But in the midst of the
legal battles against Standard Oil, the Federal government,
fearful of the power inherent in the great Rockefeller fortune
(which was hovering close to the $1-billion mark), scru-
tinized Rockefeller philanthropy for evidence of self-interest.
Thus Rockefeller forces encountered resistance in 1910 when
they attempted to obtain a charter in the Congress for a new
fund, to be capitalized initially at $50 million and called the
Rockefeller Foundation. The procedure was similar to the
chartering of the General Education Board. But now presti-
gious elements within the Federal government opposed granting another Rockefeller fund "a public character."

The Rockefeller forces themselves provided the grounds
for opposition by refusing to define rigidly the purposes of the
new fund. To be sure, the government was to have some control. The bill to charter the fund specified that the Secretary
of the Interior receive annual reports from the fund and its
charter "be subject to alteration, amendment, or repeal at the
pleasure of the Congress." Starr Murphy, a Rockefeller
spokesman at the Senate hearings on the bill, testified that

Rockefeller was "perfectly content to leave this great foundation in the hands of Congress, that it may at any time in the future exercise its protecting power, not merely to protect his wishes, which are solely that this fund shall always be used for the public welfare and for no other purpose, but also that Congress may have the power, if at any time in the future this fund should get into the hands of men who might seek to use it for improper purposes, to exert its authority and bring this fund back again to the use for which it was intended." Murphy declined to provide specifics about what the Foundation intended to do, however, on the grounds that "it is impossible to do so, because to attempt to define would be to impose a limitation, which is exactly what he [Rockefeller] seeks to avoid. . . . He desires . . . to have a charter which will give him that . . . freedom of scope . . . that wherever there arises a human need this board may be in a position to meet it, if that shall seem wise."

Attorney General Wickersham summed up the objection to the bill in a letter to President Taft: "Is it appropriate [he wrote] that, at the moment when the United States through its courts is seeking in a measure to destroy the great combination of wealth that has been built up by Mr. Rockefeller . . . the Congress of the United States should assist in the enactment of a law to create and perpetuate in his name an institution to hold and administer a large portion of this vast wealth? Never has there been submitted to . . . any legislative body such an indefinite scheme for perpetuating vast wealth as this."

The 1910 bill calling for a Congressional charter for the Rockefeller Foundation was withdrawn, but a second bill was introduced in Congress in 1912. Meanwhile, Standard Oil had lost its appeal on the 1909 antitrust ruling. In May 1911, the

United States Supreme Court, by majority verdict, held the combination in violation of the Sherman Anti-Trust Act and ordered it broken up into smaller corporations (which are still the giants in the field—Standard Oil of New Jersey remaining the largest oil corporation in the world: Mobil, formerly Standard Oil of New York, being the third largest; and Standard Oil of California, Standard Oil of Indiana, and Marathon Oil being in the top ten).

The new bill passed the House in 1913, but floundered in the Senate, although Rockefeller forces accepted the following restrictive amendments: the Foundation's total property would be limited to $100 million; income would not be accumulated; the Foundation's property would be distributed, either after fifty years, upon a vote of the trustees, or after a hundred years, at the discretion of Congress; new trustees would be approved by a majority vote among the President of the United States, the Chief Justice, the President of the Senate, the Speaker of the House, plus the presidents of Harvard, Yale, Columbia, Johns Hopkins and the University of Chicago; not more than one-tenth of the Foundation's property could be invested in a single corporation.

Despite these amendments, which granted Congress additional controls over the Foundation, the bill never got out of committee. But Rockefeller spokesmen had made it plain that the Foundation would be set up whether or not Congress chartered it. On May 14, 1913, a charter without any restrictive amendments was secured from the New York State Legislature. The Foundation's broad statement of purpose read: "To promote the well-being of mankind throughout the world."

The Rockefeller Foundation ran into trouble immediately. The situation was a muckraker's dream: Rockefeller Junior, who was working with Gates at the Rockefeller philanthropies in New York, was the absentee owner of 40 percent of the stock of the Colorado Fuel and Iron Company at Ludlow, Colorado. The company's workers and their families lived in company houses—under agreements that leases could be terminated on three days' notice—and shopped in company stores. The company barred union organizers, blacklisted employees suspected of union activity and supervised their schools and churches.

In September 1913, thousands of workers struck for higher pay, shorter hours, better working conditions, safety precautions and the right to organize. The strike lasted until December of the following year. Strikers were attacked by armed company guards in the fall of 1913. Men were shot, clubbed, jailed and deported from the state. The next spring, the state militia, sent by the Governor upon demand of the company, invaded a strikers' camp and burned shacks and tents. Women and children were killed in what became known as the Ludlow Massacre.

Throughout the bloody strike, Rockefeller Junior refused to go out to Ludlow. His letters to the company's managers, made public later by a Congressional commission, revealed his full backing for an uncompromising position. "We feel," he wrote, after the massacre, "that what you have done is right and fair and that the position which you have taken in regard to the unionizing of the mines is in the interest of the employees of the company. . . . Whatever the outcome may be, we will stand by you to the end." His defense of his inaction was based on his assertion that he was ignorant of labor conditions at the company.

This did not end with Rockefeller Junior's indiscretions,

however. After the president of Colorado College and the dean of the College of Liberal Arts at the University of Denver had obtained signatures on a "public manifesto" demanding that the strikers return to work and charging them with provoking violence and acting in bad faith, the schools each received unrestricted grants of $100,000 from the Rockefeller Foundation and the General Education Board. The Foundation also financed Canadian Mackenzie King's widely publicized study of labor relations in the United States, even though a Congressional commission headed by Frank Walsh of Missouri inquiring into the Ludlow affair was at work at the same time. Walsh accused the Rockefellers of trying to supersede his inquiry and using money designated for philanthropic purposes to perpetuate nineteenth-century labor practices. The commission recommended that the Foundation be dissolved and its money, accumulated "by means of economic pressure, violation of law, cunning, violence practiced over a series of years by the founder . . . and his business associates" be disbursed to relieve unemployment and prevent sickness and industrial accidents.

This recommendation was not implemented, of course. The Foundation and the other funds established by Rockefeller Senior and Gates survived the attacks on Rockefeller and Standard Oil and the stain of the Ludlow Massacre.

By 1913-14 there had been two major Rockefeller periods. The first, which had lasted roughly from 1870 to 1890, had been marked by the formation of the Standard Oil monopoly, the founding of the great Rockefeller fortune and philanthropic giving that Gates had defined as "retail business." The second had been the Rockefeller Senior-Gates period of "wholesale philanthropy," when a series of great philanthropic institutions, whose initial work was in medical science, public and higher education, and public health, had been founded; the period had been marked also by the climax of the attacks on Rockefeller Senior and Standard Oil.

During the next period—the third—which extended from World War I to the mid-1930s, a combination of agents assembled. The Rockefeller Institute for Medical Research, the General Education Board and the Rockefeller Foundation (which soon absorbed the Rockefeller Sanitary Commission) became great funds like those Gates had envisioned. While the Rockefellers and their philanthropic institutions continued to hold controlling blocks of stock in Standard Oil,* it

* Shortly before World War II, the Senate Temporary National Economic Committee (TNEC), which had subpoena powers, looked into the distribution of ownership of shares in major nonfinancial companies as of 1937-39. According to the study, around the end of 1937 Rockefeller holdings in the Standard Oil companies were:

	Percentage of shares held by the Rockefellers personally	Percentage of shares held by the Rockefeller Institute, the General Education Board and the Rockefeller Foundation	Totals
Atlantic Refining	1.16	—	1.16
Consolidated Oil	5.71	—	5.71
Continental Oil	—	0.84	0.84
Ohio Oil (now Marathon Oil)	9.83	9.69	19.52
Socony-Vacuum Oil (now Mobil Oil)	16.34	—	16.34
Standard Oil of California	11.86	0.46	12.32
Standard Oil (Indiana)	7.83	3.53	11.36
Standard Oil (New Jersey)	8.69	4.82	13.51

It should be noted that with Standard Oil of Indiana ownership of stock in Standard Oil of New Jersey, the Rockefellers' personal voting soon began to fade as the trademark of Rockefeller financial power. (The new trademarks would be Rockefeller Center, the grand midtown-Manhattan commercial and cultural complex which Rockefeller Junior began to construct at the beginning of the Great Depression; and the Chase National Bank, now the Chase Manhattan Bank, which the Rockefellers have controlled since 1930.*) Rockefeller Senior had long since retired from Standard Oil; Rockefeller Junior had resigned as a director in 1910. Then Rockefeller Senior even retired from philanthropy. Among his institutions, he was a trustee of only the Rockefeller Foundation and never attended a board meeting. Gates and Rockefeller Junior pre-

---

power in the latter company—in assets the largest industrial enterprise in the world—was actually 15.38 percent, enough to give them practical control.

The current overall extent of Rockefeller holdings in the Standard Oil companies is not known, except for the philanthropic institutions, which now hold much lower percentages of Standard Oil shares than in 1937. The Securities and Exchange Commission does not require publication of personal holdings of less than 10 percent in a company (unless the shares are held by an officer of the company). Of course, Rockefeller personal holdings in any company can be split up so as to hide the extent of Rockefeller ownership.

* The current overall extent of Rockefeller holdings in Standard Oil companies is smaller now. For example, members of the Rockefeller family own 1.02 per cent of Exxon; 2.01 per cent of Standard Oil of California; and 1.74 per cent of Mobil. Similarly, the oil stock holdings of the Rockefeller philanthropic institutions have been reduced. But control of industrial corporations is thought to be indirect today— through controlling interests held by money-lending institutions such as banks and insurance companies.

sided over the growth of the Foundation and the Rockefeller Institute for Medical Research. Gates was chairman of the board of the Foundation until 1917 and of the Institute until 1928. Rockefeller Junior was president of the Foundation until 1917, then succeeded Gates in both chairmanships.

In the first decade or so after 1914 this fortuitous and powerful combination worked great changes on the Rockefeller family's public image. The philanthropies were the most important agents of the transformation. A considerable portion of the family's fortune was being disbursed through these highly visible institutions. With their growing records of good works* the family's public esteem rose from the low level that had persisted throughout the early years of the twentieth century to a level high enough to mask the sinister aspects of the reputations of Rockefeller Senior and Standard Oil and to bleach the stains of the Ludlow Massacre.

With a positive image, the Rockefeller family now had a name that was as much an attraction as it had been formerly an object of hatred. As a result, Rockefeller beneficences could be accepted now with open gratitude. The consequences were enormous, for this improved reputation granted the family new powers.

The Rockefellers—that is, Rockefeller Junior; his wife,

---

* Under the guidance of the General Education Board, 1,600 public high schools were established in the South by 1922. The Rockefeller Foundation eradicated hookworm disease in the South; established the nation's first schools of public health and hygiene at Johns Hopkins and Harvard, contributed to county health budgets in rural areas and was an active partner in the establishment of the first full-time county health officer system; and became the first world health organization, conducting surveys and disease-control programs in a battle against malaria and yellow fever in tropical regions overseas.

Abby Aldrich Rockefeller; and their children—could not have assumed new burdens on the basis of the family fortune alone. Public esteem, earned by Rockefeller philanthropy, was required; without it, the Rockefellers could not have become the great public benefactors they are. If John D. Rockefeller's intention had been to establish his monumental philanthropic institutions not only to discharge a deeply felt philanthropic responsibility, but also to earn public esteem for his family, esteem that could be converted to power, he had done a magnificent job. For such was the impact of his philanthropy that within a couple of decades his family had passed from an era of controversy over its motives for giving to the beginning of an era when it would enjoy power in an ever-expanding range of activities. The equation was: Profit times Philanthropy equals Power.

The third Rockefeller period, which lasted from 1915 to the mid-1930s, was Rockefeller Junior's. Now middle-aged, he became the major family figure. Throughout these years, except for building Rockefeller Center, he devoted himself almost exclusively to philanthropy. In large part, two circumstances of birth were the mainsprings for his vocation. For one thing, as he put it himself, "I was born into money. It was there like air or food or any other element." For another thing, he was born into religion. His family was immersed in it. His father had given so much money, time and labor to his Baptist church as a teen-ager in Cleveland in the late 1850s, that he was elected one of its five trustees as soon as he reached his twenty-first birthday. Years later, the Rockefeller family's home on West Fifty-fourth Street in Manhattan was the scene of temperance lectures and prayer meetings. Ministers, missionaries and charity workers were constant visitors. Mrs. Rockefeller worked with boys from the Fifth Avenue Baptist Church. Alta, their daughter, managed the church sewing school and taught boys' Sunday school. Rockefeller Junior taught the men's Bible class for eight years around 1900. "I got a great deal out of the experience," he told Raymond B. Fosdick, his biographer. "We talked about very concrete things; for example, 'Is a lie ever justified?' We tried to find out what we ought to do in the presence of certain types of very practical problems. . . . All I could do was find out how individuals in the Bible had dealt with the problems that we faced and pass on to the members of the class such information as I could obtain by study."

Religious work was a major outlet for Rockefeller Junior's philanthropic responsibility. In the third Rockefeller period, with his family's public esteem moving upward, he was able to devote himself to it and related passions without restraint. No one would object to his wishes on the grounds they reflected self-interested motives; whatever he did was held to be in the spirit of philanthropy. Thus he need place few limits on his contributions to the spiritual needs of the members of the church where he worshiped. In 1925 he invited Dr. Harry Emerson Fosdick to become pastor of the new Park Avenue Baptist Church. But Dr. Fosdick replied that he could not accept the invitation, for although associate membership in the Park Avenue church was granted to unimmersed Christians, baptism by immersion was required for full membership, and he was unwilling to conduct a pastorship under such a condition. Furthermore, because the congregation numbered only 800 people and the church was located in one of New York's poshest residential neighborhoods, Dr. Fosdick believed that

if he presided there he "would be justifiably accused of sur-
rendering a real opportunity for public influence to become
private chaplain to a small group of financially privileged people." Rockefeller Junior's immediate reply to these objections
was to offer a new church on a new site, uptown on Morningside Heights, overlooking the Hudson. Membership would be
open to the entire Protestant community. Dr. Fosdick found
the proposal incredible, for the Park Avenue church had been
only recently built. He was still reluctant to accept, as he told
Rockefeller Junior, because "I do not want to be known as
the pastor to the richest man in the country." Rockefeller
Junior parried this comment: "I like your frankness," he told
Dr. Fosdick, "but do you think that more people will criticize
you on account of my wealth than will criticize me on account
of your theology?" Later, to Dr. Fosdick's "immense surprise," the Park Avenue congregation, under Rockefeller
Junior's leadership, "met all the conditions so unanimously
that it opened a door I could not refuse to enter." This door
led to the building of the nondenominational Riverside
Church, with Rockefeller Junior the major contributor.

His concern for the spiritual needs of his fellow man extended far beyond the needs of the membership of his local
churches. After World War I he offered personal and financial support to the Interchurch World Movement, a campaign
of the evangelical churches of North America "to Christian-
ize the world" with a series of worldwide surveys of missionary enterprises, a publicity campaign, which was to include
a month-long "Christian Pageant" at Madison Square Garden,
and a financial campaign, whose projected figure came to
$336,777,572. In the words of Raymond B. Fosdick, the move-
ment was a twentieth-century crusade. Dr. Earl S. Taylor,

who became its head, was uncompromising in estimating the hardships and dedication its workers had to look forward to: "It is going to cost life somewhere. It is going to take life blood to put this thing through and the men are not going in lightly at all. I do not find anybody that has any preconceived ideas as to *how* it ought to be done. We find deep conviction that it *ought* to be done." John R. Mott, a worker in numerous ecumenical organizations, spoke of the magnitude of the undertaking: "We shall shake the United States of America to a degree that has never before been done in any piece of planning which has been conceived; but it means not only that, but we shall bring within our view, within our surveys, within our intensive studies, the entire inhabited earth. We are summoned to nothing less than this large plan. . . ." Woodrow Wilson supported the effort, saying that "once more in the providence of God America has opportunity to show the world that she was born to serve mankind."

Fosdick wrote that Rockefeller Junior saw in the movement "the culmination of all his earlier ideals and beliefs in interdenominational cooperation . . . [and he] threw himself into its activities with fervor and earnestness." He was elected to the movement's executive committee and made public speeches in New York, Rochester, Pittsburgh and Chicago. In April 1920, he began a fourteen-day tour of fifteen cities with several other leaders of the movement.

The Interchurch World Movement was a failure. It ran up a deficit of $7.5 million, despite contributions of more than $1¼ million from the Rockefeller family. The movement was criticized for its "conversion of the Christian spirit to the materialistic methods of modern business and advertising." But Rockefeller Junior had become interested in the stud-

ies—concerned not only with churches but also with the relationship of religion to economic, educational and racial factors
—that had been undertaken, and he supported their completion
over the period of a dozen years under a new organization, the
Institute of Social and Religious Research. Late in 1930 the
Institute of Social and Religious Research dispatched a corps
of "fault-finders" to study the missions of seven denomina-
tions. In September 1931, a Commission of Appraisal, a large
bundle of data in hand, set out on a year's tour of missions in
the Orient. The result was a controversial book, *Re-Thinking
Missions*, which was published in the fall of 1932. The book
stressed people-to-people contact and a sort of Peace Corps
approach to missionary work, whereby a deeper appreciation
of alien cultures and a turning away from evangelistic preach-
ing to such activities as education, medicine and agriculture
were recommended. Many churchmen rejected the commission's recommendations and it did not effect large-scale
revisions in missionary policy, but Rockefeller Junior enthusiastically approved.

In addition to his ecumenism and his approval of an enlightened approach to religious missionary work, however, Rockefeller Junior was a moralistic crusader. Throughout his life he
was devoted to liquor prohibition, a family cause since the
middle of the nineteenth century, when his maternal grand-
parents, the Harvey Buel Spelmans, worked and prayed in
Cleveland and Brooklyn for strict abolition. According to
Raymond B. Fosdick, Grandmother Spelman "encouraged
John in his interest in temperance: 'I am glad that you are
interested in the children's temperance meetings. I hope I shall
sometime hear you speak "The Price of a Drink." ' " By the
time he was ten years old, John had signed a pledge to abstain

from "tobacco, profanity and the drinking of any intoxicating beverages." He and his sisters became members of the Loyal Legion Temperance Society in New York. They attended temperance lectures and got people to sign pledges. A couple of decades later, when Rockefeller Junior was in his late twenties, he was "disgusted" when a female friend attending his sister Alta's wedding refused to sign a pledge.

The Rockefellers directed their anti-liquor campaign toward securing the Constitutional amendment prohibiting the manufacture and sale of liquor. In 1883 Rockefeller Senior served on an advisory committee in Cleveland organized for an attempt to pass such an amendment. From 1900 to 1919, according to Rockefeller Junior's own account, the family contributed $350,323.67 to the Anti-Saloon League, $85,000 of which was spent in 1918 during the final battle for the amendment. (Rockefeller Junior justified the contributions to the League on the grounds that its "aim is for the benefit of the nation." He announced that "it is a matter of conviction to me that any problem confronting the country can best be solved by earnest, sober men and women. Therefore, any movement that contributes to a better degree of self-control on the part of the people as a whole challenges my attention and makes a strong appeal for my support." But by 1926 the militant League became a liability to the Rockefellers' image, and they transferred their financial support for prohibition to the more proper National Citizens Union of a Thousand on Law Enforcement.)

The Eighteenth Amendment was ratified on January 16, 1919. Afterwards, Rockefeller Junior allowed a letter to be given to the press. "I take this occasion to express my feeling of the vital importance of law observance and law enforcement as essential to the permeance of our free institutions. The question of the wisdom and propriety of National prohibition is no longer at issue, having been decided by the adoption of the Federal constitutional amendment and sustained by the United States Supreme Court. It is now the law of the land, predicated upon a constitutional amendment, which is the most solemn form of legislation possible under our form of government. To fail in the observance of such a law strikes at the very foundations of orderly government, and is in that way an attack upon civil liberty, for in a republic there can be no freedom for the individual if there is no respect for an enforcement of the laws which have been enacted in the manner prescribed by the people themselves in the constitution which they have adopted."

But while some people considered Prohibition—which went into effect on January 16, 1920—a wise and proper law, others held it to be an infringement of their private rights. Masses of people violated the law, and it was a failure. Rockefeller Junior took action to disavow it. In June 1932, he issued a letter announcing his support for repeal of the Prohibition amendment. "When the Eighteenth Amendment was passed I earnestly hoped—with a host of advocates of temperance—that it would be generally supported by public opinion and thus the day be hastened when the value to society of men with minds and bodies free from the undermining effects of alcohol would be generally realized. That this has not been the result, but rather that drinking generally has increased; that the speakeasy has replaced the saloon, not only unit for unit, but probably twofold if not threefold; that a vast army of lawbreakers has been recruited and financed on a colossal scale; that many of our best citizens, *piqued* [emphasis added] at what they regarded as an infringement of their private rights, have openly and unabashedly disregarded the Eighteenth Amendment; that as an inevitable result respect for all law has been greatly lessened; that crime has increased to an unprecedented degree—I have slowly and reluctantly come to believe."

While the "noble experiment" had failed, the crusade had to go on. Rockefeller Junior commissioned a worldwide study on methods of liquor control. In the introduction to the report, "Toward Liquor Control," published in the fall of 1933, he wrote: "It is my earnest conviction that total abstinence is the wisest, best, and safest position for both the individual and society. But the regrettable failure of the Eighteenth Amendment has demonstrated the fact that the majority of the people of this country are not yet ready for total abstinence, at least when it is attempted through legal coercion. The next best thing—many people think it is a better thing—is temperance. Therefore, as I sought to support total abstinence when its achievement seemed possible, so now, with equal vigor, I would support temperance. . . . To develop the habit of temperance in individuals, to take up again the slow march of education—this is the real and fundamental approach to the problem of alcohol."

Rockefeller Junior never abandoned the anti-liquor crusade. At the age of eighty he lectured a club at Seal Harbor, Maine. "For some twenty years [he wrote] I ran it myself, giving earnest attention to every detail. . . . One of the important reasons why it has been such a unique and attractive family center for parents and children alike is because never has liquor in any form been provided at the club, nor has its use by those who may have wanted to bring it in been permitted. Being now the sole owner of the club . . . I may say to you quite frankly that if there is any deviation from this policy, the lease which has run on from year to year will automatically terminate."

Rockefeller Junior's anti-liquor crusade can not be relegated to a bygone, less complicated era. It was more than simply the reaction of a moralist to a situation he found personally repugnant. His persistent willingness to use his considerable power to advance his crusade was a manifestation of a deeply felt responsibility for the well-being of his fellow man. Discharging this responsibility was so important that he condoned the infringement of private rights. He felt it so deeply that he asserted a belief that he knew better than other people how they should conduct their lives; he felt justified in using his wealth in an effort to control them.

ii   The Cornerstone of
a New Garden of Eden:
Rockefeller Center

Since World War I there have been two major Rockefeller periods—the third, when Rockefeller Junior was the dominant family figure, and, beginning in the mid-1930s and lasting through this writing, the fourth, when his sons, the Rockefeller brothers (John D. 3rd, born in 1906; Nelson, 1908; Laurance, 1910; Winthrop, 1912; and David, 1915), became dominant. During the third period, Rockefeller Junior and his wife, Abby Aldrich, extended the family's interests beyond religious work and the initial activities of the Rockefeller Senior-Gates philanthropic institutions. Through their efforts, the Rockefeller name became associated with conservation, the arts and monumental construction projects. Rockefeller Junior contributed to the establishment and maintenance of National Parks from Maine to California; in addition, he donated land tracts for parks in Cleveland and New York City. In 1925 he supplied the Metropolitan Museum of Art in New York with a collection of medieval art objects; several years later, in order to display the collection and related objects properly, he undertook construction of the branch of the Metropolitan known as the Cloisters. In 1927 he began the restoration of Colonial Williamsburg, one of several restorations he financed in the United States and Europe. Late in 1928 he undertook construction of his most ambitious project, Rockefeller Center. In the spring of 1929 Abby Aldrich Rockefeller, a collector of both modern art and American folk art, founded (as the leader of a group of her friends) the Museum of Modern Art. Within these projects were the seeds of major commitments that the Rockefeller brothers would attempt to fulfill during the fourth period. With the construction of Rockefeller Center, the Rockefellers entered into a commitment to construct colossal public projects. With the founding of the Museum of Modern Art, they entered into a commitment to refining the public's taste in art, architecture and applied design. With their contributions to the National Park system they entered into a commitment to conserve and develop our natural resources. These commitments complement the philanthropic vision Gates set forth in his famous letter to Rockefeller Senior in 1905. In the late 1920s and early 1930s the Rockefeller family, informed by its powerful philanthropic responsibility, became committed to the creation of a new Garden of Eden.

Rockefeller Center was the first in a lengthening series of construction projects undertaken by the Rockefellers. After it came Morningside Gardens, a middle-income housing complex, begun in 1949 under David Rockefeller's leadership; Lincoln Center for the Performing Arts, begun in 1955 under John D. Rockefeller 3rd's leadership; the Chase Manhattan Bank and Plaza and the redevelopment of the entire financial district in Lower Manhattan, begun in the mid-1950s under David Rockefeller's leadership; resort hotels in Wyoming, the U.S. Virgin Islands, Puerto Rico, Hawaii, Vermont, etc., begun in the mid-1950s by Laurance Rockefeller; the Albany South Mall, begun in the late 1950s by Nelson Rockefeller upon his election as Governor of New York; the development of entirely new cities and towns, begun in the late 1960s by Nelson Rockefeller in New York State and throughout the United States by David Rockefeller.

Rockefeller construction projects reflect in a basic way the commitment to create a new Garden of Eden. For by undertaking them, the Rockefellers meant, among other things, to clean up around themselves. The Albany South Mall, for instance, replaced a slum that lay between the Capitol and the governor's mansion. With the redevelopment of Lower Manhattan, the district around the Chase Manhattan Bank and Plaza is meant to be rehabilitated. Lincoln Center replaced a slum on Manhattan's West Side, not far from Rockefeller properties in midtown. Morningside Gardens replaced another slum, this one in the shadow of four Rockefeller-endowed institutions in the Morningside Heights area of Manhattan—International House, Riverside Church, the Interchurch Center, and the Union Theological Seminary. One is not meant to look out over decaying territory from a Rockefeller-endowed institution. The Rockefellers will not be charged with enriching or beautifying an island in a sea of trouble.

The Rockefellers entered into this aspect of their Garden-of-Eden commitment with Rockefeller Center. It occupies land first developed by Dr. David Hosack, professor of botany and *materia medica* at Columbia College and a founder of the College of Physicians and Surgeons. In the early 1800s he bought twenty acres three miles north of what were then the city limits for $5,000. There he spent some $100,000 to construct the Elgin Botanical Gardens, a teaching aid and tourist attraction, with over 2,000 different plants and a small pasture. When he could no longer meet the expenses for maintenance of his project he petitioned New York State to buy the property. Appraisers for the Legislature fixed the price at $74,-268.75. The act authorizing the purchase specified that no public funds were to be spent on maintenance and that doctors and students were to have free access. The College of Physicians and Surgeons was appointed manager of the lands and leased them to one of the gardeners, but the place fell into disrepair when he devoted himself to raising marketable produce.

Columbia College, located downtown on Park Place, had been petitioning the Legislature for financial aid. In 1814 New York State gave Columbia Hosack's lands on condition that the college must move there within twelve years and must furnish exotic plants to other colleges. Columbia was released from these obligations in 1819, and all remaining plants were given to hospitals. A paying tenant was found in 1823, but after a decade farming the property was abandoned. In 1850 Columbia's trustees decided to subdivide the property in separate lots for one-family houses to be constructed in a specified style and size.

Columbia's property was bounded on the east by Fifth Avenue, which was the only road leading north from the main portion of the city. After Central Park was completed in 1876 the avenue entered into its glorious years. It became the route for most of New York's great parades. At the turn of the century hotels were built along it; department stores and specialty shops began to leave Broadway and Sixth Avenue to settle on it.

The value of Columbia's land increased dramatically. Valued at $7,500 in 1819, $550,000 in 1856 and $7 million in the 1880s, it was estimated to be worth more than $62 million in the 1920s. But the land was essentially underdeveloped. While rents on the rest of Fifth Avenue climbed by as much as 600 percent between 1900 and 1920, Columbia's rents remained at disappointingly low levels. The institution netted only about $300,000 a year from 199 lots. Leases that had been renewed during the depression year of 1907 were not due to expire until 1928 to 1931.

In the latter 1800s Rockefeller Senior had moved his family into a home with garden and stables at 4 West Fifty-fourth Street, just off Fifth Avenue. Some years later, during National Prohibition, when Rockefeller Junior and *his* family lived at 10 West Fifty-fourth, the homes on Columbia's property, three blocks to the south, were turned into speakeasies and brothels. So both Columbia and the Rockefellers became anxious to find a more suitable use for this property, Columbia in order to realize greater profits, the Rockefellers in order to clean out a nest of vice in what was virtually their own back yard.

In the late 1920s the Metropolitan Opera Company, which had been looking for a site for a new opera house for many years, became interested in Columbia's property. The Met's architect, Benjamin Wistar Morris, proposed that the new house be combined with an office building, its income to defray the company's production expenses, and that this complex be set off by a luxurious plaza. But the first available sites had been too far removed from the fashionable areas where the opera's patrons resided. These sites had been too small, furthermore; an office building large enough to support a grandiose opera house and a plaza would have dominated them. Columbia's property offered the solution. Its midtown location was ideal. The tract was huge, taking up three full blocks, bounded by Forty-eighth and Fifty-first Streets on the south and north and by Fifth and Sixth Avenues on the east and west.

The size of this tract enabled Morris to devise a more grandiose plan. The opera house was to be positioned on a broad open plaza with a monumental arcade forming the approach from Fifth Avenue. Seven office buildings, three of them skyscrapers, would flank the house and plaza on the north and south, the lower buildings forming a buffer between the skyscrapers and the opera complex. The office buildings would be connected one story above street level by broad promenades lined with shops. The land assigned to the opera house and plaza was priced by Columbia at $6 million; the cost of constructing the house was set at $8.5 million. Real estate experts considered the Met's plan financially sound.

Rockefeller Junior became involved in the plan during the ensuing fund-raising campaign. In December 1928, he formed the Madison Square Corporation, which was to develop Columbia's property for the opera house; theaters for music, drama, variety, comedy and movies; shops, luxury hotels, department stores and offices; and landscaped plazas and promenades. A lease was signed in 1929. The agreement specified that Rockefeller Junior had an option to buy a 500-foot-wide strip of land on the western boundary of the property, from Forty-ninth Street to Fiftieth, for $6 million.

The Met would use the proceeds from the sale of its old house to build a new house on a portion of the land Rockefeller would purchase from Columbia. Boxholders would pay

him ground rent of $3.6 million. He would use the rest of the
land for a plaza which he would present as a gift to the city.
The land he had leased from Columbia he would in turn lease
to other parties to erect hotels, department stores, etc., in conformity with Madison Square Corporation's design concept.

The Met was asking $13 million for the old opera house,
although current opinion held that $8 million was the most
the sale could realize. Then on October 29, 1929, the market
crashed and the Met despaired of finding a buyer for the old
house at a workable price. When Rockefeller refused the
Met's plea that he sublet his site rather than sell it—on the
grounds that he did not wish to support the opera company
financially—the Met quit his project.

The Met was out, and so was everybody else. For who but
a Rockefeller could dare embark on new building projects
during the early years of the Great Depression? Rockefeller
Junior had to proceed alone. He had to construct enough rentable space to cover the costs of the leases he held. He could not
scrimp on the project, despite the fact of a depression; only
a commercial and entertainment complex magnificent enough
to lure the best tenants would save his investment. But he
would go beyond that: He would construct a monument to
catch the eye of the world.

Rockefeller took out a mortgage of $45 million at 5 per-
cent interest from the Metropolitan Life Insurance Company
and put up the rest of the estimated $125 million construction
cost himself. He spent more than $5 million for land on Sixth
Avenue that Columbia had sold in the past. Buying up leases
on Columbia's property required more than $6 million. (Some
leaseholders doubled their prices, and not everyone sold out,
at that. Some old-timers refused to depart their quarters and

were allowed to remain until they died. Others set prices that were too high, so several old buildings remain amid the new.)

The Rockefellers became determined to build a cultural center, with or without the Metropolitan as principal tenant. Word reached the Radio Corporation of America, the young giant of the communications industry. RCA was then housed in a new building on Lexington Avenue at Fifty-first Street, only three blocks away from the northeast corner of the Rockefeller Center land. Rockefeller offered RCA enough space for a radio metropolis that would include business offices, radio broadcasting studios, television studios, and at least two, and possibly as many as four, theaters suitable for variety shows and movies. On June 4, 1930, RCA signed an agreement which called for the rental of four theaters (two of which might be dropped) and space for its other activities in two office buildings for $4,250,000 per year. RCA was also given the right to name its portion of the Rockefeller project. The name "Radio City" was chosen.

Rockefeller Center had its principal tenant and was on the road to financial success. But the road was rocky, for in the 1930s New York did not *need* the Center. At the start of the Great Depression, commercial building in New York was in a queer position. Paradoxically, as rents declined the number of buildings increased. Construction had developed so much momentum that for four years after the stock market crash, buildings continued to be thrown up in the Grand Central Station zone, the heart of midtown Manhattan. Financing had been completed and contracts let, so nothing could be done about halting skyscraper construction.

In 1930, seventeen new office buildings with 6,299,000 square feet of rentable space were added to the city. In 1931 twenty-five buildings with 7,630,000 square feet were opened. There were 1,966,000 square feet in the Empire State Building alone. It was known as the Empty State Building; despite having Alfred E. Smith as its president (at $65,000 a year) it was one-third empty for years. The millions paid by sightseers who rode to the top of the building, where King Kong had carried Fay Wray and battled against the air force, saved it from financial ruin. In 1932 only 995,000 square feet were added to the city's office-building-rental rolls. But in 1933 Rockefeller Center weighed in with 2,285,000 square feet, bringing the dread total for the first four years of the Depression to seventeen million, slightly less than a third of the total of choice office space available in all of Manhattan.

Businesses either cut back on space or moved out altogether. In those days you could walk through empty corridors and find no or possibly one or two tenants per floor. In the Grand Central and Wall Street zones rents fell from a $7.50-per-square-foot top in 1929 to $3.75 four years later, when Rockefeller Center went into business. Buildings were torn down in order to permit their owners to avoid income and inheritance taxes based on pre-Depression assessments. (Buildings were taxed then based on what they had cost, not what they could be sold for; now they are taxed based on their market values.) The rush of elderly people to unload their real estate holdings depressed prices at a quickening pace. Estates were forced to sell their properties to more affluent investors at small fractions of what they had cost. The Ritz Carlton Hotel, for example, had cost at least $25 million; it was bought for $750,000 with $100,000 worth of liquor in it. Buildings thrown up by speculators who were mortgaged beyond their capabilities to ride out the Depression were taken over by court-appointed receivers who were accountable only for real estate taxes and employee payrolls. Since operating costs were cut sharply, rents could be cut as well. In order to maintain fees for himself, a receiver would set rents at an absolute minimum, thereby preventing profits from rising high enough to enable a building to recover and be brought out of receivership. This unfair competition ruined buildings held by more conservative mortgagers; these buildings soon would be in receivership, as well. In order to survive, landlords engaged in body-snatching, a practice that ruined entire districts surrounding their buildings. A landlord would convince a company to abandon its quarters in another building for space in his property at a lower rent. He would then take over his new tenant's former lease and rent out the space for less than the lease called for. Other tenants would get wind of the lower rent and demand their rents be similarly reduced. Thus rental income on an entire building would be depressed. Estimates at the time held that displacing 50,000 square feet would depress rents for one million square feet in the same district.

In 1934 the Rockefellers were accused of such tactics. August Heckscher, a leading real estate tycoon and philanthropist, sued them for $10 million in damages on six counts. He alleged that they used coercion, threats, agreements, promises or other inducements to lure away his tenants; paid money "or other valuable things" to cause desertions; assumed leases or made credits; quoted prices less than adequate to cover the payment of taxes, interest and operating costs on their property; offered space in *his* buildings, taken over on assumed leases at prices inadequate to cover taxes, interest and operating costs on these buildings; and were just plain unfair in weaning away his tenants. In addition, the suit attacked the bonded warehouse privilege on imported goods that the Rockefellers had obtained by special act of Congress. Heckscher charged that whereas the act was intended to cover the free importation of foreign goods for the sole purpose of exhibiting them to the general public, the privilege was advertised as a vehicle for allowing "far-flung merchandising" without the need for capital to cover payment of import duties. Importing firms were thereby enticed into Rockefeller Center's British and French Buildings. The suit named as defendants Rockefeller Junior; his brother-in-law, Winthrop W. Aldrich, head of the Chase National Bank; various Rockefeller associates; companies interested in Rockefeller Center; and Nelson Rockefeller, who ran a company engaged in renting space in the Center.

The Rockefellers held that their practices were the norm in New York real estate. They remained cool under fire. An executive from Rockefeller Center told an interviewer from *Business Week* that he wasn't worried about the Heckscher suit. "It's good advertising," he said. "We haven't been on the first page of the papers since that row over Diego Rivera's murals." The Rockefellers denied that they used improper methods to lure tenants into their development. The Heckscher case against them was dropped before it came to trial.

Bruce Bliven summed up the Great Depression case against Rockefeller Center in the pages of *The New Republic:* "We are confident [he wrote] that the desire to make money did not lie behind the creation of Radio City. John D. Rockefeller, Jr., wanted to leave behind him a monument; he thought of himself as a modern member of the Medici, and there is no doubt that among his chief impulses was the wish to do something for New York. And hasn't he just! It would be unfair to say that he sent into bankruptcy most office buildings within half a mile in every direction, for probably most of them would have gone bankrupt. . . .

"It hardly needs to be pointed out that Radio City is typical not only of the anarchy of modern capitalist society, but of America in particular. Capitalism exists elsewhere, but there is not a city in Europe where Mr. Rockefeller would be permitted to build his monument, nor would have, anytime this past fifty years. If I am right in believing that in the future the world will not allow the creation of such vast fortunes as Rockefeller Senior accumulated, and that it certainly will not tolerate such a piece of gargantuan exhibitionism as Radio City, then perhaps it is just as well to have one such monument to the follies of a past age, as a reminder and warning. . . . At least, for a few years."

During the 1930s Rockefeller Center ran deficits of about $4 million a year. It began to operate in the black in the 1940s, but its financial position was still not secure after World War II, when it was only 60 percent rented, according to developer William Zeckendorf. In his autobiography he mused about Rockefeller Junior's motives in purchasing and donating to the United Nations seventeen acres Zeckendorf controlled along the eastern boundary of midtown Manhattan. He claimed that the $8.5-million purchase deterred him from building his "X City," a commercial development that would have threatened the economic health of Rockefeller Center. ("X City" would have extended seven blocks north from Forty-second Street and two blocks west from the East River. Four large office buildings, an airlines terminal, a major modern hotel, a residential community and a new home for the Met were envisioned for it. Zeckendorf began serious negotiations to line up tenants with the Mutual Benefit Life Insurance Company of New York; Time, Inc.; and the Aluminum Corporation of America.)

By 1947 Rockefeller Center's federal income taxes were substantial, and in the next few years gross income climbed to $20 million a year. By the early 1950s 1,100 tenants occupied the Center's current collection of buildings, and there was a waiting list of 1,500 firms wanting space. The average rent had gone up to $4.50 a square foot. By the mid-1960s, after Rockefeller Center had pushed beyond the boundaries of Columbia's lands, there were 9,600,000 square feet rented, the assessed real estate valuation of Radio City alone was $245,-600,000, and the Center was still growing.

The Rockefellers had not intended to run their gigantic development at a loss and they took every precaution to prevent that. Operations that could not pay their own way were dropped. Ralph Hancock, an authority on gardening who installed all the Rockefeller Center gardens, attempted to run a Horticultural Hall on the tenth floor of the RCA Building, in conjunction with a three-quarter-acre Garden of Nations. He rented space in the hall and charged admission to the garden, but when the enterprise did not prosper financially it was terminated.

Rockefeller Center was not constructed to provide the Rockefellers their livelihood, however. It was constructed to illustrate the family's ability to marshal great energies and powerful forces. It says: "See what the Rockefellers can do." When we enter it we encounter Rockefeller power. We Americans cultivate bigness. We are meant to be astounded by the size of the Center and its statistics—the number of windows, doors, locks and telephones; the length of the elevator shafts; the size of the maintenance staff and the quantities of cleaning supplies consumed; the quantities of building supplies used to make this city within a city.

We are meant to enter a part of the new Garden of Eden here. There are art works and decorations to marvel at: the eighteen-foot gilded bronze statue of Prometheus at the skating rink; the bronze Atlas on Fifth Avenue; the sculptures and bas reliefs over the entrances to the buildings; the murals; the floral displays in the channel leading from Fifth Avenue to the skating rink; the Christmas tree and other seasonal decorations; the rooftop gardens.

We are meant to demand that the Rockefellers do more. And why not let them? Rockefeller Center is a marvelous place. On the second floor of the RCA Building there is a master control board which monitors the procedures of guards and watchmen; unauthorized exits by fire doors; and fire, flood and burglar alarms. The Center has its own police force to deal with emergencies. You can buy anything you might need in the Center—all your meals, clothing, books, newspapers, tobacco, greeting cards and prescription drugs. There is someone to entertain you, clean your clothes, repair your shoes, process your film, bank your money, cut your hair, get you a passport or take you on a tour of the place. There is night life in the Rainbow Grill. You can visit the Chase Manhattan Bank Money Museum, see a movie and a stage show at the Music Hall, attend an NBC television show. But you must leave eventually, because nobody lives at the Center and it has no cemetery.

One of the best features of Rockefeller Center is that you can traverse it on more than one level. On fine days you can stay outdoors, and in foul weather you can cross several blocks entirely underground. A long series of underground concourses can take you from the west side of Sixth Avenue at Fifty-third Street to the corner of Fifth Avenue and Forty-ninth Street, for example.

For all its size, Rockefeller Center is a human place. Curiously, however, Rockefeller Center was the instigator of one of New York's most dehumanizing projects—the rebuilding of Sixth Avenue from Forty-second Street north to Central Park, which started in the late 1950s, when the Center began to expand to the west. It teamed up with Henry Luce (55 percent to 45) to erect the Time-Life Building on the west side of the avenue across from Radio City Music Hall. A couple of years later, the completion of the Sperry Rand Building extended the old western boundary to the Center northward along the east side of the avenue. Unfortunately, these buildings are not nearly as stylish as the older structures of Rockefeller Center.

Other interests proceeded to put up office buildings on both sides of Sixth Avenue running north from Rockefeller Center. Except for Eero Saarinen's CBS Building, none of them can be approached with enthusiasm. They are metal and glass boxes designed for maximum working space per unit cost. Their skimpy plazas—some at street level, some sunken—are uninviting and have no relationship to each other. Window displays are of little interest. These buildings are rather tall, and because they are set close to the avenue they form a deep canyon through which terrible winds blow. In winter it is several degrees colder on Sixth Avenue than on either Fifth or Seventh.

Rockefeller Center did something about the condition of the new Sixth Avenue in the early 1970s. The Celanese, Mc-

Graw-Hill and Standard Oil Buildings, the trio of new Rockefeller Center Buildings lined up on the west side of the avenue
south of the Time-Life Building, are set back far enough to
allow for generous plazas with trees, fountains, pools and
benches where people actually sit throughout the day and
early evening. Together with subterranean concourses in
front of the new buildings and mid-block passageways behind
them, the plazas form the Center's western promenade.

When the $3.5-million beautification program for the plazas
was announced, Alton G. Marshall, Rockefeller Center's president, explained, "We have covenants and faith in the city and
we want to put our money where our mouth is." James R.
Kennedy, vice-chairman of the Celanese Corporation, explained that his company wanted the plazas and concourses
because "we like to live gracefully."

Rockefeller Center had instigated the mistakes on Sixth
Avenue to the north. But the Center had come to the realization that its new neighbors could tarnish its image with their
dehumanizing character. The Center had had to protect itself.
It could do so by growing and surrounding part of Sixth Avenue, then making it more attractive. Thus the Rockefellers had
instigated the ruin of the avenue, then capitalized on that condition to reinforce their image as benefactors to the quality of
urban life.

Economic circumstances had prevented the Rockefellers
from installing the Metropolitan Opera Company in Rockefeller Center. Nevertheless, the Center always has conveyed
to us an image of the Rockefellers as benefactors of culture.
Radio and television programs have emanated from the Center's RCA Building, of course. In addition, through the opera-

tion of Radio City Music Hall, its great variety theater, the
Center became the nation's landmark of popular, and uplifting,
family entertainment.

Rockefeller Center entered into a commitment to provide
uplifting entertainment with the selection of the Music Hall's
director, Samuel L. "Roxy" Rothafel, the impresario of the
Roxy Theater, "the cathedral of the motion picture," where
he had combined movies with organ and orchestral music and
stage shows. Roxy brought to his $150,000-a-year position as
"maestro of the big show" at the Music Hall* a feeling for
people he had begun to develop in his youth, when he had
drifted from job to job. "Yes, I was shiftless and a dreamer,"
he said, "but in all my shiftlessness I was building up, entirely
unknown to myself, a symposium of impressions which has
followed me through the years and left me a keener, deeper,
and more appreciative picture of human frailties and kind-
nesses." Long sea voyages during seven years he spent in the
Marine Corps gave him a craving for spectacle: ". . . nights
and days at sea, glimpses of strange lands, adventure—movement, color, strange sounds, exotic perfumes! I drank it all in
with an insatiable thirst." Operating a small silent movie theater in the dance hall behind his father-in-law's saloon in a
Pennsylvania mining town showed Roxy he could give people
uplifting entertainment. "I can say now, without affectation,

* Originally, there were two theaters at Rockefeller Center—the Music
Hall and the Center Theater, which opened in December 1932, with a
stage show and a movie on the bill. After several months, the stage
shows were dropped, and ticket prices were reduced. The theater was
closed for a long period, then reopened in 1935 for live presentations.
Popular ice shows and short-term engagements of the San Carlo Opera
Company were featured for ten years. The theater no longer exists, its
interior having been converted to office space some years ago.

that I began then to create something beautiful for people who have an unsatisfied longing for beauty." Give the people beauty, but not so much that they become bored with it. Roxy's big orchestras would play "a snatch of grand opera; a quick little silhouette scene; a few bars of a symphony; done in a normal tempo, but in such small doses that the audience wishes there were more." His simple goal commended him to the Rockefellers: "More beauty for more and more people! That's what I want."

The Music Hall got off to a terrible start. On opening night in mid-December 1932, Roxy presented an overblown extravaganza that lasted from eight-thirty until past two A.M. The audience, exhausted, straggled out before the show finally ended. The Music Hall lost $180,000 during its first sixteen days, when it ran two shows daily (movies were not on the program) with an admission charge of $2.75. While Roxy was convalescing from an illness contracted immediately after opening night, programing was changed to include movies and ticket prices were reduced drastically to thirty-five cents before one P.M., fifty cents in the afternoon and seventy-five cents in the evening. The novelty of the new format wore off (only eight of the total of forty-seven movies shown in 1933 did better at the box office than the first one*). Money was

* The first movie shown at the Music Hall was *The Bitter Tea of General Yen*. I saw it at another Rockefeller theater, the auditorium of the Museum of Modern Art, years later. Barbara Stanwyck plays the role of a young woman who has arrived in China to become the bride of a missionary. After the wedding the couple is separated during a storm. The bride is rescued by General Yen, who is the chief protagonist on one side of a civil war raging throughout the countryside. The rest of the movie is an Oriental-Occidental will-she-or-won't-she? Although at one point Miss Stanwyck demands that Yen "Take your hands off me, you yellow swine"—the line got a big laugh at the

scarce in 1933, after all; during the bank holiday tickets were sold for scrip, postdated checks, IOUs or any other paper—anything to help fill the Music Hall's seats.

A month after the Music Hall opened RKO, the RCA subsidiary, went bankrupt, and its leases on the two Rockefeller Center theaters were terminated. A committee of three representatives from the Center and three from RCA took over. Later, the Radio City Music Hall Corporation was formed; it was run jointly by the two groups. Poor Roxy resigned in 1934. He died two years later, at fifty-three. The Music Hall survived him. By 1935 it had begun to show a profit.

The Music Hall became more than a source of profits. It became an American institution, one of New York City's major tourist attractions. Pageants presented as part of the stage shows at Christmas and Easter became traditional holiday entertainment. The Rockettes, whose precision tap-dance routine is the focal point of the stage shows, became an institution in themselves.* The Music Hall became the country's pace-

museum in 1969—she finally yields to his embrace. Circumstances of a political and military nature force Yen to do himself in, and Miss Stanwyck comes to learn what true love is all about. The role of the Chinese general was played by a white actor in slant-eyed makeup, perhaps so 1933 audiences would feel more at ease watching miscegenation.

Coincidentally, Abby Aldrich Rockefeller's sister Lucy, a deaf spinster of fifty-five, had been seized by Chinese bandits during a train trip through China in the spring of 1923, ten years before *The Bitter Tea of General Yen* opened at the Music Hall. She had been held captive for a weekend, and had lived to tell about her experience in *The Atlantic Monthly* later that year.

* The Rockettes have been the most honored of Music Hall performers. After they had danced at the 1937 Paris Exhibition (tickets for their sixteen-minute performance had gone for as much as $50 apiece), they were awarded the Grand Prix de la République, France's highest

setter in motion picture entertainments. Booking a movie there guaranteed bookings at other good houses. (So distributors courted the Music Hall; it was the only theater in the country able to get a look at a movie before booking it.)

The Music Hall has always felt a responsibility toward its audiences. A screening committee was set up to determine whether a movie was "a Music Hall picture," that is, as a Music Hall official put it in an interview in *Business Week* in the mid-1960s, if it were a "well-made, good picture" that was "big enough" to be shown on the huge Music Hall screen. As for a movie with sex in it, management would "accept sex only if it's incidental to a broader theme," the Music Hall official said. "Especially at Christmas and Easter we feel a responsibility. After all, people come from as far away as Baltimore to see the Nativity."

The ideal Music Hall picture has been a big musical, and unless distributors insisted on a reserved-seat, high-price-ticket policy, the Music Hall could get any musical it desired. And why not? *The Unsinkable Molly Brown* packed in 21,000 people a day and grossed close to $2 million during a ten-week run in the mid-1960s. *The Great Caruso* grossed $1,390,043. *Fanny* grossed $1.5 million. Doris Day was the ideal movie queen. *That Touch of Mink* (with Cary Grant) grossed $1,885,335 during its 1962 run. The Walt Disney organization has been cultivated always, starting with the animated car-

---

honor. But they have not been so well rewarded at home. They were the backbone of the strike by 103 performers against the Music Hall in September 1967—the first strike in its history. The strike lasted only a week. The terms of the settlement were not disclosed. The Rockettes had been making between $99 and $126.50 a week; they had asked for a 40 percent increase and had been offered 15.

toons of the 1930s. Although the usual rental fee for one of Disney's shorts was $150 a week in any other first-run house, the Music Hall paid as much as $1,500. Management demonstrated its faith in Disney by booking his first feature-length cartoon, *Snow White*, sight unseen. (Some people claimed the movie was too violent and frightening for kids, however. Dr. Benjamin Spock would tell an apocryphal story about it: "Nelson Rockefeller told my wife a long time ago that they had to reupholster the seats in the Radio City Music Hall because they were wet so often by frightened children.") When the Disney studios began to make profitable movies with live actors portraying spotless, God-fearing folks, the Music Hall exhibited them, too.

The Music Hall did not intend always to be so square. Unfortunately, however, the Rockefeller name could interfere with the selection of a movie. After having helped George Schaefer become president of RKO late in 1938, Nelson Rockefeller urged him to hire Orson Welles, then the "wonder boy" of the "War of the Worlds" broadcast that had created a nationwide uproar. Schaefer was rewarded amply when Welles directed and played the lead in the monumental *Citizen Kane*, which was based loosely on the life of William Randolph Hearst. The Hearst organization immediately applied pressure where it could to prevent the movie's exhibition. Frightened that Hearst would mount a campaign charging them and the entire movie industry with immorality, the Hollywood moguls offered Schaefer a large profit on his firm's investment if he would destroy all prints and negatives. He turned them down, and the movie was scheduled to open at the Music Hall on February 14, 1941. Although it was the showcase for big RKO pictures and its manager was enthusiastic about *Citizen Kane*, the Music Hall suddenly declined to show it. Schaefer put in a call to Nelson Rockefeller to find out why. "Rockefeller told me," Schaefer said, "that Louella Parsons [Hearst's Hollywood gossip columnist] had warned him off it, that she had asked him, 'How would you like to have the *American Weekly* [Hearst's Sunday magazine] run a double-page spread on John D. Rockefeller?' "

The Music Hall is a philanthropic enterprise. Its champions assert that it serves a basic need of the American family. As the *New York Daily News* editorialized at the end of the musicians' strike that darkened the theater for a short time in 1972, "Along with its stage shows—featuring the incomparable Rockettes—the theater specializes in wholesome, family-style movies—the kind they seldom make any more . . . the rare blockbusters suitable for Mom, Dad and the kids." Management's aim is to raise our spirits. Shortly after yet another assassination attempt on an American politician (George Wallace, in May 1972), *The New Yorker*, speaking wryly of America's "waking up once again to the importance of just plain old-fashioned smiling," cited the Music Hall, "where thousands pack in nightly [and during the May 1972 stage show] the audience joins in singing 'Smile' as the lyrics are projected on a scrim. The last lines are, 'You'll find that life is still worthwhile,/If you'll just smile.' "

Sneering at Radio City Music Hall is an American's birthright. But who can sneer in fairness at Rockefeller Center? It is a splendid achievement in city planning, harmoniously combining tall buildings, shorter buildings and open spaces, and containing a multiplicity of functions in a pleasant and serene city within a nerve-racking city. It is an admirable place. Yet it bothers me.

The Rockefellers' building projects give us confidence in their ability to handle other tasks. The very design of the buildings in Rockefeller Center propels us toward this conclusion. Look at them: They are slabs of nonuniform heights and widths. The RCA Building, the tallest, is a composition of slabs. The overall effect is reminiscent of a bar graph, a device used to chart an institution's progress. The Center represents the Rockefellers' progress toward creating a new Garden of Eden. There are open spaces where we can look up at how high the bars rise on the graph of accomplishment. We are meant to understand that if the Rockefellers could construct this wonderful city within a city, they could build a better world.

An inscription at Rockefeller Center reads:

JOHN D. ROCKEFELLER, JR.
1874-1960
Founder of Rockefeller Center

If we take the root of the word *founder* to be that of *fund*, we read in the inscription that in founding Rockefeller Center, Rockefeller Junior was laying the foundation of an enterprise that was meant to grow. It was meant to grow far beyond the boundaries of the Center itself, for with the Center the Rockefellers were entering into a commitment to create a new Utopia, to be furnished with more great construction projects, and to be promoted not only with the Rockefellers' own funds, but also with other private funds and with public funds. The projects would serve a multiplicity of functions, and would be freighted with philanthropic intentions. One project would provide facilities for New York's major orchestra, opera and dance companies, and a new repertory theater. Another would be built as symbol of the importance of state government within the federal system. Some would be built as focal points for the rehabilitation of decaying sections of Manhattan, while others would provide wholly new communities throughout the nation. With these projects, the Rockefellers would mean not only to benefit those people immediately affected, but also to fashion models to be emulated by other builders elsewhere. Yet despite this philanthropic orientation, the projects spawned by the success of Rockefeller Center would not be as socially useful as it became. For they would be monuments. Too often, they would be built to satisfy the ego of the builder rather than the needs and desires of the public. In addition, there would be an element of financial self-interest in the Rockefellers' new Garden of Eden. Their projects would primarily be vehicles of private profit, rather than stimuli of public benefit. So what is bothersome about Rockefeller Center is that it gave the Rockefellers room to pursue their personal vision of creating a new Garden of Eden in America with monuments that are said to be, but are not, in the public interest.

iii   Postwar Construction Projects

Between 1855 and 1934, Rockefeller Senior gave $531 million to various organizations, including $387 million to Rockefeller philanthropic funds and $60 million to the Rockefeller Institute for Medical Research. Nearly all the rest of his fortune was transferred to his son, Rockefeller Junior, virtually intact. (Before 1914 there were no gift taxes; between 1924 and 1930 tax rates were low; and during the 1930s stock prices were depressed.) When Rockefeller Senior died in 1937 at the age of ninety-eight, he left an estate of only $26 million, 60 percent going for state and federal taxes, the rest going to the Rockefeller Institute and, eventually, Lincoln Center for the Performing Arts.

Within a few years of Rockefeller Senior's death, the third Rockefeller period came to a close, as Rockefeller Junior, the dominant family figure of the period, reached the age of sixty-five. The Sealantic Fund, which he founded in 1938, and Jackson Hole Preserve, which he founded in 1940, were among his last major accomplishments, although he was to live until 1960. (Between January 1, 1917, and December 31, 1959, he gave $474 million to various organizations, including $111.5 million to Rockefeller philanthropic funds, $56 million to Colonial Williamsburg, Inc., and related projects, and $6 million to the Rockefeller Institute. He left an estate of only $150 million, half going to his widow, Martha Baird Rockefeller, and half going to the Rockefeller Brothers Fund, which the brothers founded in 1940.* The remainder of the Rockefeller fortune was transferred to the third and fourth generations through a large number of trust funds.†)

The Rockefeller brothers came of age in the third period. They completed their formal schooling‡ and embarked on careers. John entered his father's office and began to devote himself to philanthropy full-time. Nelson was at the Chase National Bank for a short time, and also became engaged in a series of small enterprises, including one that arranged business deals between large companies. He transformed this enterprise

* See Appendix for descriptions of these philanthropic funds.
† According to the TNEC study (see footnote, p. 34), around the end of 1937, with stock prices depressed, the Rockefellers held somewhat less than $300 million in the 200 largest nonfinancial corporations, nearly all of it in oil stocks. Such holdings are worth around $4 billion at current prices. Assuming that the Rockefeller investment portfolio has been managed carefully, this figure, which does not account for family holdings in real estate, banks and other financial institutions, can be used as a conservative estimate of the size of the Rockefeller fortune.
‡ They all attended Ivy League Colleges. John graduated from Princeton, Nelson from Dartmouth. Laurance graduated from Princeton and attended Harvard Law School for two years ("two misspent years," he called them later). Winthrop attended Yale. David graduated from Harvard, attended the London School of Economics and received a Ph.D. in economics from the University of Chicago. His doctoral thesis, published in 1940, is entitled "Unused Resources and Economic Waste."

into Special Work, Inc., which was a rental agent for Rockefeller Center. In 1937 he began to involve himself in United States Government and business policy toward Latin America. He became executive vice-president of Rockefeller Center and, a year later, its president. Laurance entered the aviation business on two fronts. In 1938 he and Captain Eddie Rickenbacker, the World War I flying ace, bought into North American Aviation, then part of General Motors, and formed Eastern Airlines;* in 1939, Laurence began an association with J. S. McDonnell, Jr., a St. Louis aircraft designer who established the McDonnell Aircraft Corporation with Rockefeller backing. Winthrop worked in the oil fields for a while, then returned to New York and spent a year as a trainee at the Chase National Bank. He then joined the foreign department of the Socony-Vacuum Oil Company and also became an industrial relations consultant at Rockefeller Center. David served for eighteen months as a secretary to New York Mayor Fiorello H. LaGuardia.

The brothers spent World War II in government service. John joined the Navy and served three years in Washington, first in the Bureau of Naval Personnel, then in naval military government. Nelson was appointed Coordinator of the Office of Inter-American Affairs by President Roosevelt in 1940, then served as Assistant Secretary of State with jurisdiction over Latin American affairs from December 1944 until August 1945. Laurance served in the production division of the

* He has owned about 3 to 4 percent of Eastern's stock (the Chase Manhattan Bank, the airline's principal bank, is now the second largest stockholder, with 6.4 percent of the stock), and served as a director of the airline until 1960. Among the current directors (as of 1970) are Rockefeller family employee Harper Woodward and family associate Rosewell Gilpatric.

Navy's Bureau of Aeronautics. Winthrop enlisted in the Army about a year before the attack on Pearl Harbor; he eventually served as a supply officer in the Pacific theater, where he was wounded in 1945. David enlisted in the Army in 1942; he spent two years in North Africa, mostly in intelligence work, and after the war ended he spent six months as an Assistant Military Attaché in Paris.

After the war, the brothers came back to New York. John resumed his career in philanthropy. Nelson began to divide his time between philanthropic projects in New York and government service in Washington. He was appointed head of the International Development Advisory Board by President Truman in 1950, head of the Presidential Advisory Commission on Government Operations by President-elect Eisenhower in 1952 and Undersecretary of Health, Education and Welfare in 1953. Laurance became head of Rockefeller Brothers, Inc., the collective venture-capital enterprise established in 1946. He also became involved in numerous defense-oriented aviation and electronics companies, including the Piasecki Helicopter Company, of Philadelphia; Reaction Motors, of New Jersey; Marquant Aircraft Company, of Los Angeles; Laboratory for Electronics, of Boston; Airborne Instruments Laboratory, of Long Island; Aircraft Radio Corporation, of New Jersey; and the Glenn L. Martin Company. Winthrop returned to his desk at Socony-Vacuum. (He eventually became the only brother to leave New York; he moved down to Arkansas, where he was twice elected governor.) David entered the foreign department of the Chase National Bank in 1946. At the end of four years he became a vice-president; he supervised the bank's business in Latin America and established an economic quarterly—*Latin American Business Highlights*. In 1952 he became a senior vice-president; he provided general supervision for the economic research department, supervised customer relations and was in charge of all bank branches in the New York City area.

By 1953 the brothers had established themselves as philanthropists; they had assumed positions of authority at the Rockefeller institutions of the second and third periods. Since the late 1930s Nelson had been the dominant trustee at the Museum of Modern Art; David had become chairman of the board of the Rockefeller Institute for Medical Research in 1950; John had become chairman of the Rockefeller Foundation in 1952; Winthrop became chairman of Colonial Williamsburg in 1953. They had founded an entirely new series of philanthropic institutions: the Rockefeller Brothers Fund (1940); the American International Association for Economic and Social Development (1946); the Population Council (1952); the Council on Economic and Cultural Affairs (1953)*; and the Government Affairs Foundation (1953).† The brothers also had participated in numerous other philanthropic projects, including fund-raising campaigns such as the Greater New York Fund and the promotion of organizations such as the National Urban League.

By the early 1950s, when the Rockefeller brothers were in their thirties and forties, the fourth Rockefeller period reached a critical juncture. Based on their parents' activities, the brothers' name had become associated not only with philanthropy

---

* See Appendix for descriptions of these funds and other funds established after 1953.
† The Government Affairs Foundation, which financed and published studies on local, state and federal government operations, was dissolved in 1968.

but also with building, the arts and conservation. At this point, the brothers were ready to take full advantage of all aspects of their reputation, to extend the scope of Rockefeller activities and exercise their own brand of influence on America through philanthropy.

The brothers would do so without the great disbursements of funds their father and grandfather had made; the philanthropic projects the brothers would promote would be subsidized by outside sources of funds, both private and public. The brothers believed, as John, the oldest, put it:

> that we—the third generation—were in a quite different position than Father and Grandfather. They could give large sums of money for work others carried on. Today the character of philanthropic operations has changed because you have, generally, more givers but they give less. Giving, of course, is essential, but it seemed to me that in our approach the most important thing was our personal effort.

The brothers' chief contribution would be personal effort. Of course, it had its risks. It was one thing to supply funds for scientific, medical and educational projects to be carried out by the skilled professional staffs at the philanthropic institutions Rockefeller Senior had established. It would be quite another thing for the Rockefeller brothers to undertake philanthropic projects on their own. On the other hand, success was in their blood. Standard Oil, their grandfather's gigantic enterprise, had made billions; the good works of his philanthropic institutions had rewarded his family with admiration. And by the 1950s, Rockefeller Junior's greatest enterprise, Rockefeller Center, could be considered a personal triumph, both commercially and artistically, in no uncertain terms. So

the Rockefeller brothers could undertake large-scale philanthropic projects with some confidence that personal effort
would meet with success. And on what better grounds to do
so than to undertake great construction projects in emulation
of Rockefeller Center?

The year 1953 was important for the Rockefeller brothers.
It was marked by the first stirrings of the Lincoln Square
urban renewal project, an ambitious undertaking which covers
a huge chunk of Manhattan's West Side, running north from
West Fifty-ninth Street to West Seventy-second and west
from Central Park to the Hudson River. This was a mixed
neighborhood of 20,000 people, about a quarter of them members of minority groups—mainly black and Puerto Rican. It
contained 110 rooming houses, all built before 1902. There
were problems of delinquency, crime and disease, of crowding
indoors and congestion outdoors. Urban renewers saw Lincoln Square as a slum that had to be done away with.

The overall project was the brain-child of Robert Moses,
who between 1949 and 1960 promoted $5 billion of redevel-
opment construction in New York City under the Title I
Urban Redevelopment Act, whereby a city could exercise its
right of eminent domain to buy at fair market value land considered blighted and then sell the land at below cost to developers who would build low- and middle-income housing and
other structures. Moses wanted Lincoln Square to be rede-
veloped by "several substantial sponsors" who "would provide
for housing, a hotel or hotels, and other improvements, including, perhaps, such quasi-public institutions as the Engineering
Societies, Metropolitan Opera, Philharmonic, etc." He wrote
to a member of the Met's executive committee to inquire
whether the Met would "have enough money to buy, let us

say, three acres at a written-down cost and enough funds left to be sure of completing a building within four years. . . ." The Met's board chairman was opposed to Moses' plan, and by August 1954, Moses was counting the Met out of any Lincoln Square deal.

In 1955, however, Robert Moses' Lincoln Square proposal received the backing he desired. The Met, under new leadership, agreed in October to raise $1.5 million to cover the purchase of land (12,000 square feet at $8 a square foot), drafting of preliminary plans for a new opera house, demolition of buildings and relocation of dislodged residents. At about the same time, the New York Philharmonic, having been advised by the managers of Carnegie Hall that its lease could not be renewed after 1958 because the building was scheduled to be demolished (a citizens' group later saved it at a cost to the city of only $5 million, however), agreed to purchase an acre at Lincoln Square (also at $8 a square foot). A group headed by theatrical producer Roger L. Stevens proposed that a legitimate-theater complex be built on the block between West Sixty-fifth and Sixty-sixth Streets. The $35-million plan called for six theaters, five of them under one roof, plus landscaping, commercial buildings and coffee shops. Broadway theater owners objected vigorously enough to kill the plan, however. Nevertheless, a center for the performing arts had been founded.

An exploratory committee for a musical arts center was formed on October 25, 1955. Some months later, on June 22, 1956, Lincoln Center for the Performing Arts was incorporated as a nonprofit membership organization with responsibility for financing, building and coordinating policy for a performing arts center to be located in the Lincoln Square complex. The Center was to raise $50 million for land and buildings—which turned out to be less than a third of the amount required—and $10 million for commissions of new works and for educational projects, to be spent over a ten-year period. The plan contemplated four buildings for opera, music, dance and drama, plus a school, library and museum. The Philharmonic became a constituent of the Center in November 1956. The Juilliard School of Music and the Metropolitan Opera Association achieved similar status in February of the following year, and the New York Public Library did likewise in 1959. The Lincoln Center Repertory Association was formed in February 1960.

John D. Rockefeller 3rd was chairman of the exploratory committee, and when Lincoln Center was formed he became its president. Although he had no prior involvement in the performing arts, he was the logical choice for leader of the Lincoln Center group, for with a Rockefeller at the helm, the project had a comfortable safety factor: his family's wealth guaranteed the project's completion in the event sufficient funds could not be raised from non-Rockefeller sources. With this guarantee, these sources would be encouraged to contribute to the Center, and the performing arts institutions themselves would be encouraged to sign on board.

There were powerful motivations for Rockefeller's undertaking building the Center. For one thing, the huge Lincoln Square slum was an excellent subject for his family's Garden-of-Eden commitment. For another thing, by building Lincoln Center he would be carrying out his father's wish to place a magnificent opera house at the focal point of a great complex of buildings. (In fact, Wallace K. Harrison, the architect of the Metropolitan Opera House at Lincoln Center, also had been one of the chief architects of Rockefeller Center. His rendering of the opera house and plaza proposed initially for Rockefeller Center and the Rockefeller-directed realization at Lincoln Center bear remarkable similarities that underscore this desire.) Furthermore, the Rockefeller family had long been advocating a performing arts center. Back in the late 1930s they had proposed a municipal music and arts center to link up Rockefeller Center with the Museum of Modern Art, installed in quarters two blocks to the north in 1939. The value of the connecting real estate was about $9 million. The city owned $1 million worth, the Rockefellers $300,000 and other private parties the remainder. According to Robert Moses' view of the situation in 1938, those third parties were "a menace to the entire Rockefeller program." Several "attempted to hold up the Rockefeller group for tremendous prices far in excess of the city's assessed valuations." The deal did not go through, but the Rockefeller family remained an enthusiastic supporter of the idea of placing New York's performing arts institutions in a setting where they could stand aloof from the city's turmoil, rather than, spread throughout the city, remaining part of its tempestuous daily life.

Lincoln Center became a Rockefeller project. The architects assigned to it had ties to the Rockefellers. Harrison was a relative by marriage and had been associated with family projects since the late 1920s. Max Abramovitz, assigned to Philharmonic Hall, was his partner. Philip Johnson, assigned to the theater for dance, had been associated with the Museum of Modern Art and the Rockefeller family for more than twenty years. Gordon Bunshaft, assigned to the library and museum, was also the architect of the new Chase Manhattan Bank. Eero Saarinen, assigned to the theater for drama, had been honored by the Museum of Modern Art for his building and furniture designs.

A considerable portion of Lincoln Center's construction fund came from Rockefeller sources. The Rockefeller Foundation contributed $2.5 million in 1957, $7.5 million in 1958 and $5 million in 1963. Rockefeller Junior contributed a total of $10,805,656 in 1958 and 1960. In 1965 the Juilliard School received $8.9 million from a trust fund that Rockefeller Senior had established for his daughter, Edith Rockefeller McCormick. (A part of the fund eventually had been left by Mrs. McCormick's daughter to four adopted children, all under six years of age when she died in 1959. Her estate contended that the adopted children were legal "issue" under terms of the original fund, but a trust committee headed by John D. Rockefeller 3rd and supported by the Chase Manhattan Bank, acting as the committee's trustee, contended that the children did not meet the terms. After a five-year legal battle, the case was settled out of court, with the four children receiving $3.1 million, and Lincoln Center the bulk of the contested portion of the original fund.)

With Harrison in a state of semi-exhaustion (this was soon after he had completed the United Nations Headquarters), John D. Rockefeller 3rd assumed direction of Lincoln Center's overall design. He announced that the project would have far-reaching significance. "Our desire," he said, "[is] that the completed center be a dynamic, exciting and beautiful whole greater than the sum of its parts. We look to this group of architects to combine their talents, to work together to achieve another notable example for our city and our nation."

Unfortunately, Lincoln Center was first notable for poor design. The acoustical performance of Philharmonic Hall, the first building to open (on network television for all America to see), was terrible. New York-based critics saw to it that the problem assumed the proportions of a national disaster. Many solutions were offered, but improvements were not immediately forthcoming. Indeed, Philharmonic Hall's acoustics were worked on for seven years, and more than $1.5 million was expended on several patching-up jobs.

Philharmonic Hall is Lincoln Center's most notable architectural disaster. Eero Saarinen's Vivian Beaumont Theater, which contains two houses—the Beaumont, with 1,140 seats, and the Forum (underneath the Beaumont) with 299 seats—is the Center's outstanding architectural achievement. It has been consistently praised for its seating arrangements and for its magnificent backstage accommodations. Among its admirers has been Clive Barnes, dance and drama critic of the *New York Times*, who has called the Forum "the most beautiful small theater in the nation." It is "a gem" and "cannot be duplicated," according to Barnes. There have been those who have wished to remodel the Beaumont, however, and with good reason.

In the fall of 1971 the Vivian Beaumont was at the center of controversy. One of Lincoln Center's problems had been the Repertory Theater, which was always in trouble, both artistically and financially. Over the six seasons from 1965 to 1971, when the Rep's expenditures came to $13,267,000, its cumulative deficit totaled $4,300,000. In early 1971, following initiatives by the Lincoln Center executive committee and the City Center of Music and Drama, the Finance Committee of the New York City Council had recommended that the Vivian Beaumont be sold to the city for one dollar and that the city spend $5.2 million to rearrange the interior of the building. Three small movie theaters and a film museum would be installed in the space currently occupied by the Forum, which would, in effect, be moved to the large area backstage of the main theater (41 percent of that backstage area would be lost). Management of the Vivian Beaumont would be turned over to the City Center group. The program director of the new movie theaters, which would show fifteen feature films a day, seven days a week, all year round, would be the celebrated Henri Langlois, who presides over a collection of 60,000 films at the Cinemathèque in Paris. In addition, the City Center had been given permission to demolish its theater on Fifty-fifth Street and erect in its place a high-rise office building with a 3,000-seat theater.

The plan was in the tradition of combining profitable and unprofitable enterprises in order to make up the deficits of one with the surplus earned by the other. But legitimate-theater people were disturbed by the very thought of movies subsidizing stage plays and afraid that prospective subsidies of legitimate theater in other communities would be cut back if the Lincoln Center Repertory Theater's failure were admitted. Rallying around the architectural excellence of the Vivian Beaumont, they formed an *ad hoc* Committee to Save Theater at Lincoln Center, with Dore Schary, playwright, producer and politician as top banana. "My main concern," he said, "is that the Forum—a ten-year-old house and a beautiful place—not be destroyed. Three movie houses plus a screening room plus the Henri Langlois museum—that's a moveable feast. The Forum is not. There's plenty of room for more houses all through Lincoln Center. We're willing to compromise on everything except the Forum. You simply can't move a theater."

The committee pressured the Repertory Theater's board

into withdrawing its support for installing movie theaters in the Vivian Beaumont. The board offered a substitute, three-part plan: Propose to the legitimate-theater unions that their members accept lower minimum wages and permit reductions in numbers of personnel required at performances; discuss fund-raising plans with members of the City Council; find 500 people willing to donate $1,000 apiece in exchange for attending social functions with theater people.

A further blow at the City Center takeover was the assertion by a member of the City Council, Eldon R. Clingan, Liberal of Manhattan, that the Rockefeller family, as owners of a building with garages and offices next door to the City Center Theater on West Fifty-fifth Street, would realize a "financial windfall" from the erection of an office building on the City Center site. Either the garage building would be sold to provide additional land for the new office building or, if it remained intact, its value would increase appreciably. "The Vivian Beaumont proposal is a classic sweet deal," Clingan said. "First, Lincoln Center will unload a white elephant that costs them $750,000 a year; second, the City Center will acquire new facilities; third, a new commercial building will be built on the present City Center site and on adjacent parcels of land."

The City Center's board chairman, Richard Clurman, pooh-poohed Clingan's third point: "If we needed the [adjacent] property," he said, "we would expect to ask [the Rockefellers] to donate it, but we don't need it."

The real problem behind the Repertory Theater's difficulties, brought out by the Clingan-Clurman debate, was part of the tradition of Lincoln Center: that the constituents have no external means of support other than handouts from private and public philanthropies. The Rep's $517,000 deficit for the 1970-71 season had to be made up by donations from private persons, foundations and government agencies.

The Repertory Theater was a creature of Lincoln Center. It was a new institution, unlike the Metropolitan Opera, but the financial positions of these two Lincoln Center constituents were woefully similar. According to a white paper issued in September 1971, the Met's expenditures were rising faster than its income. In the decade from 1961 to 1971, income from ticket sales and other sources rose to only two and a half times the 1961 level, but expenditures tripled. Whereas the deficit in 1961 had been $900,000, the deficit in the fiscal year ending on July 31, 1971, was $4.3 million (against an income of $20 million). The Met, like the Repertory Theater, had no major external means for producing profits to help make up its deficits (other than the $250,000-a-year ground rent on its old site). It was dependent on income from ticket sales (which, at a $17.50 top, hardly could be forced to higher levels) and on philanthropic subsidies. What had become of the old idea of combining the opera house with an office building?

In the last fiscal year covered by the white paper, most of the Met's deficit had been made up by philanthropic contributions from private sources. About half a million dollars, or 10 percent of the total deficit, had been contributed by government agencies, most of it by the New York State Council on the Arts, an organization Governor Nelson Rockefeller and the State Legislature had established in 1960-61. This latter sum was simply not enough. The Met contended that unless government subsidies were raised to between $1 and $2 million, services would have to be cut back. But the question was, would this higher level of government subsidy be enough? For Lincoln Center was in grave financial trouble.

John D. Rockefeller 3rd was president of Lincoln Center until 1960, when he moved up to a newly created position, chairman of the board, and General Maxwell Taylor was brought in to help marshal contributors to the building fund. After less than a year, however, Taylor resigned and composer William Schuman, president of the Juilliard School, became the Center's president.

Schuman resigned in December 1968. When he did, a financial crisis at Lincoln Center was revealed, with both the Center's superstructure and its constituents in trouble. His regime had been activist. The more events the Center's superstructure itself had staged, however, the worse matters had become. It had run Summer and Film Festivals that both had lost money, for example. In fiscal 1968, income had been less than $5 million against expenditures of a little over $8 million. (In addition, the Philharmonic's deficit had been $800,000 and the Met's $3,533,000 before contributions.) So the third Summer Festival, set for 1969, had to be canceled, and the Center's commitment to the New York Film Festival had to be terminated. (An independent group took over the Film Festival's operation.) For unless the Center stopped playing entrepreneur, it would have to compete with its hard-pressed constituents in raising a considerable amount of money. It seemed better to retrench.

After Schuman resigned, the naming of a new president was deferred. Why bring in someone who might want to start new programs and create more financial difficulties? The Center's administrative staff was cut from eighty to fifty; three vice-presidents resigned and were not replaced. The operating budget for fiscal 1969 was cut from $1.9 to $1.4 million. The budget for fiscal 1970 was projected at under $700,000, less than a tenth of what it had been in fiscal 1968. Lincoln Center was disappearing. Only the buildings would remain, with independent constituents inside them.

Rockefeller was chairman of Lincoln Center's board until mid-1970, when he retired and chose as his successor Amyas Ames, chairman of the Philharmonic's board. Rockefeller was confident about Lincoln Center's future. "The arts are such a terribly important factor in our lives," he said, "that I cannot conceive that the American public will not respond to the situation over a period of time. The problems will be faced forthrightly and progress will be made." He announced that Ames would be responsible for "reorganization and retrenchment."

Lincoln Center's financial problems derived in part from fund-raising difficulties that Ames and Schuman attributed to individuals' and corporations' directing their philanthropic contributions in recent years toward alleviating urban, racial and educational problems, rather than to the arts. As for the Center's ambitious promotions in the face of reduced contributions, Ames said: "I even think it was good to be ambitious." He added that "Lincoln Center perhaps needed to try for programs that would give it an identity of its own."

"An identity of its own" is something Lincoln Center's defenders want it to have. But what is the Center, except a location where halls have been built for organizations in business long before it was conceived? It provides nothing else for its constituents. It provides no major sources of auxiliary income for them; they have to depend on box office revenues and philanthropic contributions. It has no power to control their expenses. The Met, for example, grows more flabby, despite its financial troubles: Star singers command outrageous fees; hideous and expensive sets are the rule. As for the services Lincoln Center provides to New York City, the public obtains nothing it could not get without the Center. The constituents do not need an entity like the Center in order to take their student programs to the public schools, for example. Arts festivals held in the Center's plaza could be held in other public places. Any project the Center boasts about could be held without it.

What Lincoln Center provided was an opportunity for the Rockefellers to build a monument—the fulfillment of a long-standing desire to install the Metropolitan Opera in a new house in a grand setting. Unfortunately, the Center is no more than a monument—a great white elephant of a monument. By leading its building, the Rockefellers did not lead its constituents into an era of guaranteed support. Even the continuing arrival of large Rockefeller contributions does not guarantee good economic health at the Center. When Martha Baird Rockefeller (Rockefeller Junior's widow, a patron of the opera and a former musician) died in 1971, she left the Center $10 million, the Metropolitan Opera $5 million (the largest gift it had ever received) and the Philharmonic $1 million.*

* Martha Baird Rockefeller's other bequests were: Colonial Williamsburg, Inc., $5 million; the Martha Baird Rockefeller Fund for Music, Inc. (See Appendix), $5 million; the Metropolitan Museum of Art, $5 million; Brown University, $1 million; the Riverside Church, $1 million; the New England Conservatory, $1 million; Occidental College, $1 million; the Boston Symphony Orchestra, Inc., $500,000; the Osteopathic Hospital and Clinic of New York, Inc., and the Foundation for the New York Academy of Osteopathy, Inc., $500,000; the American Red Cross, $250,000.

But while Amyas Ames called her bequest "a turning point," the fear was expressed that such large gifts might mislead potential contributors about the economic health of the Center and its constituents. He had much to fear. In 1971, when Lincoln Center box offices took in $25 million, the total deficit came to $13 million. And his fears were realized, for shortly after the Repertory Theater's 1972-73 Forum season opened, it had to be canceled on account of insufficient funds.

The cost of constructing Lincoln Center was $185 million. It was an ambitious project, but it was far from being enough to satisfy the Rockefeller family's Garden-of-Eden commitment. The Rockefeller brothers undertook other, more ambitious projects, even as Lincoln Center was being built. The second brother, Nelson, the leading contender for the heavyweight building championship of the fourth Rockefeller period, promoted a project whose cost dwarfs the cost of Lincoln Center.

During his college days at Dartmouth in the latter 1920s, Nelson Rockefeller talked about becoming an architect. His mother wrote to him that she was "glad" if he felt "absolutely sure." She also admonished him to think over his responsibilities as member of the Rockefeller family. "There are so many fine things that it is possible for you to do and so many things that seem necessary for someone to do," she wrote. "I am eager that the high standard of citizenship set by your father shall be maintained by you boys. It seems as if all of you would have to join in the battle for righteousness in all walks of life, business, church, professions and private life, no small or easy job. This has always been the dream of my life, but of course each of you will have to work out your own salvation and, as we trust you, so we can have faith in your futures."

Nelson did not become an architect; instead, he pursued careers in business and public service. But perhaps he felt that in not becoming an architect he had deprived himself of his true mode of self-expression, for three decades after his graduation from college he seized an opportunity to design and build a great project and promoted it with such abandon that he appeared to be releasing half a lifetime of frustration.

Rockefeller served in the Eisenhower Administration from 1953 to 1956, first as Undersecretary of Health, Education and Welfare, then as a Special Assistant to the President. Back in New York in 1956, he was appointed chairman of the State Commission for a Constitutional Convention, which was charged with studying legislative reapportionment and proposed changes in the state constitution. In this role he met politically involved people throughout the state. In August 1958, with the backing of Republican Party State Chairman L. Judson Morhouse, Rockefeller won the nomination for Governor at the Republican state convention. He ran a splendid campaign, received an excellent reception in the press, and beat incumbent Averell Harriman by 530,000 votes.

When Rockefeller went up to Albany to take over the governor's office, the area between the state capitol and the governor's mansion was a warren of shabby stores and tenements housing some 3,000 families, most of them poor and black. There was one spot where you could hear good modern jazz, but the district was known primarily for its bordellos. It was called the Gut. Rockefeller later recalled that during his first term in office he had to ride through the Gut with Princess Beatrix of the Netherlands, who was visiting the city. "There's no question that the city did not look as I think the Princess thought it was going to," he said.

The Gut was an embarrassment to Rockefeller. It had to be

cleaned out. But what should be built in its place? The Gut's location suggested the answer: a complex of public buildings connecting the capitol with the governor's mansion. This was not to be simply a collection of functional spaces, however. The project was to be much more ambitious; a monument, an uplifting symbol of government, was to be built. As Rockefeller put it himself, here was an opportunity to transform Albany into "the most spectacularly beautiful seat of government in the world."

Wallace K. Harrison, the Rockefeller family's long-time associate, was designated chief architect of the new government complex, which came to be called the Albany South Mall. Governor Rockefeller pursued an active role in the Mall's design; architects in Harrison's office received sketches he had done. The design became the product of a collaboration between the Governor and Harrison, two men who had participated together on so many plans and projects that they were able to anticipate each other's reaction to the aesthetic qualities of a work of architecture.

The South Mall, designed to be a huge, expensive and ambitious undertaking, covers ninety-eight acres. It has eleven buildings, including five high-rise office buildings: four twenty-three-story agency buildings and the forty-four-story office tower, the tallest building in the state outside New York City. There are three office buildings with relatively low profiles: the Justice Building, the Legislative Building and the quarter-mile-long Motor Vehicles Building. There are several special-purpose buildings, including a meeting center and a cultural center, which has a library and a museum. The designs of these buildings are lavish and unusual. They are all faced with Vermont and Georgia marble. The Meeting Center is shaped like a bowl. The floors of the five high-rise office buildings have trapezoidal shapes. The buildings themselves look as if they are being held some twenty feet above ground level by giant "C" clamps. But the most expensive and ambitious feature of the Mall is yet another construction, called the Main Platform, a colossal construction 1,440 feet long and 600 feet wide, which has five levels and is surmounted by the five high-rise office buildings and the Meeting Center. The Platform's three lower levels contain mechanical and storage areas, garage space for 3,300 cars and a tunnel for a four-lane highway; the fourth level contains a concourse with offices, cafeterias, shops, meeting halls, exhibition areas and a bus terminal; the top level has landscaped plazas with fountains, pools and walkways; the Platform also houses a health laboratory and a 13,000-square-foot fallout shelter.

The method used to finance construction of Governor Rockefeller's South Mall was more unusual than any aspect of its design. Under an arrangement put forward by Albany Mayor Erastus Corning* (who once had called the plan for the Mall "hasty and ruthless . . . unnecessary and inhuman," but had reversed his position), bonds to cover the construction of these state-occupied buildings were issued not by the

---

* Mayor Corning's arrangement, which Governor Rockefeller called "most interesting, most ingenious," is a lease-purchase agreement between New York State and Albany County whereby the state agrees to become the county's agent for the purpose of erecting the South Mall. The Legislature appropriates operating expenses, which are called first-instance funds. The county sells bonds and reimburses the state on a quarterly basis for the first-instance funds. The state pays the county an annual rental equal to the principal plus the interest due on the bonds and also makes supplementary payments to the county for its trouble. When all the principal and interest on the bonds have been paid off, the state takes title to the Mall.

state but by Albany County. The arrangement was undertaken for several reasons. For one thing, unlike a state bond issue, a county bond issue did not require approval by the voters. For another thing, while the arrangement had to be approved by the Legislature, its approval of the Mall project *per se* was not required. The Governor could construct the Mall by executive order. He could ignore objections to the design of the project and to any aspect of its construction.

The South Mall project became more than a vehicle for Nelson Rockefeller's architectural ambitions. It became a symbol of a deeply felt responsibility for fulfilling a familial commitment to create a new Garden of Eden. For the Governor became demonic about the project. He promoted it in a manner that bespoke a feeling that the more monumental the Mall was and the sooner it became a reality, the sooner the world would enter the new era.

Design work on the huge South Mall project went ahead as tenements were torn down and the site became a parking lot. In 1966 Albany County began selling bonds to finance the first stage of construction. The pace of work accelerated during the latter months of that year, when Governor Rockefeller was up for reelection to a third term and the *New York Daily News* straw poll, which is usually highly accurate, showed him losing to the Democratic candidate, Frank O'Connor. Although plans, schedules and designs for the Mall were as yet incomplete,* there was great pressure to have construc-

* The slowness probably was caused by New York State laws requiring that the state act as its own general contractor for buildings. The trouble was that the state bureaucracy was incapable of handling a project as large as the South Mall. The Office of General Services (OGS) acted as general contractor for the Mall only until 1966. A point was reached that year when the scope and amount of work be-

tion contracts signed before the end of the year. Harrison's architects' telephones were kept busy by contractors frantic to have specifications and drawings on which to base bids.

Rockefeller survived the election and entered his third four-year term as Governor. Construction of the South Mall was underway. It was put on a tight schedule, with completion set for 1971. But there would be major delays arising from the rush to let contracts. When contracts were awarded for the foundation of the Main Platform, for example, only its southern half had been designed. The state hoped that the northern half would be a twin of the southern half, but foundation work in Albany is treacherous, and the halves did not turn out to be twins. Construction of the northern half was unexpectedly complex and difficult, and although the foundation had been scheduled for completion in 1968, it was still unfinished three years later. Work on the superstructure of the Main Platform, originally scheduled to start in April 1968, could not be undertaken until December of the following year, and then only on a limited basis. More delays occurred, so that although completion of this work had been set for 1971, it was only 10 percent finished by the end of the year. The scheduled completion date had to be moved back five years.

The overall concept of the South Mall's construction created delays. In order to meet the 1971 completion date, the state had decided that instead of completing the Main

---

came overwhelming. Rather than expand OGS's staff and upgrade its expertise, the state hired the George A. Fuller Construction Company to manage the Mall's superstructure contracts, while OGS continued to manage the foundation contracts. This dual command structure was maintained until late 1968, when Fuller was given responsibility for administering and supervising the entire project.

Platform first and then constructing the buildings that sur-
mount it, simultaneous construction of the Platform and
buildings would be undertaken. As a result, about 2,000 employees of some forty to fifty prime contractors and close to
200 subcontractors were swarming over the site by the middle of 1968. Problems were created as work crews got in each
other's way. Work on the office tower's superstructure had
begun before work on the Platform's foundation had, for example, and by the time both jobs were in operation, tower
workers clashed with platform workers over space on the site
crucial to both crews. Both jobs suffered. Scheduled construction on the tower lagged as its workers were denied convenient access to the site. At one point, rubbish was being
dumped from the tower on the platform workers below; they
refused to work under such conditions, shifts had to be scheduled on nights and weekends and the sequence of work had to
be changed.

Contractors and construction unions could not escape blame
for delays on the project. The state charged contractors with
failing to provide adequate supervision, failing to provide sufficient manpower and failing to cooperate with the state and
among themselves. The state also charged that poor workman-
ship had necessitated many design changes that had resulted in
delays. Jurisdictional disputes between rival unions resulted in
work stoppages. (In 1970 an argument between the Teamsters
and the Operating Engineers Union over who should hold the
nozzle of the hose used to refuel equipment caused more than
twenty-five work stoppages.) There were strikes. Contractors charged that featherbedding and low productivity were
extraordinary.

By January 1971, the Albany South Mall was some five and

a half years behind schedule. Cortland V. R. Schuyler, the re-
tiring General Services Commissioner who had supervised the
project, admitted that the state had been responsible for the
delay. "The state was at fault," he said. "There was more
complexity to the project than we realized. People got in each
other's way, there actually wasn't enough room for contractors and there was not enough labor to meet our requirements." At a news conference held a couple of days later,
however, Governor Rockefeller, then in his fourth term, contended that the concept of simultaneously constructing the
Main Platform and the buildings surmounting it had saved
five years and thereby halved the project's cost. Construction
delays had been caused by the necessity of removing "a volume of mud equal to the weight of each building."* This, according to the Governor, had affected every other phase of
the work for every contractor. In addition, there had been labor problems and a lack of qualified bidders. When "you get
into some of the huge buildings and huge contracts . . . some
of the eligible contractors haven't had the experience to do
this kind of work," the Governor said.

The initial estimated cost of construction of the South Mall
is said to have been $250 million by everyone except Governor
Rockefeller. He has contended that $250 million was merely
"an off-the-cuff figure" provided by an architect and that the
state's first estimate was $480 million, nearly twice as much.
Whichever the estimate was, it was a poor one. From the outset, contract prices far exceeded estimates. For example, the
contract price for the Main Platform's superstructure (the

---

* To be sure, a lot of mud *did* have to be removed from the site; in
order to build the foundation of the Main Platform, for example,
2,700,000 cubic yards of gelatinous blue clay were hauled away.

largest contract in the project) was $97.8 million against an estimate of only $76.4 million. Then came the delays in construction. The trouble with them was not that the Mall's scheduled completion date had to be put off, of course, but that they were expensive and someone had to pay for them. The Legislature determined that the state had to assume some responsibility, and in 1969 the Equitable Adjustment Act, which applied only to the Mall, was passed. The act gave contractors the right to charge the state for losses incurred when "the performance of all or any part of the work has been suspended, delayed or interrupted for any extraordinary and unreasonable period of time by an act or omission of the . state not expressly or impliedly authorized by the contract." Benefits were handsome. The contractor for the Main Platform's foundation received $27 million more than the contract price of $37 million. The initial price of $97.8 million for the Platform's superstructure rose to the neighborhood of $149 million. The contractor for the agency buildings' superstructures received $37.6 million against a contract price of $23.9 million.

At one point, Albany County had agreed to issue $480 million in bonds to finance the Mall's construction. As the cost of construction rose, the county had to issue more bonds. Funding was increased to $670 million in 1969, then to $850 million in 1971, when interest charges on the bonds were calculated at $537 million. (Because the county has a lower credit rating than the state and pays a four-tenths-of-one-percent higher interest rate, about $44 million of these charges are due to the "interesting, ingenious" financing scheme itself.) By December 31, 2004, when the state will take title to the Mall, the total cost will exceed $1.5 billion.

The citizens of New York State would have reason to disapprove of the South Mall. It was an outrageous extravagance, whose cost was being driven up by a ridiculous construction schedule. By early 1971, the cost of the office space, for example, was becoming three times as expensive as office space built by private interests elsewhere in Albany at the same time. Costs for facilities throughout the Mall were becoming two and three times higher than prevailing costs for similar facilities elsewhere. And was the Main Platform, at $300 million, necessary? But perhaps the public eventually would be persuaded that the Mall was not an extravagance. Governor Rockefeller *had* cut corners here and there. An early plan which had provided for low-income housing in the Main Platform for 500 families displaced by the Mall had been canceled when the cost rose from $10 to $20 million. The Governor had called it "way out of line." And perhaps the public eventually would be persuaded that the Mall was necessary. The Governor had faith. In his January 1971 news conference on the delays and increasing construction costs at the Mall, he predicted that it would "turn out to be the greatest thing that has happened in this country in a hundred years."

In the mid-1950s, at the same time the Rockefellers were undertaking construction of Lincoln Center on Manhattan's West Side, they directed their Garden-of-Eden commitment toward another part of New York City—the financial district in Lower Manhattan, where the main offices of the Rockefeller-controlled Chase Bank are located. The opportunity arose because the district was decaying and was threatened with abandonment. Little office space had been built there since the 1920s, and corporations were moving to midtown, where building was booming. The 1954 question in Lower Manhattan was, Would the banks follow the corporations uptown? The Chase provided the answer when it decided to remain downtown, for if the Rockefellers' bank were willing to gamble on a real estate situation, other banks, mindful of the lesson of Rockefeller Center, would make the same bet.

According to William Zeckendorf, David Rockefeller was responsible for the Chase's decision to move out of offices inconveniently scattered in eight separate buildings and to construct large new headquarters on a site at the corner of Liberty and Nassau Streets, a couple of blocks north of Wall Street. Zeckendorf asserts in his autobiography that the Chase was not aware that bids on the desired site were due on the very day he was called in to a meeting of the bank's leaders to discuss their real estate prospects. He informed them that they had to commit themselves immediately. "David had been quietly directing the meeting," Zeckendorf writes. "He did this *sotto voce*, because that is his manner and because many of the older men in that room were more powerful than he within the bank, but it was David who personally guided Chase's gamble on the stabilization of Wall Street."

It also was David who subsequently took charge of the redevelopment of the entire Lower Manhattan district. He announced his intentions in 1956, when he invited fifty-five men from the district's large institutions to join with him in founding the Committee on Lower Manhattan. In 1958, when this group merged with the older Downtown Manhattan Association (founded in 1937) to form the Downtown-Lower Manhattan Association (DLMA) with Rockefeller as chairman, he became Lower Manhattan's chief planner.

In the 1960s, both David Rockefeller and Lower Manhattan

moved up. In 1962 Rockefeller became president of the Chase Manhattan Bank; in 1969 he became chairman and chief executive officer. Concurrently, a dramatic growth in the district's commercial space began. Only two and a half million square feet had been built between 1950 and 1957, but in the first ten years of the Downtown-Lower Manhattan Association 14 million square feet were built, including the $120-million Chase Manhattan Bank headquarters (completed in 1960). By the end of 1972, 28 million more were added.

The major contributor to this expansion is the World Trade Center, which has 9 million square feet of office space in twin 110 story towers and six shorter buildings, 200,000 square feet of retail-store space surrounding a five-acre plaza, plus parking for 2,000 cars. Among the Center's tenants are importers and exporters; domestic and foreign manufacturers' representatives; freight forwarders; Custom House brokers; international banks; federal, state and overseas development agencies; trade associations; and transport lines.

The Center is the invention of the Downtown-Lower Manhattan Association. Early in 1960 DLMA requested the Governors of New York and New Jersey and the Mayor of New York City to authorize the Port of New York Authority, which is charged with coordinating facilities for commerce in the New York metropolitan area, to undertake a feasibility study of a center for international commerce. The Port Authority became eager to build the Center, and in 1962 New York and New Jersey enacted legislation empowering it to do so.

The World Trade Center, like Lincoln Center, is a Rockefeller monument. But unlike Lincoln Center, the World Trade Center will not be a white elephant. Instead, it will be a financial success. Such optimism is indicated by the Center's immediately attracting tenants, despite opening in the early 1970s, when there was a glut of office space in New York City.* Tenants came for reasons of convenience and cost. Shipping companies and other maritime enterprises left buildings on lower Broadway's Shipping Row for the Center because it houses consulates, insurance companies, tugboat operators and other firms essential to the shipping industry, and because the Center is near the new Customs House.† Because the Center is funded by tax-free, low-interest bonds and is exempt from real estate taxes (the Port Authority pays New York City $6.5 million a year in lieu of taxes of more than $28 million), it is able to offer its space at lower rates than privately owned buildings must charge in order to make a profit. In 1969, as part of New York State's effort to consolidate its major Manhattan-based offices, the state's Office of General Services (OGS) searched through Lower Manhattan for optimum prices on 2 million square feet of space. OGS found that whereas rentals in privately owned buildings were quoted at an average of $9.35 per square foot per year for the required 2 million square feet of space, the annual cost in the World Trade Center is $8 per square foot for the first forty years of a ninety-nine-year lease and only maintenance and upkeep thereafter. "We can't tell what maintenance costs will be in forty years," a state official told a *New York Post* reporter in the fall of 1971, "but we figure that we'll be saving a lot in the

---

* In the fall of 1971, 15 million square feet of prime office space in Manhattan's business districts was empty. This is 12 percent of all such space that had been built since the end of World War II.
† One estimate held that the vacancy rate on Shipping Row had climbed to 20 to 25 percent by the latter half of 1971.

long run." (At 1971 rates, maintenance and upkeep would be $4 per square foot.) The state made plans to move 8,000 employees from fifty leased offices around the city to fifty-eight floors in the Center's South Tower; Governor Rockefeller would move his Manhattan office from the building he owns on West Fifty-fifth Street to the Tower's eighty-fifth floor. Thus, about one-quarter of the Center's space would be guaranteed by the state government.

This now led into the construction of another Rockefeller monument in Lower Manhattan. The process began in 1966 with an agreement between the Port Authority and New York City requiring the Authority to deposit in the Hudson River material excavated from the Center's site, with ownership of this considerable landfill going to the city. In June the City Planning Commission announced a twenty-year effort— involving removing piers, demolishing a portion of an elevated highway and replacing it with a depressed highway, and adding more landfill—to develop Manhattan's Hudson River waterfront as a human-scaled residential community for 80,000 to 100,000 people. But the plan for the greening of the Lower Manhattan waterfront had been upstaged in May, when Governor Rockefeller released his own plan, prepared by Wallace K. Harrison, for a "Battery Park City." *New York Times* architecture critic Ada Louise Huxtable later wrote that this plan—which called for housing for 14,000 families, a 2,200-room hotel and two sixty-seven-story office towers—"was a heart-chilling cliché of standard towers in a nonenvironment of vacuous spaces, a familiar formalism grown weary and stale since the 1930s when it was hot from Le Corbusier." This was, of course, a plan for a monument. In 1968, after a struggle between the Governor and New York Mayor Lindsay, a compromise version of Battery Park City was announced. It called for four neighborhoods for 14,000 families at the northern end of a ninety-one-acre landfill development, the neighborhoods to be joined by a multi-level spine of facilities to a towering commercial complex at the southern end, where there will be more than 7 million square feet of office space. In the compromised version, Battery Park City still will be a monument.

While Nelson Rockefeller worked up his plan for Lower Manhattan's western flank, David Rockefeller worked up a plan for a counterpart to Battery Park City on the eastern flank. His plan was made public in April 1972, when he and Mayor Lindsay announced that the Downtown-Lower Manhattan Association and New York City would work together to obtain government loans and private financing for a $1.2-billion development, to be called "Manhattan Landing," for Lower Manhattan's East River waterfront. This huge construction project would contain 9,500 luxury apartments, 6 million square feet of office space, a new building for the New York Stock Exchange, a 400-room hotel, an oceanographic museum, the restored South Street Seaport, an indoor sports complex, a park, a 1,000-car municipal garage and a marina.

Mayor Lindsay hailed the proposal, which had been in the works in one form or another for fifteen years, as "a strong affirmation of faith in the city's future by the planners who conceived it, the financial community who will back it and the developers who will build it." David Rockefeller called his own proposal "ambitious, imaginative and practical." But, he asserted, "it's going to be difficult to execute, as any plan as elaborate and costly as this must necessarily be." His warning was well-founded, for the proposal soon encountered objections, particularly in regard to the proposed use of public funds to cover part of the high construction costs of the luxury housing.* Bronx Borough President Robert Abrams urged city authorities to refuse to allow "severely limited city tax subsidy and housing monies to be used for the construction" of this luxury housing. Manhattan Landing would be "the wrong project, in the wrong place, at the wrong time," he said. Subsidizing "a Gold Coast for the financially elite while housing deterioration is destroying sound neighborhoods [elsewhere in New York City] reminds me of a man who buys a Cadillac while his children are starving. . . . We will be subsidizing new housing for executives who earn $60,000 a year, while middle-income families earning $9,000 to $12,000 a year search fruitlessly for decent housing at rents they can afford."

The Manhattan Landing proposal was defended on the grounds that the development would produce large tax revenues that would "trickle down" to benefit other communities in New York City. "But the priorities of this city have a tragic polarity," the *New York Times* editorialized a couple of days after the proposal had been announced. "It is hard to make a moral reconciliation of the urgency of poverty and the adequacy of the tax base. Significantly, support for the plan is being solicited on the premise of the use of its revenues to better the human condition in other parts of the city, and specifically to build more housing elsewhere. Is that pitch also an easy political panacea? And will the business community and the administration commit themselves equally to the city's poor?"

* Subsidies were needed to enable rents to be set at levels that would attract tenants. But at an estimated rent of $120 per room per month only the rich would be able to live in Manhattan Landing. The high cost of landfill—$40 per square foot—ruled out construction of low- and middle-income housing.

To be sure, the Rockefellers had attempted to meet such objections. Poor people had been included in the Garden-of-Eden campaign; a construction project had been undertaken in a decaying district in New York City with the avowed purpose of benefiting the poor directly. But the nature of a Rockefeller-style urban rehabilitation project is such that the poor are not its principal beneficiaries. In order to attract development capital, such a project must be designed for maximum profitability. This means that office buildings and upper-income housing must predominate; low-income residents and small entrepreneurs, who depend on cheap rents for survival, must be removed. And whatever is done by way of benefiting them—by relocation, say—it becomes evident that the neighborhood is no longer theirs, that it belongs to development interests, and that these interests, not the members of the community, will receive the principal benefits arising from the renewal project.

The announcement of a Rockefeller construction project can produce fear and, ultimately, conflict. The seeds of a typical battle were sown in September 1966, several months after the unveiling of the Battery Park City plan, when Governor Rockefeller announced a project for the heart of Harlem—on one of the centrally located blocks on 125th Street, the district's major thoroughfare. A state office building and an adjoining cultural complex, which was to have shops and facilities for theater, music and conventions, were to be built. The Governor was enthusiastic about the project's future benefits for Harlem. "I would like to predict," he said, "that this is the start of a major surge of growth in this community. It will be very exciting and a significant step in terms of the whole island of Manhattan. What I hope to see is the stimulation of other buildings and private enterprise coming in here and this will be a nucleus." Moreover, the project was to accomplish more than benefit the people in its immediate vicinity. At the unveiling of an architectural model of the state office building (designed by Ifill, Johnson & Hanchard, a black firm) in early 1968 the Governor hailed the project as a model for other communities: "As the first facility of its kind to be located in an area that some would call a ghetto," he said, "this state office building, the related cultural center—under design by the internationally famous architect, Philip Johnson—and other plans for the area currently under discussion will have a tremendous impact not only on the area itself, but on the city and, perhaps, the nation. This is a bold, imaginative effort."

Despite Governor Rockefeller's prediction, Harlem spokesmen did not support the project unanimously. While older spokesmen supported it on the grounds that any project would provide jobs and job-training for Harlem residents, younger spokesmen argued that "just situating a handful of jobs in Harlem does not stop money from continuing to flow out of the black community faster than it comes in. Nothing about this project addresses itself to the problem of black people's money (or for that matter, black people) remaining in the community and developing it." Dr. M. Moran Weston, pastor of Harlem's St. Philip's Episcopal Church and head of three nonprofit corporations that were building housing, a nursing home and a community center in Harlem, proposed that the site be sold to Harlem residents, that part of it then be leased back to the state for construction of its office building and that a shopping center, a business training center, a communications center, research laboratories and social, recreational and cultural facilities be built on the remainder of the site. "Eighty-five to ninety percent of the investment stock would be sold to, and owned by, the people of the community," Dr. Weston said. "Every boy and girl in the community would be encouraged to buy a share, and every family should own a few shares. It would become a demonstration of people's ownership."

In the midst of the argument over the project, Governor Rockefeller pressed on with it. Throughout the planning and design stage, everything went well. Clearing of the site, involving the relocation of some 300 families and the removal of some ninety businesses (mostly small shops and offices), proceeded without incident. Some shopkeepers echoed the Governor's enthusiasm. A jeweler called the project "the biggest shot in the arm" in Harlem in years. "We people on the site must yield to progress," he said. But in the summer of 1969 a group of Harlem militants interfered with the start of construction, as about 100 people moved onto the site and set up tents and temporary wooden structures.

The squatters remained until the morning of September 23, when about 150 helmeted policemen, acting on a complaint from the state Office of General Services, cleared the site. Nine persons were arrested. The action did not bring an immediate peace, however. Throughout the day and night angry crowds gathered at the perimeter of the site. They taunted police and threw rocks and bottles. Sixteen more persons were arrested. A community meeting at the nearby Hotel Theresa had to be adjourned because "emotions were too high for dialogue," according to Livingston L. Wingate, Director of the Urban League of Greater New York.

Governor Rockefeller defended the eviction on grounds that the squatters did not represent Harlem residents. "We cannot have a society where a small group which really does not have the representation can hold up the desires of the majority," he said. The Governor was unyielding in his determination to build; he would have gone ahead with the project even if opposition in the community had been total. In the face of this paternalism, discussion had degenerated into hopeless defiance. Lincoln Lynch, Associate Director of the New York Urban Coalition, contended that opposition to the project should not be brushed aside. Harlem, he told a reporter at the scene of the eviction, wanted "the power to make decisions that affect it. I am terribly disappointed in this action. I wonder who we can turn to. This is the thin edge of the wedge." A week later State Senator Basil Patterson complained that Governor Rockefeller was either "arrogantly indifferent" to the feelings of Harlem's residents or else "totally ignorant of conditions in Harlem. . . . We're trying to say to the Governor: 'You've made a mistake. Let's stop it right now. There's no loss of face. Let's sit down and reason and come up with a solution everyone can agree to.' "*

Thanks to Governor Rockefeller, New York State has a vehicle for skirting unpleasant confrontations in poor communi-

---

* Governor Rockefeller's solution was to continue; because of his determination, construction of the $35-million state office building would not be stopped. But the opposition had some overall effect on the project, for by 1972 only the office building was on the way up; plans for the remainder of the site were not yet firm. In addition, plans for what would go inside the office building had not been announced. The state was making a show of serving the community, for there were black workers on the job and two of the six prime contractors were black-owned firms. There was a state information office on the eastern edge of the site. When I visited the office its sole occupant did not know much about the project, except that many people did come by to ask about it. If I wanted more information I could write to the state, he told me, but he did not know the proper address.

ties. He announced it in 1968, as he proceeded with the Harlem state office building project. In late February he sent the Legislature a bill calling for the creation of the New York State Urban Development Corporation (UDC). This new superagency was to have the power to decide what any community, town, city or region in the state needed in the way of housing and facilities for business, industry, education, recreation and culture, decide how to provide such things, and then do so. It was to have the authority to issue several billion dollars in notes and bonds to finance private developers. In a case where a private developer could not be found, UDC itself was to proceed with the project. The most important feature of the proposed corporation was to be its "drastic" power to override local objections to any projects, to condemn property and ignore local zoning and building codes at will.

The drastic-power feature of the proposed corporation became the focus of debate over Governor Rockefeller's bill. Mayor Lindsay called this feature "encroachment on home-rule rights of localities." He offered a substitute proposal which would authorize state and local governments to make direct loans and payments to public and private groups to cover construction of housing and other facilities. The state could undertake a project without local approval "only where local government has failed to develop its own programs to accomplish the purposes of the proposed state programs, or fails to do so within a reasonable time as prescribed by law." State Senate Republican Majority Leader Earl W. Brydges summed up the case for the drastic-power feature. "No community has any inherent sovereignty," he said as he closed the debate. "They're creatures of the state. If they don't do their job, we'll have to do it for them."

The debate was interrupted by the assassination of Dr. Martin Luther King, Jr. Soon afterwards, Governor Rockefeller went on television to urge quick passage of pending legislation "vitally affecting the lives of all our Negro citizens." The Urban Development Corporation was to be a slum-clearance memorial to Dr. King. Despite this lobbying, the State Assembly rejected the bill by a vote of eighty-five to forty-eight while the Governor was in Atlanta for Dr. King's funeral. (Upstate Republicans voted against it because they saw its major benefits going to New York City; the city's Democrats objected to the attack on home rule.) New strategy was required. The Governor provided it by telephone from Atlanta. The Assembly was recessed for three hours while legislators were called into the offices of party leaders and were harangued by leaders' aides in the capitol's corridors. Promises were extracted. At around ten P.M. the Assembly was reconvened and debate resumed. As a new vote was being taken, leaders' aides remained on the Assembly floor to remind legislators of their promises. At around eleven-thirty, approximately seven hours after the bill had been turned down, it was passed by a vote of eighty-six to forty-five.

As Governor Rockefeller signed the bill into law in an elaborate, crowded ceremony on the day after the vote, he explained that the large number of switched votes could be accounted for by his threats to stop doing "personal favors" for legislators, such as signing pet bills or appointing friends to jobs. "Now I don't like to take this position," the Governor said, "but I think that one has to use whatever authority one has when something of major importance to the people comes before you."

The work of the Urban Development Corporation would

justify these Godfather tactics. Long after Governor Rockefeller and his brothers would be finished building grand monuments marking the entry into the new era, UDC would be undertaking great construction projects.

The greatest of them would involve building entirely new
communities modeled on the classic "new town" concept.*
This would be an ambitious program. In *New Communities
for New York,* a sumptuous brochure published in 1970, UDC
recommended building housing for 2.5 million people in new
communities by the year 2000. The program would be so
large that UDC would be operated on the "seed money" principle, as if it were one of the Rockefellers' private philanthropic institutions. UDC would sell bonds to cover the purchase of land, installation of water and waste-removal systems,
and construction of schools, transportation facilities, police
and fire departments, clinics and hospitals, and community
centers, public parks and recreation facilities. It was estimated
that expenditures of $1.8 billion for such items would generate
private expenditures of $7.3 billion for construction in the
new communities.

This was only a beginning, for the Rockefellers soon began
to promote the development of new communities throughout

* The idea of "new towns" began with a book, *Garden Cities of
Tomorrow,* published in England around 1900 by Sir Ebenezer Howard, a London court reporter whose hobby was community planning.
He proposed that self-contained new towns—with one area for industry; another for housing, schools and open spaces; and the center
for jointly owned shopping, cultural and recreational facilities—be
built in the London countryside. Each new town would be encircled
by a permanent green belt to block expansion beyond the original
borders; every aspect of development—how land could be used, what
could be built, how many people could live in the town—would be
controlled by a paternalistic public authority.

the United States. In February 1971, David Rockefeller called for the development of 110 new cities by the year 2000. He proposed the creation of a new federal corporation or agency which "would deal with the problem of land acquisition—and perhaps guidance in terms of national land-use planning . . . with additional powers for planning and obtaining sites for new towns." The public corporation would work with a private or quasi-private corporation created to raise $10 billion in seed money for acquiring the land. Then "private developers would take over both the financing and construction of buildings after the private corporation had arranged long-term loans for land-acquisition and predevelopment costs."

The Rockefellers have promoted the development of new communities by example: David Rockefeller sponsored Columbia, Maryland, a new city twenty miles northeast of Washington and seventeen miles southwest of Baltimore. The Chase Manhattan Bank, the Connecticut General Life Insurance Company and the Teachers Insurance and Annuity Association have invested $80 million in this five-by-nine-mile city which has office buildings, stores, a community college and a hospital in a downtown section surrounded by seven villages, each with a maximum population of 15,000. The centers of the villages are about a mile from downtown. Each village has its own plaza, meeting hall, restaurants, stores and planned neighborhoods clustered around day-care centers, grade schools, swimming pools and small grocery stores. Scattered around the perimeter of the city are industrial parks, including General Electric's $350-million appliance park, which can employ 12,000 people in a plant half again as big as the Pentagon. There are lakes, golf courses and walkways in Columbia. The city is meant to be complete unto itself.

This new city has a philanthropic orientation. The developer, Jim Rouse, is a devoted member of an experimental church which is involved in social issues. "No matter where he is or what he's doing, he gets back to that church of his every Tuesday night," an associate has said of Rouse. He has been called "a religiously driven improver of man." Rouse, for his part, has called Columbia "a garden for the growing of people." What he might mean by this description is indicated by the fact that there is more racial integration in Columbia than in nearby suburbs. In late 1971, the proportion of blacks in Columbia was estimated at between 15 and 20 percent, which was about double the proportion in the Washington suburbs and about triple the proportion in the Baltimore suburbs.

But Columbia's most important feature is its profitability. While the development lost $619,000 in 1970, it made a fine profit of $3,656,000 in 1971. An outstanding profit was predicted for 1980, when development was scheduled for completion. According to one estimate, the developer's overall profit before taxes would be $70 million and the investors' would be $80 million. Profitability is important, because Columbia is meant to be a model for other new cities, "and making a profit," Rouse has said, "is the surest way to see that that occurs."

To be sure, development of a new city is expensive. A developer is faced with difficulties from the beginning, when large land tracts must be assembled. Huge investments then are required to provide streets, utilities and sanitation systems. Nevertheless, a long list of corporations has entered the new-city field: Standard Oil of New Jersey and Shell in the Houston, Texas area; Texaco in Anaheim Hills, California; Bethlehem Steel in Chicago, Illinois and Birmingham, Alabama; El Paso Natural Gas (with Diversified Properties, Inc.) in Tempe, Arizona. International Telephone and Telegraph (ITT) is planning a new city for swampland on Florida's east coast. Ford is building a new town within the 4,000-acre Ford farm, Fairlane. Costs for the 2,310-acre new town have been estimated at between $500 million and $750 million, to be spread over a fifteen-year period.

Corporations are entering the new-city field not principally to discharge a Rockefeller-style Garden-of-Eden commitment, but to make profits. So one end result of the Rockefellers' discharge of their philanthropic responsibility is profit. This idea should not strike us as strange. Return to Lincoln Center, a typical Rockefeller monument, and ask the question: Who has benefited from the accumulation of some of New York's major performing arts institutions in the Center? Several answers to the question have been rehearsed. According to one, America's image is said to have benefited. In the early days of construction, John D. Rockefeller 3rd spoke of the Center as a symbol:

> When one travels [he said in 1956] one so often hears it said that the emphasis in our country is on the material side. Our feeling is the Center will be a tangible indication to other peoples of the appreciation of art in our lives. Aaron Copland said it could be a symbol of American regard for the arts.

It has also been said that the performing arts will benefit. In the late 1960s Richard Rodgers, whose musical comedy productions were the only profitable endeavors at the Center, said:

I think those people who think bricks and mortar mean nothing to the artist are just cockeyed. Once you build a center like this, it's an instrument, ready to be used. An artist will want to use it. . . . You will see the real value of Lincoln Center. . . . There will be a wonderful exchange of creative ideas . . . the beginning of a wonderful new era in the performing arts.

The Center's constituents are said to have benefited. Amyas Ames has alluded to the fact that the Center's constituents have saved money by being able to share the costs of heating, cleaning, maintenance and security. All of these answers show Lincoln Center to have been built in the spirit of philanthropy. But a visitor to the Center's environs receives a rather different kind of answer, for he is surrounded by new apartment and office buildings of sizes and styles that are hymns of praise to the real estate fast buck. West of the Center are the Lincoln Towers apartments which have 3,859 units. Across Broadway from the Center is One Lincoln Square, a huge business and residential bulwark that is ugly, menacing and contrary to limitations on the use of air space in the special zone finally set up around the Center. Running north from the Center is a line of huge, homely apartment buildings; one takes up an entire city block; another is over forty stories tall. South of the Center is the Gulf and Western conglomerate's forty-four-story office building; its position and height often combine to create winds of terrifying velocities. Lincoln Center's builder, John D. Rockefeller 3rd, and the men who have sat on the boards of the Center and its constituents—bankers; lawyers; restaurant, motel, sugar and bedding executives; and one performer, actor Robert Montgomery, who gained a place in the Establishment by coaching President Eisenhower for his television appearances—created a real estate boom with the Center.

With the construction boom created by Lincoln Center, capital began to flow. And with the flow, the Rockefellers profit, for with their billions the Rockefellers are so vested in business and finance that when a large amount of construction capital flows, the tides of profit must wash up on them. They need not be concerned with profit directly. All they have to do is discharge their philanthropic responsibility by promoting a huge, attractive enterprise like Lincoln Center and they will be enriched. They need not even spend their own money in order to enrich themselves. They are so influential that they can involve government agencies in improving Lower Manhattan or in building new cities and towns, for example, and profit again. So the philanthropy the brothers discharge through giving money and through personal effort is, at bottom, self-interested. The Rockefellers do not give away something for nothing. In addition to the old equation, Profit times Philanthropy equals Power, there is a new equation: Power times Philanthropy equals Profit. To be sure, the philanthropy in the new equation is real: benefit from the Rockefeller construction projects does trickle down to the public.

iv   Art: Collecting, Exhibiting and Tastemaking

John D. Rockefeller's principal avocations were sportive. He was devoted to driving, ice skating and, especially, golf, which was introduced in the United States in the late 1880s. He took his first golf lesson out of the glare of publicity on a remote field in New Jersey in 1899, when he was nearly sixty years old. Two months later, on his first round, he shot 64 on a nine-hole, 2,800-yard course. The next day, he shot 61. Encouraged by his performance, he soon built a twelve-hole course on his estate in Westchester County, New York, and a nine-hole course on his estate at Forest Hill, Ohio. In order to improve his game, he hired a photographer to take a series of pictures of his stroke; hired a boy to shout "Hold your head down! Hold your head down!" on tee shots; used a wire croquet wicket to secure his feet on long shots. He provided bicycles for himself and his golfing partners, and when he grew older had his bicycle pushed. "I like to play golf as much as possible," he said, "so I save up my energy."

He was not involved much with the arts. He seldom attended the theater. Except for the Bible and a few favorites, such as Lew Wallace's *Ben Hur*, he cared little for literature. He did not collect art objects.

Rockefeller Junior, in contrast to his father, was involved with art. He became a dedicated collector of objects which nurtured a passion he had developed for formalism, craftsmanship, precision and detail. He thus was attracted to J. P. Morgan's Chinese porcelain collection, which was exhibited at the Metropolitan Museum of Art. When Morgan died and art dealer Joseph Duveen acquired the collection, Rockefeller Junior became determined to buy it. But the price was high, and he had to ask his father for a loan of more than a million dollars. "I have made many visits to the museums," Rockefeller Junior wrote in pleading his case, "and have studied carefully the most important pieces. I have sought expert advice regarding them. Such an opportunity to secure the finest examples of Chinese porcelains can never occur again, and I want to avail myself of it." But Rockefeller Senior was suspicious of the deal for the porcelains. "I confess frankly," he argued, "I feel afraid of it. This may be because I am not so well informed in regard to their value, present or prospective. . . . It would seem to me that it would be wiser not to make this investment now. . . . I would at least defer the consideration of so important a step for the present." But Rockefeller Junior would not be dissuaded by such cautiousness. He presented his case again:

> I have never squandered money on horses, yachts, automobiles or other foolish extravagances. A fondness for these porcelains is my only hobby—the only thing on which I have cared to spend money. I have found their study a great recreation and diversion, and I have become very fond of them. This hobby, while a costly one, is quiet and unostentatious and not sensa-

tional. I am sure that if I had the actual cash on hand, you would encourage rather than discourage my development of so innocent and educative an interest. The money put into these porcelains is not lost or squandered. It is all there, and while not income-producing, I have every reason to believe that even at a forced sale I could get within 10 percent of what these would cost, while a sale under ordinary circumstances would certainly realize their full cost value, and, as the years go by, more. . . .

Upon hearing this plea, Rockefeller Senior did not lend his son the money. Instead, he made the Morgan porcelains a gift.

In the 1920s Rockefeller art collecting took a wide turn into modernism. Rockefeller Junior and his wife had begun to buy Italian primitives that they had been given to study by Duveen when "all of a sudden," as Rockefeller said later, "my wife, who was very catholic in her tastes and loved all sorts of beautiful things, became interested in modern art. I said to her, 'Here I have spent years trying to cultivate a taste for the great primitives, and just as I begin to see what they mean, you flood the house with modern art!' " It was hardly a flood. The lower floors of their home overflowed with Oriental porcelains, traditional painting, statuary, rugs and tapestries, and the adjacent building had to be refurbished to house the excess. Abby Aldrich Rockefeller's collection of modern art was kept in the children's playroom on the top floor.

In deference to her husband's opinion, Abby Aldrich Rockefeller spent only "Aldrich money" on modern art. She chose small pictures for her collection, usually limiting herself to spending no more than $1,000 on any single work. (At least once, however, she spent considerably more; she paid $20,000, for example, for a tapestry portrait of the Rockefeller family outside their summer home at Seal Harbor, Maine.) Despite her restraint, her collection grew as she became a patron of artists. During the Depression she commissioned Ben Shahn to paint portraits of the Rockefellers' horses at $250 apiece. She commissioned Stefan Hirsch to paint a view from her window and Charles Sheeler to portray buildings at Colonial Williamsburg. While she favored the photographic realism of Sheeler and the romanticized realism of Burchfield and did not like social-consciousness painting, abstraction or surrealism, she bought Shahn's documentary Sacco and Vanzetti series and Peter Blume's almost surrealist *Parade*.

In 1929 Abby Aldrich Rockefeller began to collect American folk art. (New York art dealer Edith Gregor Halpert had convinced her that a folk art collection would provide background for her modern American art collection.) Eventually this collection amounted to some 400 objects, many of which she had bought from sculptor Elie Nadelman and his wife. Mrs. Rockefeller's favorite was a carved wooden eagle that had cost only $750, including her agent's fees. It was valued eventually at $20,000.

The passion for collecting was passed down to the third Rockefeller generation. Winthrop collected antique automobiles and rare books. Laurance bought paintings. In the early 1950s John became an important collector of Asian art objects. His wife Blanchette became an important collector in her own right; in addition to accompanying her husband on treasure hunts to such places as Japan, India, Nepal, Indonesia, Cambodia and Thailand, she bought abstract-expressionist works in New York galleries. The largest collections, however, were assembled by David and Nelson. David's, which emphasizes paintings by French Impressionists and post-

Impressionists, consists of several hundred objects. It is large enough to require the services of a curator, and its undisclosed value is well into the tens of millions of dollars. Exactly how large and valuable it is, no one will say.* Nelson amassed two large collections. One, consisting of primitive art objects from Oceania, Africa and the Americas, appreciated enormously in value over the years.† By the early 1970s it was valued at $20 million. The other collection consists of about 1,500 twentieth-century art objects—European painting and sculpture from the first half of the century; contemporary American painting (Nelson Rockefeller was among the foremost collectors of abstract-expressionist painting in the 1950s); post-World War II American sculpture; prints and illustrated books. This is the collection of an enthusiast with an open purse, the product of what Nelson Rockefeller called "a weakness for collecting." When he wanted something, he got it, no matter what its price. For instance, when he badly wanted a Modigliani nude, but was unwilling to pay the dealer's top price, and was told that he was being given first crack at the picture, but that fourteen other eager customers were lined up behind him and that he would get a second chance at a lower price only if none of the fourteen would pay the top price, he paid it rather than risk losing the picture. In 1956 he took a fancy to Picas-

* The curator, Olive Bragazzi, would fend off requests for estimates with the statement that David Rockefeller and his wife "are very discriminating buyers. I couldn't really say how many pieces there are [in their collection] because their tastes are so broad. It's not just paintings and sculpture, but porcelains and furniture of museum quality. What do the values of these things mean? Insurance? Market value? There's no way to tell."

† A Tarascan dog, for example, which could be bought in Mexico for $2 and in New York for $25 in 1927, cost between $250 and $400 in 1948, and a first-class piece brought $1,500 in 1957.

so's 1910 Cubist painting, "Girl with a Mandolin," which was priced at $98,000. He hesitated, but finally paid what was the highest price that had ever been paid for a Cubist painting up to that time. (It could not have been a poor investment. In 1969 dealer Sidney Janis estimated that a Cubist Picasso or Braque painted between 1900 and 1912 and measuring no more than forty inches high would cost $500,000. Although Nelson Rockefeller would complain that such paintings were "too expensive . . . way out of reach," *his* Picassos and Braques had appreciated along with everyone else's.)

I mean neither to sneer at the Rockefeller brothers for being wealthy nor to suggest that they have collected art objects strictly for financial investment. To be sure, they long ago became acquainted with art collecting's financial potential; indeed, it has helped make collecting attractive to them. But their involvement with art has given pleasures beyond profit. Aline Saarinen described in her book, *The Proud Possessors*, how Nelson Rockefeller would pause while dressing to play with some of the dozens of four-inch pre-Columbian figurines arranged in a shallow bureau drawer in his Fifth Avenue apartment. She also wrote that during his service in the Eisenhower Administration—when he is said to have worked very hard (he ate his lunch of a sandwich, ice cream and a chocolate brownie at his desk most days and expected subordinates and visitors to discuss business as they shared his meal)— "he frequently telephoned René d'Harnoncourt, the director of the Museum of Modern Art and his mentor in primitive art, and asked him to bring down some 'stuff.' D'Harnoncourt . . . would arrive in Washington with a suitcase full of paper-thin Peruvian gold pendants, little bowlegged Tarascan dogs, a suavely curving ceremonial paddle from Easter Island.

Green and exhausted, Nelson Rockefeller became visibly refreshed and revitalized during a half-hour spent selecting the 'stuff' he wanted to buy."

There always has been something besides private moments of aesthetic appreciation: philanthropic responsibility. It has been a powerful element of the Rockefellers' involvement with art; they have been devoted to sharing the enjoyment of art objects with the general public. There was that time in 1919, for example, when Rockefeller Junior received a letter from the dealer Kelekian saying that he had been unable to find an American buyer for the great Assyrian winged bulls from the palace of Ashur-nasir-apal and was taking them to Europe. Two days later Kelekian bumped into Rockefeller Junior as he was on his way to the dealer's gallery. The transaction for the winged bulls was completed on a street corner. Rockefeller Junior then gave the bulls to the Metropolitan Museum.

It became well known that Rockefeller Junior was at least as devoted to art philanthropy as to collecting, and on occasion museum personnel were quite bold in playing on his generosity. After having given the Metropolitan $1 million to obtain a collection of medieval sculpture, tomb slabs and architectural elements, including fragments of French monasteries, that sculptor George Gray Barnard had assembled in Europe and housed in his "cloister museum" in New York City's Washington Heights section; after having supplemented this collection with forty more objects; after having given $2.5 million for the design and construction of a new museum—the Cloisters, a branch of the Metropolitan; after having assumed responsibility for landscaping fifty-six-acre Fort Tryon Park in upper Manhattan, where the Cloisters was built . . . after all this giving, Rockefeller Junior wrote to James Rorimer of the Metropolitan that Rorimer was never to "feel under the slightest embarrassment in giving me your frank opinion of any object belonging to me which I may submit for the consideration of the museum as a possible gift to it." Later, while studying the architectural drawings for the Cloisters, Rockefeller saw that one of the rooms was to be called the "Tapestry Hall." What, he wanted to know, did Rorimer intend to install there? "I was thinking of something like the Unicorn Tapestries," Rorimer said. "What?" Rockefeller asked in disbelief. The tapestries covered the walls of Rockefeller's favorite room in his home on West Fifty-fourth Street, a room which he often visited alone. Nevertheless, they were installed in the Cloisters in time for their opening in 1938. And that, befitting the Rockefeller philanthropic responsibility, is where the tapestries belong. Rockefeller spoke of a connection between his responsibility and art at the Cloisters' opening ceremonies:

With the changes that time has brought, the wholesome and profitable use of leisure, now so startlingly prevalent, is one of the great problems of the day. In its solution the cultural and uplifting value of beauty, whether apprehended with eye or ear, is playing an increasingly important part. . . . May it well not be that the Cloisters . . . surrounded by nature at her best, will become another stimulating center for the profitable use of leisure? If that should prove to be true, if what has been created here helps to interpret beauty as one of the great spiritual and inspirational forces of life, having the power to transform drab duty into radiant living; if those who come under the influence of this place go out to face life with renewed courage and restored faith because of the peace, the calm, the loveliness they have found here; if the many who thirst for beauty are refreshed and gladdened as they drink deeply from this well of beauty, then those who have builded here will not have built in vain.

With a deeply felt responsibility to put things on public view, Rockefeller Junior and his wife were liable to turn any of their private collections into exhibitions. Part of Mrs. Rockefeller's magnificent collection of American folk art found its way into a house within her husband's restoration at Colonial Williamsburg. But the collection was out of place there. For one thing, because almost all of the paintings in the collection had been done about a century after the Colonial period, they were not consistent with the painstaking authenticity of the restoration. For another thing, the collection's velvet paintings and plaster sculptures were being ruined by Williamsburg's climate. Rockefeller Junior had to move the collection. Predictably, he chose to build an appropriate home for it himself. Since the latter 1950s his wife's folk art collection has resided in a fully air-conditioned nineteenth-century-style mansion just outside the restoration.

The responsibility to transform enthusiasms for collecting into exercises in philanthropy was drummed into the Rockefeller brothers; they became dedicated to it. Accordingly, Nelson Rockefeller's first acquisition of a primitive object—a Sumatran knife handle in the form of a human head, hair and all—when he was passing through the Dutch East Indies on his honeymoon in the early 1930s marked the beginning of an exercise in art philanthropy. Several years later he acquired some pre-Columbian objects in Mexico, and in 1939 he offered the Metropolitan Museum money to cover an archeological expedition. But the Metropolitan's director flatly refused the offer. The museum simply was not interested in primitive objects. Rockefeller continued to build his collection, and by the early 1950s his Fifth Avenue apartment was crammed with primitive objects. He and René d'Harnoncourt then began to lay the groundwork for turning the private collection into a public one. D'Harnoncourt prepared a set of five notebooks, one for each geographical area of primitive art. He made a map of each tribal area, then drawings of all objects needed for a great public collection. For those pieces in the Rockefeller collection of top aesthetic quality, drawings were removed from the notebook and photographs of the Rockefeller pieces were inserted. Rockefeller made additional purchases to meet the demands he and D'Harnoncourt had set. By 1954, photographs outnumbered drawings, and the collection was deemed suitable for public display. Rockefeller opened the Museum of Primitive Art in 1957 in a brownstone on West Fifty-fourth Street, with himself as president, D'Harnoncourt as vice-president and Robert Goldwater as director. The Primitive remained a rather small museum, and with fewer than 30,000 admissions per year, it did not pay its own way; Rockefeller had to guarantee its operating expenses from out of his pocket. But the existence of the Primitive had a powerful effect on the Metropolitan. A little more than a decade after the Primitive had been established, an exhibition of 664 objects from the Rockefeller collection was mounted at the Metropolitan. This was the Metropolitan's first showing of objects from primitive cultures. More important, when Rockefeller offered to donate the Primitive's collection of some 4,000 objects to the Metropolitan, his offer was accepted, even under the condition that the transfer would not take place until space had been built for the collection. And a new Department of Primitive Art has been formed at the Metropolitan—the first such department at a major art museum. It had taken more than three decades, but now this Rockefeller exercise in art philanthropy was complete.

.

The Rockefellers brought their enthusiasms for art to the decoration of their business institutions. In 1932, Diego Rivera, the controversial anti-bourgeois Mexican painter whose work Abby Aldrich Rockefeller admired despite its themes, was commissioned to paint the principal mural in the great hall of the RCA Building at Rockefeller Center. His mural was to cover the large wall opposite the main entrance (which is on the short private street that runs parallel to Fifth Avenue, between Forty-ninth and Fiftieth Streets). He was to be paid $21,000, by Great Depression standards a handsome fee—high enough to permit him to hire a large number of assistants to prepare the wall, grind colors and make tracings of his sketches and stencil them on wet plaster. He planned to do only the final painting himself.

Here again the Rockefellers intended to combine their artistic enthusiasms with their philanthropic responsibilities. The mural not only was to decorate the hall, it was to convey an important philosophical message to anyone passing by. The instructions the Rockefellers transmitted to Rivera read, in part:

> The philosophical or spiritual quality should dominate. . . . We want the paintings to make people pause and think and to turn their minds inward and upward. . . .
>
> Our theme is NEW FRONTIERS. . . .

Man cannot pass up his pressing and vital problems by "moving on." He has to solve them on his own lot. The development of civilization is no longer lateral; it is inward and upward. It is the cultivation of man's soul and mind, the coming into a fuller comprehension of the meaning and mystery of life.

Rivera's sketches for the mural were accompanied by a commentary which read, in part:

> My painting will show, as the culmination of [the development of the ethical relations of mankind], human intelligence in possession of the Forces of Nature, expressed by the lightning striking off the hand of Jupiter and being transformed into useful electricity. . . . Below, the Man of Science presents the scale of Natural Evolution, the understanding of which replaces the Superstitions of the past. . . .
>
> My panel will show the Workers arriving at a true understanding of their rights regarding the means of production, which has resulted in the planning of the liquidation of Tyranny, personified by a crumbling statue of Caesar, whose head has fallen to the ground. It will also show the Workers of the cities and the country inheriting the Earth. . . .
>
> The Worker gives his right hand to the Peasant who questions him, and with his left hand takes the hand of the sick and wounded Soldier, the victim of War, leading him to the New Road. On the right of the central group, the Mothers, and on the left, the Teachers, watch over the development of the New Generation, which is protected by the work of the Scientists. Above, on the right side . . . a group of young women in the enjoyment of health-giving sports, and on the left, a group of unemployed workmen in a breadline. Above this group . . . an image of War, as in the case of Unemployment, the result of the evolution of Technical Power unaccompanied by a corresponding ethical development.

Rivera worked on the mural into the spring of 1933. When newspaper reporters went to Rockefeller Center to inspect the work, they registered outrage at what they saw. RIVERA PAINTS SCENES OF COMMUNIST ACTIVITY AND JOHN D. JR. FOOTS BILL shouted the headline of Joseph Lilly's article in the *New York World-Telegram*. Lilly had seen "microbes given life by poison gases used in war . . . germs of infectious and hereditary disease . . . so placed as to indicate them as the results of a civilization revolving around nightclubs . . . a Communist demonstration . . . iron-jawed policemen, one swinging his club. . . . The dominant color is red—red headdress, red flags, waves of red . . . in a victorious onsweep. . . ." According to Lilly, Rivera had said that "Mrs. Rockefeller said she liked my painting very much. . . . Mr. Rockefeller likes it too. . . ." The Rockefellers' reaction to the mural was "remarkable," according to writer Geoffrey Hellman, who wondered why they did not object to the mural's showing "a Soviet demonstration before the Kremlin as one of civilization's brightest features, war as a product of capitalism in contradistinction to sport as a product of Communism, and a bridge game the precursor of venereal disease."

But the Rockefellers began to like Rivera's mural less when the head of "the Worker" turned out to be a likeness of Lenin! The Rockefellers' enthusiasm for art and Rockefeller Center were being violated. Rivera was informed by Nelson Rockefeller that while he was still enamored of the "beautifully painted" mural, the inclusion of a portrait of Lenin "might seriously offend a great many people. If it were in a private house it would be one thing, but this mural is in a public building and the situation is therefore quite different." Rivera was asked to substitute the face of an unknown man for Lenin's. When he refused to do so, he was ordered off the premises. The mural was covered over; no photographs were allowed.

There was a great uproar; committees of artists agitated for and against the mural. On May 12 the *World-Telegram* reported Rockefeller assurances that "the uncompleted fresco of Diego Rivera will not be destroyed or in any way mutilated, but . . . will be covered, to remain hidden for an indefinite time. . . ." The Rockefellers allowed the mural to remain on the RCA Building wall only until Saturday, February 9, 1934, however. At midnight they destroyed it. They paid Rivera the $21,000 fee in full and hired another muralist.

The Rivera affair had no noticeably deleterious effects on the Rockefellers' enthusiasm for installing art works in their business institutions. Under David Rockefeller's leadership in the 1960s, the Chase Manhattan Bank became, in *New York Times* art critic John Canaday's words, "the leader in the golden age of collecting by business," as the bank spent $800,-000 for 1,500 paintings, sculptures and graphics. Nor did the Rivera affair give the Rockefellers an evil reputation among artists. The Rockefellers' continuing support was appreciated; when David Rockefeller arranged a "thank you" dinner at Chase headquarters in April 1969, 125 artists from around the world showed their appreciation for his enthusiasm by attending. (One West German, who could not attend in person, mailed a life-sized, cardboard-backed photograph of himself that was set up in a chair pulled up to a dining table.) But the Rivera affair was a lesson. As a result of it, the Rockefellers turned away from the notion of adorning their business institutions with art works meant to convey philosophical statements. In the $2.5-million art collection assembled after World

War II by the Chase Manhattan Bank under David Rockefeller's personal leadership, the emphasis has been on nonrepresentational American art of the 1950s and '60s, art which is abstract, which makes no philosophical statements about such things as "new frontiers" to those whose eyes it catches in the bank's offices. Art still has an important place in the Rockefellers' business institutions, but merely as decoration.

The most important artistic outlet for the Rockefeller family's philanthropic responsibility was founded by Abby Aldrich Rockefeller. She began by turning what had been the children's playroom on the top floor of her home in Manhattan into a private gallery of modern art. In the late 1920s she decided to go public, and by 1928, as she wrote to her son Nelson, her mind was "full of ideas for a new Museum of Modern Art in New York." That winter she bumped into Lizzie P. Bliss—one of the new breed of twentieth-century collectors, men and women of inherited wealth who had been influenced by the Armory Show of 1913 and bought modern art*—while Miss Bliss and her niece were passing through Jerusalem. At lunch, according to what the niece, Mrs. Elizabeth Bliss Parkinson, has told us, Miss Bliss and Mrs. Rockefeller

    began talking quite seriously about a museum of modern art in
    New York. Well, that May—it was 1929—Abby Rockefeller

* Lizzie P. Bliss was the daughter of Cornelius N. Bliss, who had made a fortune as a selling agent for New England textile firms and was briefly McKinley's Secretary of the Interior. Her art collection, which included a group of Cézannes and representative works by Seurat, Gauguin, Redon, Rousseau, Matisse, Picasso and Modigliani, was devoted mainly to French painting.

gave a small luncheon in her home. . . . Lillie [her family called Lizzie Lillie] was there, and Mrs. Cornelius J. Sullivan, and A. Conger Goodyear. Mr. Goodyear was from Buffalo, where he'd been in banking and lumber and had started the Albright Gallery. The ladies asked him to help them create a gallery for modern painting and sculpture. He agreed, and brought in Frank Crowninshield, the editor of *Vanity Fair*, and Peter Grimm, the real estate man. By early summer they had a provisional charter, six rented rooms in the old Heckscher Building on Fifth Avenue, and a name, the Museum of Modern Art. Dr. Paul Sachs of Harvard had joined them. It was he who suggested hiring Alfred Barr, Jr. Alfred was only twenty-seven then, but Dr. Sachs spoke so highly of him that he was hired anyway. So the museum had a director, and was opened to the public by November.

The art at the Museum of Modern Art (MOMA) was not to be limited to painting and sculpture. Alfred Barr, who had been dubbed "the very modern Mr. Barr of Cambridge and Wellesley" by Boston art critics, had devoted a portion of the groundbreaking course in modern art he taught at Wellesley College—it was the first course in modern art in the United States—to excursions into music, photography, theater, movies, architecture and the design of articles sold in dime stores. Soon after he had been selected as MOMA's director, he said that "in time the Museum would probably expand beyond the narrow limits of painting and sculpture in order to include departments devoted to drawings, prints and photography, typography, the arts of design in commerce and industry, architecture (a collection of *projets* and *maquettes*), stage designing, furniture and decorative arts. Not the least important collection might be the *filmotek*, a library of films, with a projection room such as is already maintained in Moscow, where the score or so finest films of the year would be preserved and shown."

Barr was bent on educating MOMA's trustees, on broadening their artistic interests. He sent postcards recommending films he considered works of art to Mrs. Rockefeller and Mr. Goodyear; he took Miss Bliss to see *The Passion of Joan of Arc* in an attempt to pursuade her that movies are an art form. And MOMA itself went beyond painting and sculpture in order to discharge its "primary purpose [which] is to help people enjoy, understand and use the visual arts of our time." In MOMA's first decade—in addition to a major Van Gogh exhibition, surveys called "Cubism and Abstract Art" and "Fantastic Art: Dada and Surrealism" and a huge Picasso retrospective—there were major exhibitions devoted to the International Style of architecture and "Machine Art" (which included such items as a ship's propeller, a cross-section of undersea cable and a gasoline pump) and film and photography departments were established.

One of the most important exhibitions at MOMA during its first decade was the 1932 architectural exhibition in which Philip Johnson and Henry Russell Hitchcock promoted the work of Frank Lloyd Wright, Walter Gropius, Le Corbusier, J. J. P. Oud, Mies van der Rohe, Raymond M. Hood, Howe and Lescaze, Richard J. Neutra and the Bowman brothers. (The exhibition also promoted Lewis Mumford's solutions to current housing problems.) In the introduction to the exhibition's catalogue, Alfred Barr asserted MOMA's intentions in a most direct manner: "Expositions and exhibitions," he began, "have changed the character of American architecture of the last forty years more than any other factor." Barr illustrated his point by recalling that the Chicago Columbian Exposition of 1893 had produced a Classical Revival: Colonial houses, Gothic college dormitories and Spanish country clubs had become fashionable. And more recent competitions and exhibitions had signaled the end of the Classical Revival. Although, for example, the 1922 competition for the *Chicago Tribune* Tower design had been won by Raymond Hood with a Gothic design, Finnish architect Eero Saarinen's second-prize entry, which had been a departure, had been received enthusiastically by American architects and made them doubt that historical styles were sufficient for modern purposes. The 1925 Paris Exhibition of Decorative Arts had delivered another blow to American confidence in historical styles when architectural exhibitions from the United States were ruled out on the grounds that they were out of step with the times.

According to Barr, American architecture was currently in a state of confusion. The facades of office skyscrapers—a form in which the United States was preeminent—were either Renaissance or Roman or Gothic. But the "more advanced" American architects, who were influenced by "modernistic" decoration in vogue in Amsterdam, Paris, Stockholm and Vienna, were embellishing these skyscrapers with "zigzags and chevrons instead of Gothic crochets and Classical modelings." The result was that the avenues of the great American cities had become an uncertain conglomeration of styles. But "the present exhibition," Barr wrote, "is an assertion that the confusion of the past forty years, or rather of the past century, may shortly come to an end." Since the early 1920s "the ideas of a number of progressive architects have converged to form a genuinely new style which is rapidly spreading throughout the world. Both in appearance and structure this style is peculiar to the twentieth century. . . . It has been called the International Style."

The architectural style Barr was heralding was meant to give skyscrapers (and other buildings, such as factories, schools and libraries) a light, clean look. The old design concepts gave skyscrapers a heavy, messy look: exterior walls were made of heavy masonry, upper floors were set down on heavy bases composed of three or four floors, and exterior walls were topped by heavy cornices; the lower floors and cornices were outlets for architects' talents for ornamentation, and walls were cluttered with more ornamentation. But the International Style—in which a skyscraper is constructed by hanging a thin, lightweight shell of exterior walls on a skeletal steel framework—affords freedom of design. "The modern architect," Barr wrote, "feels it unnecessary to add an elaborate ground floor or an elaborate crowning decoration to his skyscraper. . . . He permits the horizontal floors . . . to repeat themselves boldly without artificial accents or termination."

In the International Style, the paramount considerations are the choice of building materials and the proportions and composition of the elements of a design. Walls are flat surfaces; windows and doors are flush; moldings and ornamentation (including modern ornamentation, which Barr derided as "usually crass and machine-manufactured") are gone, lest they "mar rather than adorn the clean perfection of surface and proportion." Anything that is nonutilitarian is forbidden.

Barr was championing more than the International Style of architecture. He was describing a general theory of applied design. It was summed up at MOMA as the principle of *or-*

ganic design: "a harmonious organization of the parts within the whole, according to structure, material, and purpose . . . [with] no vain ornamentation or superfluity, but [with] the part of beauty . . . none the less great—in ideal choice of material, in visual refinement, and in the rational elegance of things intended for use." This principle became the touchstone of a philosophy of applied design which was meant to influence not only architects, but also industrial designers. In a 1941 booklet called "Organic Design in Home Furnishings," Eliot Noyes, Director of MOMA's Department of Industrial Art, described MOMA's effort to influence the design of everyday furniture:

> Obviously the forms of our furniture should be determined by our way of life. Instead, for the most part, we have had to adapt ourselves uncomfortably and unreasonably to what has happened to be manufactured. For several years the Museum of Modern Art has been studying this problem in order to foster a collaboration between designer, manufacturer, and merchant, to fill this strange gap in the conveniences for modern existence.

"Organic Design in Home Furnishings" was a report on a design competition that MOMA had inaugurated in October 1940. The prizes awarded to the designers were contracts with furniture manufacturers. MOMA had recruited twelve major department stores in large cities from coast to coast to sell the prize-winning designs.

The purpose of the competition was to engage designers in the task of creating a streamlined household environment; they were to apply the principle of *organic design* to the ordinary functions of sitting and storage. Accordingly, the prize for chair design was won by architects Eero Saarinen and Charles Eames with a chair which provided the basic function of sitting without any decorative frills whatsoever. The seat of this new chair was a shell molded so as to give the body continuous support. The shell was formed by laminating strips of wood veneer in a cast iron form of the appropriate shape. The shell was covered with a thin foam rubber pad, in order to cushion the body, and was mounted on four straight, non-ornamental legs. These purely functional chairs were less than half as heavy as traditional, overstuffed chairs of comparable size.

The solution to the problem of streamlining storage was the unit furniture system, in which pieces such as bookcases, chests of drawers and cabinets were units of standardized dimensions. Thus, they could be combined in any way desired, either horizontally or vertically. Bases, which could be used as low tables and benches as desired, could also be used to raise storage units off the floor; accordingly, it would be easy to clean the units, they would be more accessible and wall protrusions could be avoided. The units had no ornamentation: surfaces were flat and clean, as in the International Style; drawer pulls were either recesses or grooves; legs, either straight or tapered, were without decoration. The units could be used anywhere in the home—in either the living room, dining room or bedroom. MOMA called the unit-furniture concept the twentieth century's one completely fresh idea in furniture storage.

Gifts from three women—Lizzie P. Bliss, Abby Aldrich Rockefeller and Mrs. Simon Guggenheim—became the nuclei of MOMA's collection of painting and sculpture. Miss Bliss bequeathed her collection of French painting to the museum in 1931. In 1935 Mrs. Rockefeller donated a collection of 181 mostly American paintings and drawings, including groups of watercolors by Burchfield, Demuth, Hart and Pendergast and oils by Blume, Sheeler and Weber. In 1935 and 1936, when prices were very low, she gave Alfred Barr several thousand dollars to purchase abstract and surrealist works in Europe. She gave the museum its first large purchase fund in 1938. With it, the museum bought Lehmbruck's *Kneeling Woman* (1911), Matisse's *The Blue Window* (c. 1912). Klee's *Around the Fish* (1926) and Kane's *Self Portrait* (1929). In 1938 Mrs. Guggenheim began to provide the museum with large purchase funds. The next year, Mrs. Rockefeller gave the museum two collections: thirty-six pieces of modern European and American sculpture, including works by Maillol, Despiau, Lehmbruck, Lachaise and Kolbe, and examples of American folk painting and sculpture, including one twentieth-century work—Pickett's *Manchester Valley*.

As a result of such generosity, visitors to MOMA's collection of painting and sculpture in the 1940s encountered an illustrated history of modern European art. The effect on the art world was of great significance. "The fact that good European moderns are now here is very important," Jackson Pollock told an interviewer in 1944, "for they bring with them an understanding of the problems of modern painting." In MOMA's galleries American artists could apprehend the artistic revolution that had been centered in Europe during the past several decades, and the museum became a major factor in the shift of the center of artistic influence from Paris to New York in the 1940s.

The effect of modern European art had been far wider: the

twentieth-century European painting styles exhibited in MOMA's galleries had been a potent influence on the work of architects and designers. This influence was proclaimed in an exhibition called "Modern Art in Your Life," mounted for the museum's twentieth birthday celebration in 1949, which showed how the inventions of twentieth-century European painters were reflected in the appearances of skyscrapers, houses, furniture and its arrangement, table settings, tapestries, rugs, fabrics, the Kleenex Tissues box, radio sets, newspaper advertisements, magazine covers, title pages of books, book and record jackets, posters and store window displays. In a monograph written for the exhibition by Robert Goldwater in collaboration with René d'Harnoncourt, it was noted that

> modern art plays an important part in shaping the world we live in. Sensitive to the conditions of the modern world, it has transformed and remade much of the outward appearances of familiar scenes. Whether we are aware of it or not (and whether we like it or not), it helps to produce the environment of our daily lives.

With periodic exhibitions devoted to illustrating applications of the principle of organic design, and with continuous exhibition of modern European painting and sculpture, the Museum of Modern Art assumed its role in American life. MOMA's broad program was directed toward a specific goal: to persuade. The museum set out to influence the work of artists, architects and designers and to build public demand for the new work. The key words in the museum's statement of purpose are "help people use . . . the visual arts of our time."

In this role, MOMA fulfilled a basic Rockefeller need. For

whatever could have been done with art by way of collecting it, supplying it to museums and adorning business institutions with it—all of this would not have been sufficient to have satisfied the artistic demands of a commitment to create a new Garden of Eden. After all, how many art objects could the Rockefellers buy and in how many places could the objects be put on public view? In any event, installing art objects in public places would be a rather tedious method for beautifying the world. Besides, what about the total environment? No place could be made into a part of what was supposed to be a Garden of Eden if while you beautified one patch someone else put something ugly or inharmonious on another patch. The commitment required a potent tastemaker under whose influence architects and designers throughout the United States would produce a uniformly beautiful, harmonious environment. The Museum of Modern Art, located in the country's center of artistic activity, filled this requirement. As Alfred Barr once put it: "The Museum of Modern Art has a few times set out deliberately to be a tastemaker. It did a great deal to accelerate revolutionary changes in American architecture and probably affected the design of American furniture, too." Indeed, the International Style has dominated the design of our office buildings for many years. And the Saarinen-Eames chair (now commonly made of molded plastic, rather than wood, with aluminum legs) and the unit-furniture concept have achieved tremendous popularity.

Members of the third Rockefeller generation have held positions of authority at MOMA since the 1930s, when Nelson Rockefeller became an enthusiastic trustee, working diligently on membership drives and raising funds for a building on West

Fifty-third Street, where the museum has been located since 1939. When the building opened, he was president of the board of trustees and had become a dominant figure at the museum. In 1949, the year after his mother's death, he hand-picked the museum's second director, his colleague in primitive art, René d'Harnoncourt. Since then, either Nelson, his sister-in-law Blanchette, or his brother David has sat as chairman or president of the board of trustees.

From the beginning, MOMA's tastemaking has been beneficial to the Rockefeller brothers. In the early 1950s Joe Alex Morris wrote in *Those Rockefeller Brothers*, which he subtitled *An Informal Biography of Five Extraordinary Young Men*, that when Laurance Rockefeller was furnishing a home soon after his marriage in the mid-1930s, he was introduced by Harmon Goldstone, an architect in the employ of Wallace K. Harrison, to the modern furniture designed by the noted Finnish architect Alvar Aalto. Rockefeller became so enthusiastic about it that he, Goldstone and Harrison decided to set up a company to import the furniture and sell it in the United States. In setting up their company, these partners had, in Morris's words, "several advantages. Mr. Rockefeller, Jr., gave them the use of an old house on Fifty-third Street. The Museum of Modern Art had an Aalto show and borrowed some of their stock, later buying it for the Museum. . . . None of the three is quite sure what might have happened had not the beginning of World War II suddenly cut off their imports from Finland. As a result they decided to liquidate New Furniture, Inc.—the company they had formed—and split up a modest profit." It was all so convenient. Not only was MOMA a tastemaker, it also became a source of profit for the Rockefellers.

This directly beneficial relationship continues. In 1969 MOMA produced a major exhibition called "Twentieth-Century Art from the Nelson Aldrich Rockefeller Collection," and published a 140-page book which called his assemblage of modern painting and sculpture part of "one of the most glorious [collections] ever assembled." Such praise cannot help but increase the value of the collection, and it came as no surprise that when Rockefeller sold five paintings by modern American artists at an auction in November 1971, the prices commanded for works by two of the artists—Morris Louis ($50,-000) and Frank Stella ($36,000)—were record prices for those artists.

The profits accruing to the Rockefellers from their long association with MOMA have not been counted only in dollars and cents. The museum also has contributed to the Rockefellers' personal prestige, and not merely by praising their art collections. In 1971 the museum produced an exhibition called "Architecture and the Arts: The State University of New York at Purchase," and published a forty-page book which called the Purchase campus "the model for an ideal community." The $160-million campus is one of four entirely new campuses built by the New York State University Construction Fund, a multi-billion-dollar corporation set up by the Legislature on Governor Nelson Rockefeller's recommendation in 1962. The museum's exhibition and the associated book gave him an opportunity to defend his reputation as a builder at a time when the Albany South Mall, his largest single construction project then underway, was coming in for heavy criticism for extravagance. The book contains an introduction by Rockefeller in which he concluded that "the Fund has demonstrated public building programs need not result in stereotypes, mediocrity and dullness and that architectural excellence need not mean exorbitant cost." In effect, the museum was being used to certify Nelson Rockefeller's building programs.

So in addition to tastemaking on behalf of the Rockefellers' noble Garden-of-Eden commitment and enhancing the value of their private art collections, MOMA could aid the Rockefellers' reputation as builders and improve their political position. To be sure, the museum is a magnificent contribution to art in America. But the museum also has been used by the Rockefellers in ways that are not altogether benign.

V   Conservation and Development of Natural Resources

In the spring of 1875 John D. Rockefeller and three partners pooled $250,000 and formed the Forest Hill Association in Ohio; their purpose was to establish a hydropathic sanitarium. The corporation bought land Rockefeller owned at Forest Hill, which lies between the cities of East Cleveland and Cleveland Heights, and began to put up a large building on the crest of a hill with a view of Lake Erie. When hard times forced Rockefeller's partners out of the corporation, he was obliged to purchase the unfinished structure himself. He completed the building, and in the summer of 1877 he and Mrs. Rockefeller put the place to work, not as a sanitarium, but as a club hotel, hiring a manager and servants and inviting friends and their families as paying guests. After one summer, however, the Rockefellers became disenchanted with the idea. As Rockefeller told his son, "I found that guests expected Mother to entertain them and act as hostess. Therefore, we discontinued the club at the end of the first year." Over the next several years the building was remodeled, and until it burned down in 1917 the Rockefellers used it as a summer home.

159

The emphasis of Rockefeller's activities on his lands shifted eventually; his primary concern became landscaping. At the Forest Hill estate, he built over six miles of drives and paths, planted trees, cleared land for gardens and dammed a brook to form a small lake. Later, until well past the age of eighty, he worked on the landscaping of his estate at Pocantico Hills, where he had as many as 300 people on the payroll. He still continued to dabble in the use of his lands for profit. When he transplanted trees from Pocantico to another residence at Lakewood, New Jersey, he amused himself by selling himself the trees, which had cost only five or ten cents, for $1.50 to $2.00.

Around the beginning of the third Rockefeller period, when Rockefeller Junior donated 2,700 acres of the family's extensive holdings on Mount Desert Island on the Maine Coast to Acadia National Park,* set out to build sixty miles of roads and bridges for sightseers motoring on the island, and donated fifty-six acres in Upper Manhattan to New York City as Fort Tryon Park,† the primary emphasis of the Rockefeller involvement with land began to shift again. In the next several

---

* Acadia, the first national park east of the Mississippi River, was established entirely by private contributions of land and money, which Charles W. Eliot, president of Harvard, and George B. Dorr, summer residents of Maine, began to solicit in 1901.
† Rockefeller's offer of the fifty-six acres in 1916—to which he attached conditions that the city develop and maintain the land as a park and purchase a strip of land that would connect the new park to Fort Washington Park to the south—was refused. But in 1930, when Rockefeller agreed to landscape the park himself, provided that the city set aside four acres for the Cloisters, the city accepted the donation, agreeing in the bargain to close off the eastern ends of East Sixty-fourth and Sixty-eighth Streets and give the land to the Rockefeller Institute for Medical Research.

decades, Rockefeller Junior devoted a noteworthy share of Rockefeller philanthropic disbursements to promoting and developing public parks throughout the United States. He contributed to Shenandoah National Park, provided half of the $10 million required to buy the land for Great Smoky National Park, donated 216,000 acres he purchased in the Jackson Hole Territory to Grand Teton National Park* and gave $50,000 for clearing roadsides at Yellowstone National Park and $1.7 million to preserve sugar pine forests at Yosemite National Park. In addition, he established museums at Mesa Verde National Park, Grand Canyon National Park and Yosemite.

In 1940, Rockefeller Junior established Jackson Hole Preserve, Inc., a foundation whose purpose is: "To restore, protect and preserve, for the benefit of the public, the primitive grandeur and natural beauties of the landscape in areas noted for picturesque scenery. To maintain and develop historic landmarks and other features of historic or scientific interest in such areas, and to provide facilities for the public use, appreciation and enjoyment of the scenic, biological, scientific and historic features of such areas." In its early years, Jackson Hole Preserve contributed to saving Giant Sequoias in California's South Calaveras Grove; to saving the world's tallest

* This was not brought about until after a struggle that took nearly two decades. In 1943, nine years after the first attempt had been blocked by the Bureau of the Budget's objection to granting compensation for the loss in taxes resulting from the transfer, President Roosevelt declared Rockefeller's lands (plus part of an adjoining forest) a National Monument (which he could do by executive order). Congress then voted to abolish the Monument on the grounds that the area would suffer economic hardship, but FDR vetoed the bill (and Congress failed to override his veto). The lands remained a National Monument until 1950, when the transfer finally was completed.

remaining stand of virgin Bald Cypress and its historic bird rookery—the Corkscrew Cypress Sanctuary of the National Audubon Society—in Florida; to the National Park Trust Fund, the Palisades Interstate Park Commission and the Utah State Park and Recreation Commission. In 1955 Jackson Hole Preserve opened the Grand Teton Lodge Company, with 300 hotel and cottage rooms at Jackson Lake; rooms for 70 guests at Jenny Lake; log cabins accommodating more than 400 guests, stores, a cafeteria and a trailer park at Colter Bay; and a bus transportation system.

During the fourth Rockefeller period, responsibility for continuing this philanthropic work was assumed by the middle Rockefeller brother, Laurance. In the latter 1950s, when he was in his middle forties, he became a major figure in the conservation establishment, partly on the strength of his father's reputation, of course, and partly on the strength of his own contribution to the national park system and participation in public and private conservation groups. His contribution to the park system followed from a 1952 cruise through the West Indies, when he had been introduced to St. John, the least developed of the U.S. Virgin Islands. He purchased about two-thirds of the island, and then donated nearly all of this property* for the Virgin Islands National Park, which Congress

---

* On the island's western shore, he built a 130-acre resort, Caneel Bay Plantation, owned by Jackson Hole Preserve and managed by the Rockefeller Center-based Rockresorts Corporation, which also manages (and does not own) Rockefeller-built hotels and resort complexes at Dorado Beach, twenty miles west of San Juan, on the north coast of Puerto Rico; at Little Dix Bay, British Virgin Islands; at Mauna Kea Beach, on the northwest shore of Hawaii's Big Island; on St. Croix; in Woodstock, Vermont; and in Wyoming. Most of these properties were built in the 1950s. About a decade later, Laurance Rockefeller began

established in 1956. His participation in conservation groups is reflected in the 1956-57 edition of *Who's Who*, which lists him as a director of the Hudson River Conservation Society, commissioner and secretary of the Palisades Interstate Park Commission, trustee and vice-president of the New York Zoological Society, and trustee and president of Jackson Hole Preserve.

Laurance Rockefeller was well on his way to becoming what Lady Bird Johnson was to call him in her *White House Diary's* entry for February 11, 1965: "That Number One Conservationist." He received honors: the Conservation Service Award of the Department of the Interior in 1956 and the Horace Marden Albright Scenic Preservation Medal in 1957. The next year he established a new fund whose disbursements have complemented Jackson Hole Preserve's: the American Conservation Association, which has contributed to the budgets of other conservation groups and to educational, research and publishing programs in conservation. Perhaps the high point of his conservation work in the late 1950s, however, was his appointment by President Eisenhower to the chairmanship

---

to expand his vacation-resort operations. In the late 1960s he formed a partnership with Eastern Airlines, whereby he owns 20 percent and the airline 80 percent of two additions to the Dorado Beach complex—the Cerromar Beach Hotel, which has more than 500 rooms and facilities for conventions, and a development of condominiums, some of which have been sold for $160,000 apiece. In 1968 Eastern combined with Rockefeller's Olahana Corporation (also managed by Rockresorts) and the Dillingham Corporation to form the Dilrock-Eastern Company, which announced plans to develop a $250-million, twenty-square-mile vacation community at Mauna Kea, with a hotel, golf courses, homes, vacation villas, condominiums, and such Rockefeller accouterments as a community service facility and a public park.

of the Outdoor Resources Recreation Review Commission (ORRRC), the first of a series of Presidential assignments.

In an interview in the *Saturday Evening Post* in 1961, shortly before ORRRC issued a series of reports on conservation, regional planning and outdoor recreation, Laurance Rockefeller discussed natural resources. "For two centuries we fought to conquer nature," he said. "Now we must save nature before it's too late. But I don't agree with the wilderness boys who want to put these natural areas in deep freeze for future generations. I'm for conservation and *use*. . . . Less than 5 percent of Yellowstone is developed. They crowd all the tourists into this 5 percent. We need new thinking about the use of wilderness recreation lands." The people who were giving honors and forming commissions must have been impressed, for Laurance Rockefeller continued to receive honors and Presidential appointments during the next several years. He received the Special Conservation Award of the Interior Department in 1962, the Gold Seal Award of the National Council of Garden Clubs in 1963 and the Audubon Medal of the National Audubon Society in 1964. In 1964 President Johnson appointed him to the Public Land Law Review Commission, which was to spend $7 million over the next five years deliberating the fate of 724 million acres of public land (most of it in the West, only 210 million acres in national parks).* In 1965 he was named chairman of the White House Conference on Natural Beauty, which dealt with the

---

* After holding little-publicized hearings and meeting in virtual secrecy, the commission issued a 342-page report recommending that national forests be transferred for such "public purposes" as industrial and commercial expansion and that public land laws be revised to help mining, timber and agriculture interests.

beautification of America's cities, countryside and highway systems. He then was named chairman of the Citizens' Advisory Board on Recreation and Natural Beauty, which published an illustrated volume, *From Sea to Shining Sea, A Report on the American Environment—Our National Heritage*, outlining progress in environmental programs, presenting proposals and recommendations for stimulating action to enhance the environment and natural beauty, and providing guides for government and citizen action.

Laurance Rockefeller had become a leading advocate of environmental beautification programs. In an article called "Business and Beauty" in the March-April 1966 issue of *Audubon Magazine*, he wrote about "challenges" for business, which included "improving the appearance of plants and offices"; "pollution control, and this includes visual pollution of the landscape and the intrusion of excessive noise"; "maintaining a mature sense of beauty in the production business creates"; "the growing need for businessmen to take a more active part in public service for natural beauty."

The article was a typical product of Laurance Rockefeller's thinking about conservation. Implicit throughout was the idea that he was apt to go along with the development of a natural resource for commercial development as long as the plants and offices that were built were beautifully designed and decorated. But by 1966 beautification programs were not considered sufficient commitments to conservation by modern conservationists. Rockefeller was suspected of not being a conservationist at all, but merely a cosmetician apt to compromise on the side of development.

In 1967 Laurance Rockefeller turned his attention to the Adirondack Mountain region, which had posed a special problem to conservationists as far back as 1883, when New York State began an attempt to set aside 6 million acres of the region's mountains and forests as a state park. Land inside the proposed park's boundaries was to be bought and consolidated as money became available. In 1894 a "forever wild" clause was written into the state constitution to protect the forest preserve, as the lands within the boundaries are called. These lands, the clause reads, "shall be kept forever wild as forest lands. They shall not be leased, sold or exchanged, or be taken by any corporation, public or private, nor shall the timber thereon be sold, removed or destroyed." But by 1965 the state had been able to purchase only 39 percent of the designated acreage. In a report submitted to Governor Nelson Rockefeller, Laurance Rockefeller contended that "most of the public park land is in tracts so scattered that the Adirondack Mountains State Park is not, in fact, a reality—after eighty years it is largely a fiction." As for the region's future, "much of the wild forested land that people see as they drive the main highways or canoe the waterways is privately owned; it is in a wild state principally because economic opportunities and pressures have not yet brought the drastic changes that they inevitably must, if these lands continue to remain in private ownership indefinitely."

Laurance Rockefeller's report offered his solution to this problem: All the land within the park's boundaries should be purchased by the Federal government and turned into a national park, with these exceptions: "Private homes built prior to a date specified in the [park] legislation and essential surrounding land, usually not exceeding three acres, would not be subject to purchase by the Federal government except by voluntary negotiation." The same principle would apply to existing commercial properties that are "consistent with park purposes." Tracts exceeding three acres would be acquired, by condemnation, if necessary. The Park Service would co-operate with local towns to formulate zoning regulations to "help protect park values and potentialities." Five existing settlements, including those at Lake Placid and Saranac Lake, would be used to provide services for visitors to the park.

As the story came to be told, the idea had come to Laurance Rockefeller that spring, while he was in a car in Washington, D.C., with Conrad Wirth, a former director of the National Park Service and a trustee of both Jackson Hole Preserve and the American Conservation Association, who was on Rockefeller's staff. Rockefeller had turned to Wirth and asked, quite out of the blue, How about a national park for the Adirondacks? The Rockefeller report then had been prepared by Wirth, Ben Thompson, also formerly in the Park Service, and Roger Thompson, a researcher in forestry. One afternoon in late July, several members of the press were invited to the Governor's New York City office. They were not told the purpose of the invitation and wondered what the Governor was going to spring on them. When they arrived, they found the Governor, Laurance Rockefeller, Secretary of the Interior Stewart Udall, Conrad Wirth and the report, which the Governor and Secretary Udall both hailed enthusiastically. The Governor called it "most interesting and imaginative." Secretary Udall termed it a "bold proposal, which will receive careful analysis by Interior's top experts." He had directed the Park Service and the Bureau of Outdoor Recreation "to evaluate this plan in light of the conservation needs of the nation and the national interest." The timing of the report's publication was most interesting. A state constitutional convention was in progress, and the report was front-page news on the day before the "forever wild" clause in the constitution was up for debate.

The *New York Times* expressed reservations in its editorial columns about turning the Adirondacks into a national park and published two letters against Laurance Rockefeller's proposal during the summer months. One letter was written by Harold B. Burton, who had been a commissioner of the Adirondack Mountain Authority since 1957. Burton argued that the Adirondacks would be better left to local control by the State Department of Conservation, which "is close to the people and inevitably more responsive to their needs than an agency [such as the National Park Service] based in Washington could be." He asserted that the state could afford the cost—estimated at $60 million—of acquiring private lands within the designated boundaries of the state park, pointing out that in a recent ballot the state had been given approval for a $100-million bond issue for parks. "What," he asked,

can the National Park Service do for the Adirondacks that the Conservation Department does not do? Build public campsites? There are dozens of them now. Build hiking trails or horse trails? We have them now. Build ski centers? We have two huge ski centers now, both operated by a state agency. Build scenic highways to mountaintops? We have two of them now.

The only thing the Park Service could add—and that the people of the state certainly do not want—would be more roads into presently remote areas of the Adirondacks. So the case for a National Park is a poor one. The people of the state take pride in the Adirondack Park, and it is open to all comers. Whenever a drastic change in the park structure is proposed—

such as the Adirondack Northway—they have an opportunity to vote on it. This is true democracy. It works. And it is infinitely preferable, with all respect for the accomplishments of the National Park Service, to the proposals included in the Rockefeller report.

The second letter was written by Lithgow Osborne, who had been the New York State Conservation Commissioner from 1933 to 1942. "The proposal," he contended,

> reeks of clear implications that the "forever wild" concept of the Forest Preserve, as now guaranteed in our State Constitution, will disappear. Even if the Park Service were to give assurances in this respect, it cannot guarantee what will be the policies of future Federal bureaucrats and officeholders, both executive and legislative.
>
> The issue is very clear. If New York State cedes to the Federal Government state-owned Forest Preserve lands, it is virtually certain that their wilderness character will be destroyed sooner or later.
>
> The State Conservation Department gives the Forest Preserve careful, simple, common-sense management aimed at retaining as fully as possible all the advantages for future generations of a large area of untouched wilderness.
>
> Control of the area should remain where it is.

In October, in a speech before an unusually large crowd at the Adirondack Mountain Club, Laurance Rockefeller responded to criticism of his proposal by offering to alter it in order to accommodate several "quite valid" objections that had been raised. Noting that most of the privately owned land in the Adirondacks had been kept wild by clubs and individuals despite having been under no zoning restrictions, Rockefeller now proposed that all land "where private use is consistent with park purposes," be exempted from takeover by the Federal government. He also changed his positions on lumbering and hunting, which are forbidden in national parks, but were allowed in the Adirondack State Park. In July he had contended that "the sawmill industry is a declining one . . . the hardwood timber which supported a boom immediately after World War II has been cut out." But in October he said that "the timber industry is at present a mainstay of the economy of the Adirondack counties. For the most part, in modern times cutting has been carried on in an enlightened, progressive way to achieve a substantial yield." In July he had provided statistics in an effort to show that hunting in the Adirondacks was poor. In October he recommended that the best hunting areas be kept open.

In summation, Laurance Rockefeller asserted that he had submitted his proposal in order to "stimulate thinking on an important issue—not to railroad anyone into anything." After listening to Rockefeller, the governors of the Adirondack Mountain Club voted only on his July proposal. They opposed it, sixteen to four.

Early in 1968 the State Conservation Department issued a report opposing a takeover of the Adirondack Park by the National Park Service. The report argued against changing the Adirondacks' $150-million-a-year tourist industry from back-country camping and hiking to "large-scale, high-density accommodation and recreation areas developed in linear fashion along the highway systems" in the Adirondack region—a change that the establishment of a national park would bring; contended that Federal takeover of private forest lands in the Adirondacks would seriously disrupt the twelve Adirondack counties' $150-million-a-year timber business; and contended that disruption of hunting—which attracted $4 million a year in license fees—would create overpopulation of animal herds and create starvation conditions.

The central issue, however, was the state constitution's "forever wild" clause. Some legal experts held that the clause would have to be amended before public lands within the Adirondack State Park could be transferred to the Federal government. A *Times* editorial called the Rockefeller proposal "too risky" for the Forest Preserve, on the grounds that the clause, which offered clear protection, should not be tampered with.

In January 1968, Governor Rockefeller announced that he would appoint a Temporary Study Commission on the Future of the Adirondacks. Since the commission's report was not due until the following year, observers interpreted the announcement as a quiet burial of Laurance Rockefeller's controversial proposal. The Governor proceeded slowly, moreover. He did not appoint commissioners until September. There was further delay; the commission did not begin working until December and was granted a one-year extension in the due date for reporting on its findings. Finally, more than three years after the Adirondack National Park proposal had been announced, it was buried. The commission limited itself to recommending that the "forever wild" clause be "retained without change" and that an independent Adirondack Park Agency be created with "general power over the use of private and public land in the park."

Bill Werner, the Adirondack Museum's Curator of Research, who has been involved for a long while in the region's conservation problems, believes that "the central Adirondacks should be an experimental area for demonstrating what national parks should have been." He says that he found the Rockefeller proposal "goddam revolutionary. It put ideas in my mind I have not been able to resist." According to Werner, the proposal was buried because there was "enough in it to offend everybody except the editors of *Life* [who published an editorial in favor of it]." The fact that every concerned group attacked the proposal shows that everybody *was* offended: conservationists, property owners, timber cutters and hunters alike. In some cases this was hardly a surprise. One could be sure that cutters and hunters would oppose turning Adirondack lands into a national park, for cutting and hunting then would be prohibited there. But why did conservationists oppose the proposal? After all, it was directed toward saving a natural resource that after eight decades of conservation effort still is in danger of desecration. Why did the proposal stir up powerful fears about whether the "forever wild" status of the Forest Preserve would be maintained? Were these fears triggered simply by distrust of the National Park Service? Or were they triggered by distrust of the proposal's source?

The problem with Laurance Rockefeller's proposal was that at the time he made it his reputation as a conservationist was in disrepair. This was not due merely to opposition among conservationists to his "good works" which, in keeping with his anti-wilderness attitudes, involved development of natural resources for recreation purposes. Distrust of Laurance Rockefeller ran deeper. In recent years he had compromised too often in favor of development of natural resources for commercial purposes. He had been content merely to provide cosmetic alterations.

In 1962, Consolidated Edison, the giant utility that supplies power in New York City and Westchester County, quietly announced a plan to build a $150-million pumped-storage hydroelectric plant on Storm King Mountain, a magnificent bluff that rises steeply out of the deep waters of the Hudson River in the Hudson Highlands near the town of Cornwall, about five miles north of Palisades Interstate Park, a little more than an hour's drive north from Manhattan. With this plant in operation, Con Ed would dramatically increase its capability for meeting peak power demands in New York City. During nights and weekends, when power requirements in the city would be relatively low, river water would be pumped up to an 8-billion-gallon storage reservoir on top of Storm King and adjacent heights through a two-mile-long, forty-foot-diameter tunnel cut through the mountain. During a period of peak power demand, water would be released from the reservoir to flow back down the tunnel and activate turbines. The proposed plant would be capable of generating power at a rate of 2 million kilowatts within two minutes of demand.

The Con Ed plan had its imperfections. First, the huge plant would deface Storm King, a natural resource which, in Robert Boyle's* phrase, has been "considered inviolate in the popular mind." Furthermore, construction of the Storm King plant would invite more industrial construction in the Hudson Highlands. Second, while it is true that the atmosphere would not be polluted when the pumped-storage plant was generating power, it is also true that the energy required to pump water up the tunnel to the storage reservoir would have to be supplied by other power plants which pollute the atmosphere during *their* operation. Third, Con Ed would have

* Author of *The Hudson River* (New York: Norton, 1969).

to expend one and a half times as much power to pump water up to the storage reservoir as would be generated when the water returned to activate the turbines. Fourth, the huge plant's operation would pose a grave threat to the Hudson's fish life. Eggs, larvae, small striped bass, and substantial numbers of young blueback herring, alewife, tomcod, white perch, young-of-the-year shad and bay anchovies would be killed. Some of them would be shattered on the trip up the tunnel, when river water was pumped up to the storage reservoir; survivors who needed a current to keep them buoyant would perish in the stagnant waters of the reservoir, while others would be smashed by the whirling turbine blades at the end of the trip back down the tunnel. The use of a screen with a mesh small enough to keep some varieties of marine life from being sucked up into the tunnel was hazardous, too, for fish would be sucked up against the screen itself, where they would be trapped and would die. Since the vicinity of Storm King is a spawning ground for striped bass, one result of the building of the Storm King plant would be that the Hudson would no longer be a striped bass resource.

Late in 1963, when Con Ed filed an application at the Federal Power Commission for a license to build and operate the Storm King pumped-storage plant, several conservationists, including author Carl Carmer and lawyer Leo Rothschild, established an organization called the Scenic Hudson Preservation Conference to fight Con Ed's plan. Scenic Hudson soon was joined in its battle against the utility by local experts on the Hudson's marine life, who became angered by striped bass slaughters caused by faulty design of the water intake at Con Ed's new nuclear power plant at Indian Point, fifteen miles down the Hudson from Storm King, and by misleading testimony given in Con Ed's behalf by witnesses at FPC hearings in February and May 1964. In November, while Con Ed's application was pending before the FPC, New York State's Joint Legislative Committee on Natural Resources, chaired by Republican Assemblyman R. Watson Pomeroy, jumped aboard what was becoming an anti-Storm King bandwagon. After hearing testimony from Alexander Lurkis, formerly Chief Engineer of the New York City Bureau of Gas and Electricity, who contended that environmental pollution would be minimized and that Con Ed's customers would save a minimum of $132.5 million over a fifteen-year period if, instead of a pumped-storage plant, gas turbines were used to meet peak power demands in metropolitan New York City, the committee's five members voted unanimously to oppose the Storm King plan.

Nelson Rockefeller, who was in his second term as Governor of New York State, and Laurance Rockefeller, who was chairman of the State Council of Parks and vice-president of the Palisades Interstate Park Commission, did not jump aboard the anti-Storm King bandwagon. With their family's great reputation in conservation, one might have expected Nelson and Laurance Rockefeller to have spoken out on the side of conservationists opposing the Storm King plan. But when one wrote to the Governor about Storm King, one received a bland form letter signed by the Governor's cousin and Executive Assistant, Alexander Aldrich. The body of a sample letter, dated May 28, 1964, reads, in full:

Governor Rockefeller has asked me to thank you for your recent communication concerning the proposed power developments in the Hudson Highlands area.

The application of Consolidated Edison to construct a power plant at Cornwall is now pending before the United States Federal Power Commission.

While the State itself has no direct control over this project, except for limited areas where its own lands may be crossed, nevertheless, in his dual capacity as State Conservation Commissioner and Chairman of the New York State Water Resources Commission, Dr. Harold G. Wilm and State Council of Parks Chairman Laurance S. Rockefeller have been giving careful attention to the subject. State regional park commissions have negotiated changes with the Company aimed at minimizing scenic impact and will continue to watch design plans closely. The park commissions are also cooperating with authorities of local governments having planning and zoning powers in the areas to be affected. Consolidated Edison has shown every indication of its responsibility in this critical location and of its sincere desire to cooperate constructively.

Governor Rockefeller understands your concern in this matter and appreciates your thought in writing.

The state, under Governor Rockefeller, did not watch Con Ed idly. A letter written by Alexander Aldrich to Scenic Hudson on Setpember 30, 1964—while Con Ed's licensing application still was pending before the FPC—described what the state had done with regard to the Storm King plan. The letter read, in part:

Governor Rockefeller has asked me to acknowledge your telegrams of September seventeenth and twenty-third with further reference to the proposed pumped storage plants in the Hudson Highlands.

From the very beginning, before the first proposal for the Consolidated Edison plant at Cornwall was publicly announced, appropriate agencies of the State government have kept in close touch with the plans of the utility companies. Early contact was made with Consolidated Edison by the Palisades Interstate Park Commission and was aimed successfully at obtaining an underwater river crossing,* at orienting the plant for a less conspicuous location and at design of the reservoir and retention structure so that topography and natural features would best screen its intrusive effect. This park commission has a long and distinguished history in protecting the scenic values of the lower reaches of the river and its present membership includes at least two members of the families whose outstanding contributions in money, time and energy made this preservation possible. . . .

In dealing with the utility companies in this context, these State agencies do not consider the mere existence of the power plants at river edge to be basically objectionable. They do accept fully their obligations to guide, to influence and to direct the design details so that the intrusion upon the Hudson the bridge make it more difficult to realize that goal? The state Highlands scenic resources should be at a minimum, and are confident that this desirable objective is attainable along with the economic benefits that the plants will bring to the area and the state.†

* This refers to the method for spanning the Hudson with power transmission lines.
† Among the arguments Governor Rockefeller attached to his endorsement of the Storm King project were that its construction would provide "a large number of jobs in the area" and that if Con Ed could not build the Storm King project the utility would be forced to construct a more expensive project elsewhere in the state—with the burden to be shouldered by consumers. But expert witnesses at hearings held by the New York State Joint Legislative Committee on Natural Resources argued that there would be a need for no more than 500, and probably only 300, workers to construct the huge facility, and that less than 25 percent of the work force could be drawn from the area, due to a

Scenic Hudson did not approve of all of these cosmetic changes to the Storm King plant design, however. Furthermore, even if the changes had been satisfactory in themselves, Aldrich's letter would not have quieted the conservationists. For they believed that the state had not given other important issues in the controversy thorough consideration. Accordingly, on October 14 Carmer and Rothschild telegraphed Governor Rockefeller a reply to Aldrich's letter. The telegram read, in part:

MR. ALDRICH'S REPLY . . . EMPHASIZES THE VERY CONSIDERATIONS WHICH LED US TO URGE YOUR ASSISTANCE IN OBTAINING NEW YORK STATE REVIEW OF THE PROPOSALS FOR STORM KING MOUNTAIN. WE URGENTLY REQUEST THAT REVIEW NOW. THE CONCEPT THAT THE PALISADES AND TACONIC PARK COMMISSIONS HAVE THE CON EDISON PROJECT . . . WITHIN THEIR JURISDICTION AND UNDER CONTROL DOES NOT STAND UP. APPARENTLY, THE REPRESENTATIONS MADE TO YOU ARE INCOMPLETE AND OMIT ESSENTIAL FACTS.

. . . ITEM AFTER ITEM OF SERIOUS AND IMMEDIATE CONCERN TO NEW YORK STATE . . . DOES NOT FALL WITHIN THE PURVIEW OF EITHER COMMISSION. IN FACT, UNLESS THE STATE ACTS, THESE ISSUES WILL NOT BE STUDIED AT ALL, BUT WILL BE DECIDED BY DEFAULT.

A SIMPLE INSPECTION OF THE SITE WILL REVEAL THAT THE PROPOSED PLANT IS NOT, *REPEAT NOT*, "IN A LESS CONSPICUOUS

---

shortage of skilled workers there. Con Edison itself belied the Governor's claim by letting the construction contract to a California firm and beginning to hire workers from outside New York State. And the fact that more power would be required to pump water up the tunnel to the reservoir than would be generated when the water would be released to flow back down the tunnel was of little benefit to the economic argument for building a plant at Storm King.

LOCATION" THAN ORIGINALLY SUGGESTED. IT, AND THE SCARRING
OF THE MOUNTAIN, WILL NOW BE MORE VISIBLE THAN EVER BE-
FORE FROM BOTH SHORES AND FROM EITHER DIRECTION ON THE
RIVER.

. . . THE PLANT'S ULTIMATE "INTRUSIVE EFFECTS" HAVE BEEN
AT THE VERY LEAST DOUBLED OVER THE ORIGINAL PROPOSAL PLANS.
. . .

. . . PRACTICAL ALTERNATIVES EXIST FOR SUPPLYING NEW YORK
CITY WITH NEEDED POWER. ON TOP OF THIS, IT IS NOW OBVIOUS
THAT THE ECONOMIC JUSTIFICATION ADVANCED BY CON EDISON
FOR THE STORM KING FACILITY IS FAR FROM WHAT IT WAS MADE
TO SEEM AT THE OUTSET AND MAY WELL BE FOUND DISCREDITED.

WE BELIEVE THAT ON THE BASIS OF STATEMENTS MADE BY VARI-
OUS OFFICIALS, YOU DO NOT HAVE BEFORE YOU THE COMPLETE
FACTS AT THIS TIME.

WE DO NOT ASK YOU TO OPPOSE THE PROJECT NOW. WE ONLY
URGE THAT YOU HELP TO GET ALL THE FACTS IN THE OPEN SO
THAT THE PEOPLE OF NEW YORK MAY PARTICIPATE IN AN IN-
FORMED DECISION. ONLY IN THIS WAY CAN YOU OVERCOME THE
DISTORTIONS AND MISCONSTRUCTIONS WHICH HAVE PREVENTED
FULL AND FAIR EVALUATION OF THIS PROJECT. . . .

The Pomeroy committee then cast its vote, and requested
the FPC to withhold action on the Storm King application until the State Legislature could debate the project. But Governor Rockefeller already had made up his mind. He was backing Con Ed; debate was closed. The conservationists were
annoying him, moreover. While being questioned about the
project at a meeting of the New York State Women's Joint
Legislative Forum in Albany in January 1965, the Governor
said: "I worry a little, ladies, about the fact that so many
people only get excited about doing something about something after something has happened. If there are so many

people who want to see the Hudson preserved, why don't these people band together and why don't they buy up this property and raise the money?"

In March 1965, the Federal Power Commission approved Con Ed's Storm King application by a vote of three to one. The majority opinion, written by commission chairman Joseph Swidler, stated that the Storm King plan was "far superior to existing alternatives." It would be cheaper and cleaner, Swidler claimed. He wrote that "the proposed powerhouse will not involve the destruction of any historic shrines, and its effect on the general scenic values of the area will be minimal. The powerhouse will merely add a well-landscaped, low-profile structure to the structures already in existence within the Cornwall area and visible from the river and from the opposite shore of the Hudson. It will not alter the existing environment in any conspicuous or unsightly way and, if anything, will enhance public recreation in the area." Swidler held that the huge storage reservoir would not affect scenic values because it would be visible only from the air. He held, further, that there was no evidence that building the Storm King plant would encourage more industrial construction in the Hudson Highlands.

"The Storm King project," Governor Rockefeller would write in his book *Our Environment Can Be Saved*, "is an imaginative, large-scale attempt to relieve the power shortage." Some conservationists, impressed by the Rockefeller family's reputation in conservation, were puzzled by his support of Con Ed's Storm King plan. Why was he backing it when more efficient and cleaner methods for supplying power to the New York City metropolitan area at peak demand were available?

Other conservationists attempted to supply answers. Robert Boyle, in his book *The Hudson River*, has written, "I once asked a prominent Republican why Rockefeller was so committed to Con Ed. 'The people who own Con Ed are his people,' was the reply. 'They're in the same club.'" Leo Rothschild spoke harshly of the Rockefeller commitment in the *Cornwall Local* on March 25, 1965: "Governor Rockefeller and his brother Laurance agreed to that plant through private negotiations with the company. The private agreement between the Rockefellers and Con Edison is not the kind of arm's-length transaction, conducted in public view, which has been sought by every reform effort aimed at disclosure of interests. . . . On taking office, the Governor filed a form showing he is or was a substantial Con Ed stockholder. He did not publish the extent of his holdings or those of the rest of the family. The Federal license to Storm King Mountain is potentially very valuable to the company." These comments became more interesting when the *Local* also reported that Jay Underhill, Assistant Press Secretary to the Governor, denied that Rockefeller "now or ever had interests in Con Ed." But the *New York Times* of January 19, 1965, already had reported that in filing declaration No. 109 on January 7, 1959, he had recorded investments of $10,000 *or more* in seven insurance companies, two banks and *Con Ed*. (The law did not require his listing the full extent of these investments.)*

Laurance Rockefeller saw the FPC decision as final; there was nothing that could be done about it. In May, following

---

* Around the end of 1937, the Rockefellers owned 0.28 percent of Con Ed's stock. Such a holding was worth more than $10 million in 1964.

the White House Conference on Natural Beauty, he wrote to William Osborn of the Hudson River Conservation Society:

> The suggestion of one of your directors that we request the FPC to delay granting a license to Con Edison for a year wouldn't get very far and for that reason I don't think we should try it. . . .
>
> At the White House Conference there were innumerable suggestions that the FPC, whose power of condemnation transcends the legal ability of any state to keep them from doing what they think they ought to do, should be curbed. But even if this were done it would not be retroactive.
>
> I think I should point out also that the most recent tack taken by the anti-Con Edison people which suggests that turning the Hudson River over to the Park Service would be a means of curbing the FPC and eliminating Con Edison is also a forlorn hope. The FPC's power of condemnation also transcends that of the Park Service. . . .
>
> . . . I don't see any point in going through a useless gesture.

Perhaps Laurance Rockefeller's tone of utter helplessness before the majesty of the FPC stemmed from a desire to see the Storm King facility built. In any event, it turned out that the record of the FPC's proceedings in the Storm King case should have given him pause. When other conservationists, led by Scenic Hudson, mounted an attack on the FPC's Storm King decision in the United States Court of Appeals,* a three-judge panel ruled unanimously, in December 1965, that the proceedings had been seriously deficient. The judges said that the commission had "failed to compile a record . . . sufficient to support its decision . . . ignored certain relevant factors

* An FPC decision is the equivalent of a Federal Court decision.

and failed to make a thorough study of possible alternatives to the Storm King project." According to the judges, the record failed "markedly to make out a case for the Storm King project on, among other matters, costs, public convenience and necessity, and absence of reasonable alternatives." The judges were obliged, therefore, to order the commission to "reexamine all questions on which [the court] found the record insufficient and all related matters." The words "all related matters" summed up the most important aspect of the court's ruling. For the FPC was being ordered to consider the impact the Storm King facility would have on the environment.

The ruling was a great victory for conservationists. Some years later, the New York State Commissioner of Environmental Conservation would call the ruling "the symbol of the first legal victory for the environment, a landmark decision saying you have to look at the environmental impact of a project." But Governor Rockefeller seemed to disregard the import of the ruling. The following May, as the FPC began to restudy Con Ed's Storm King application, he wrote that he was "already on record to the effect that if another solution can be found as an alternative to the Cornwall [i.e., Storm King] project, it should be." But, he continued, "my position is quite clear. I will support the Commission's decision, whether it be to relocate the project or build it at Cornwall."

Perhaps Con Ed would be stopped; perhaps the Hudson and Storm King would be saved. But the war was far from over; only the first battle had been fought. In August 1968, the FPC's examiner again recommended that the Storm King facility be built. This time, New York City objected to the proposed site, on the grounds that construction would imperil the Catskill Aqueduct, through which 40 percent of the city's water supply is carried. (Scenic Hudson pointed out that when the aqueduct was built in 1914, "a portion of the tunnel collapsed almost at the exact point where Con Edison proposed to build its plant.") The FPC examiner disposed of this objection to his own satisfaction, however, and on December 23, 1969, he renewed his recommendation. The following August, the FPC unanimously approved the project and granted Con Ed a fifty-year license to build the plant—whose cost now was estimated at $234 million. In so ruling, the commission stated that if the courts were to decide that the Storm King location threatened the aqueduct—a threat which the commission called "remote"—an alternative site downstream would be licensed. The commission held that the pumped-storage plant would be the "best use of available resources to meet the requirements for electric energy with minimum adverse impact on our environment" and that "the natural beauty of the area will not be significantly degraded."

Conservationists again sought to overturn the FPC's decision in court. This time, however, they ran into the courts' traditional reluctance to review the factual conclusions of Federal regulatory agencies such as the FPC. Judge Hays—the same jurist who had written the 1965 Court of Appeals opinion instructing the FPC to expand its proceedings—wrote a majority opinion upholding the FPC's decision. After concluding that the recent proceedings had been "exhaustive," "careful" and "thorough," he was obliged to say that "the resolution of highly complex technical issues such as these was entrusted by Congress to the Commission and not to the courts. Where the Commission's conclusions are supported by substantial evidence, the court must accept them."

Conservationists managed to postpone the start of construction at Storm King by requesting a ruling from the State Commissioner of Environmental Conservation. They argued that pumping enormous volumes of water out of the Hudson would cause ocean water to be pulled abnormally far upriver; some communities that depend on the river for fresh water thus would be hurt by the Storm King plant's operation. By way of response, the Commissioner ruled that the plant would have to be shut down if Con Ed detected any danger to the Hudson.

This ruling failed to satisfy the conservationists, and they then turned to the State Supreme Court for redress. In March 1972, Justice Forest C. Pitt handed down a decision in which he noted that the ruling did not show "reasonable assurance," as required by law, that operation of the Storm King facility would not violate water quality standards in the Hudson. He denounced the ruling as being "impractical to the point of being ridiculous." After all, it gave Con Ed the power to police its own operations.

Con Ed was "disappointed" at Justice Pitt's decision. But the conservationists had not won the war. The State Attorney General appealed the decision, and in June the Appellate Division of the State Supreme Court overturned it, holding that in the State's review of the Storm King plan there had been "no clear demonstration of any significant harmful effect upon the water quality within the State of New York." (The Appellate Division also held that if the Catskill Aqueduct were damaged by Storm King construction, the city could work out the problem with Con Ed.)

Conservationists then took their case to the state's highest court—the Court of Appeals—but, in March 1973, that court upheld the latest ruling. Nevertheless, the conservationists pledged to continue the fight, and at this writing the fate of the Storm King plan still is somewhat uncertain. It is certain, however, that conservationists attempting to block construction of other power plants will have to fight even harder, for in the midst of the war on the Storm King plan Governor Rockefeller developed a new strategy for dealing with obstructive tactics. When he had to, he used secrecy: when the State Power Authority announced that it planned to construct a $150-million pumped-storage plant—according to instructions issued by the Governor—the chairman of the authority declined to identify the proposed site or even the general area where the plant would be located. But now the Governor can override conservationists' objections in more delicate fashion. Late in 1968 he appointed Joseph Swidler—who had left the FPC chairmanship at the end of 1965 and had been practicing law—to head the state's Public Service Commission, the agency that regulates utility companies. From this position, Swidler spoke out on the question of whether private citizens should have a voice in the selection of power plant sites. In a letter to the *New York Times* on December 16, 1971, he wrote that "conferring decisional authority on unstructured private groups . . . may . . . add new levels of conflict and confusion"; selection should be controlled by a state agency. In support of this argument, the Governor had been calling repeatedly for the creation of a power plant siting board with full authority to overrule local zoning regulations and settle controversies involving utilities and environmental and community groups. In 1972 the State Legislature responded. It established a five-man board with a life of five and a half years. The board is headed by the State Public Service Commissioner, the State Commissioners of Environmental Conservation, Health and Commerce, plus a varying member chosen by the Governor from the region where the plant is to be built. The board is charged with determining whether a proposed plant is needed to meet long-range power demands. The legislation also provides for a $25,000 fund which a community wishing to block construction of a power plant can use to hire expert witnesses. This is an insignificant amount in such a battle. But what does the size of the fund matter? After all, the board is headed by Joseph Swidler, who leaves no doubt about where he stands on the question of the need for new power plants. In a May 1972 speech before a conference on New York City's power requirements, he said that the city faced a "disaster" if there were any delays in building new facilities for generating electricity.

Early in 1965, in response to the burgeoning Storm King controversy and to Governor Rockefeller's support of the Con Ed plan, several bills were introduced in Congress calling for creation of a Federal preserve in the Hudson River Valley. One proposal, sponsored by Democratic Representatives Richard Ottinger of Westchester County and Jonathan Bingham of the Bronx, called for making a stretch of the Hudson —from Newburgh south to the New Jersey line on the west bank (including Storm King Mountain) and from Beacon south to Lower Manhattan on the east bank—into a preserve to be known as the Hudson Highlands National Scenic Riverway.

Governor Rockefeller was against putting the valley under Federal control; New York State, in cooperation with existing Federal and local agencies, would do the job of protecting the river and its environs. Accordingly, he quickly established a state agency called the Hudson River Valley Commission, which was financed initially with $25,000 from his executive chamber budget and a matching grant from his brother Laurance's American Conservation Association. The Governor designated Laurance Rockefeller chairman of the new commission. The other commissioners were W. Averell Harriman; Henry T. Heald, president of the Ford Foundation; Mrs. Andrew T. Heiskell, wife of the chairman of Time, Inc., and a director of the *New York Times;* Frank Wells McCabe, president of the National Bank and Trust Company of Albany; Dr. Alan Simpson, president of Vassar College; Lowell Thomas; IBM chairman Thomas J. Watson, Jr.; William H. Whyte of Laurance Rockefeller's staff; and George Yerry, a labor union official. Conrad Wirth was named executive director. As the Legislature supplied funding, the commission hired a professional staff which included fifty-four experts in the fields of urban and rural planning, architecture, landscaping, ecology, geography, cartography, engineering, economics and graphics. The commission's job was to determine whether a proposed project would "destroy or substantially impair" natural resources in the Hudson River Valley. Start of construction could be delayed for sixty days, until a hearing was held. The commission had no enforcement powers beyond this sixty-day delay period, however.

A month after the commission had been formed, Laurance Rockefeller asserted: "It's a matter of who can best save the Hudson. The Federal government acts in default of state responsibility. The burden should not be shifted to it as long as the state demonstrates the capacity to do the job." The first step in New York State's demonstration was a report on the lower river by the State Council of Parks. The report, which was passed from Laurance Rockefeller, the council chairman, to his brother the Governor and back to Laurance, chairman of the Hudson Valley Commission, warned that "major manufacturing centers, huge power plants, transmission lines, poorly designed and cheaply built housing projects . . . are moving in on the river in uncoordinated sprawl." The report did not take the position that all development should be banned. The river's scenic-historical-recreational, residential-institutional and commercial-industrial potentials were to be given equal consideration. There is a name for this even-handed approach. it is called "compatible development."

Late in July the Subcommittee on National Parks and Recreation of the House Committee on Interior and Insular Affairs held hearings on Representative Ottinger's bill in Yonkers. Nelson and Laurance Rockefeller did not testify, but Conrad Wirth did. He said that the Hudson River Valley Commission was preparing a "plan for a plan" and that the Federal government should leave control of the valley to New York State. In order to assure the subcommittee that the state had the will to protect the valley's natural resources, Wirth pointed out that if the valley were left in the state's hands, it would be in the Rockefellers' hands. "If there is any doubt as to the intent of the state officials involved," Wirth said, "I am sure the members of this committee know that the Governor and . . . Laurance S. Rockefeller are not opposed to national park conservation, nor to the resource conservation programs of the Federal government generally. They have supported park and conservation programs in many ways throughout their lives, and their parents also supported such projects over the years. The brothers are in full sympathy with the objective of preserving as much as possible of the scenic, historic and recreational values, not only of the Palisades-Highlands region, but of the entire Hudson River and its principal tributaries, practically all of which are situated within the State of New York. At the President's request, Laurance S. Rockefeller served as chairman of the White House Conference on Natural Beauty." Wirth went on: "As a retired Director of the National Park Service I can say, without question, that the Rockefeller family has contributed more to the national park system (which includes the great national important scenic, historical and recreation areas), and to conservation in general, than any other family in our time."

About a year after the Hudson River Valley Commission had been established, Nelson and Laurance Rockefeller unveiled a plan to bring the Federal government and New Jersey into partnership with New York State for purposes of saving the Hudson River Valley from blight, planning for orderly growth and development, and preserving historic and scenic values. The three government bodies would not be equal partners, however: the permanent commission would have three members from the Federal government, three from New Jersey and nine from New York. Governor Rockefeller emphasized that the commission would not have "autocratic" or "czar-like powers." Instead, it would rely on a cooperative as opposed to "a coercive or mandatory approach" in its dealing with commercial developers in the Hudson River Valley. Thus, while the commission would have the right to review plans for major projects in the valley for a sixty-day period, it would have no veto power over any project and no authority to enforce its decisions. The sixty-day period would be used as a time for negotiations between the government commission and private interests in order to obtain voluntary conformity to an overall plan.

Laurance Rockefeller stressed the plan's pragmatic nature: "This plan isn't something we went up in an ivory tower and dreamed." He explained that he was opposed to issuing a "theoretical recommendation that could not possibly be brought to fulfillment." The plan was not directed toward treating the Hudson River Valley as a protected park. Henry Diamond, counsel to the Hudson River Valley Commission, asserted that "parts of the valley are highly populated and highly urbanized and they're getting more so, so you can't treat them as wilderness. You can't have rangers running North Tarrytown, for instance."

Secretary of the Interior Udall appeared to be dissatisfied with the Rockefellers' plan. He and Agriculture Secretary Orville Freeman had the Bureau of Outdoor Recreation draft a recommendation for a commission of three members—one each from the Federal government and the states of New Jersey and New York—with the power to disapprove all public and private construction within sight of the Hudson River banks that did not conform to a master plan for the entire valley. The commission would have power to override local zoning ordinances not strict enough to meet the requirements of the master plan and would have funds with which to buy land, primarily "as a temporary means to preserve open space, public access and scenic vantage points" until the land could be transferred to local communities or park commissions. The Bureau of Outdoor Recreation's report deplored the history of the valley's development and was highly critical of state and local government action, contending that zoning "has not prevented conglomerate development along the river because it came too late and has never been enforced. As a result, substantial portions of the shoreline, including areas with high scenic and recreation values, were unwisely developed or exploited in the name of progress, and the river itself became an open sewer for the waste and debris of the cities and factories lining the shore."

Governor Rockefeller called the report "shallow" and "self-serving." Its "conclusions and recommendations doubtlessly owe more to the season of the year than to professional substance," he wrote to Secretary Udall, as the gubernatorial elections approached. The Governor wrote that the report "invites paralysis of development" by proposing that local and state authorities "should delay major commitments in industrial, commercial and residential land use until the 'initial planning stages' are completed." According to the Governor, such thinking was the product of a "narrow view that recognized only recreation and scenic beauty as important considerations."

Congressman Ottinger continued to press for legislation aimed at making the lower Hudson a Federal preserve. Governor Rockefeller wrote President Johnson that bills like Ottinger's "would leave the valley in a state of suspended animation." Later, the Governor said: "We must stop this Federal power grab"; the bill contributes "nothing further to constructive action." Despite his protests, Congress approved a bill in September 1966 that directed all Federal agencies to consult with the Secretary of the Interior and allow him ninety days to review any federally licensed project that would affect conservation and development in the Hudson River Valley. Within three years, the Secretary would hand over responsibility for the valley to a Federal-interstate compact with enforcement powers. Conservation groups hailed the legislation. It was called a clear defeat for Governor Rockefeller. But the provisions of the bill were not retroactive, and Con Ed's Storm King plan was not affected. Furthermore, although President Nixon extended the compact several years later, the Governor managed to stall, and responsibility for the valley has not been taken out of his hands.

During 1966 Governor Rockefeller changed the membership of the Hudson River Valley Commission. Frank Wells McCabe became chairman. New members included Peter J. Brennan, then president of the New York Building and Construction Trades Council; R. Stewart Kilbourne, the State Conservation Commissioner; Mrs. Helen Hayes MacArthur, the actress; Carl J. Mays, the planning director of Orange County; Ronald B. Peterson, director of the New York State Office of Planning Coordination; Fergus Reid III, managing partner of Dick and Merle-Smith on Wall Street. Laurance Rockefeller and Conrad Wirth left the commission. The new Executive Director, at an annual salary of $29,000, was Alexander Aldrich, who had been an Assistant to the Governor since September 1963.

In fiscal 1967 the commission's budget was $447,160. Within five years it rose to $845,000. But in 1972 it was cut sharply, and the commission was absorbed into the State Office of Planning Services along with six other agencies. The commission had reviewed 397 proposals and held hearings on 36. Fergus Reid III, who had become chairman, bemoaned its demise. "What we have been," he said, "is an extraordinarily successful experiment in government by persuasion rather than fiat. Everyone's tired of being beaten up by governments telling them what they can and cannot do. It would be a shame if our innovations came to an end." But conservationists did not hold the commission in high esteem, and when the commission was broken, they did not protest.

Lack of conservationists' support for the commission dates back to 1965—the very year it was established—when Governor Rockefeller and the State Department of Public Works (DPW) quietly laid plans to build a six-lane expressway in the crowded Hudson River Valley corridor on the east bank of the river. The New York Central Railroad (as the line was called then), whose railbed is a few yards from the riverbank, provided a railbus—a vehicle that can travel both on railroad tracks and overland—for an unpublicized trip from the Bronx to a destination upriver by railroad and DPW officials and engineers hired by the Rockefellers. A route for the expressway was determined: it would be built partly on landfill in shallows along the riverbank, swing inland for a few hundred feet here and there, travel over the railbed in some places (the railroad planned to sell its air rights to the state), climb bluffs elsewhere. In May legislation was introduced in the Rules Committee of the New York State Senate calling for construction of a highway "beginning at a point on Interstate Route 503 in the vicinity of Beacon or in the vicinity of Wiccopee, to be determined by the superintendent of public works, thence in a generally southerly direction to the vicinity of Ossining and then continuing southerly, west of U.S. Route 9, along or near the Hudson River to the north city line of New York, thence generally southerly and easterly to a connection with Interstate Route Connection 512 in the city of New York, to be determined by the superintendent of public works." There were several unique aspects to this bill: one, it

was vague, in that the precise location of the highway was
not provided; two, no sponsor was listed on the bill—not even
the DPW, which usually is identified as the sponsor of this
kind of bill; three, contrary to customary practice, no preliminary plan had been announced and no public hearings had
been held prior to the bill's introduction; four, since the route
numbers used to describe the proposed highway were those
used by the DPW on its in-house maps rather than those used
on public maps, the bill was difficult for a layman to follow;
five, a supporting memorandum explaining the need for the
legislation did not accompany the bill—and was not sent to
the Legislature until after the bill had been passed.

The bill passed the Senate on May 24; the Assembly voted
its approval on the following day. Governor Rockefeller
signed the bill on May 28, the same day the supporting memorandum, dated May 14, reached the Legislature.*

* The same method was used to pass companion legislation calling for
a 3.5-mile superhighway running east-west and connecting the proposed north-south highway with Route 9A to the east. This short
superhighway, called Route 117, has been built. My first trip on it was
a shock; it was virtually empty and appeared to be a magnificent connection between two unpopular destinations. I soon discovered its purpose, however. It is an alternative to the old Route 117, a two-lane
road which meanders through the Rockefeller estates at Pocantico
Hills. The new Route 117 runs essentially across the northern borders
of the estates and does not disturb them.

The relocation of Route 117 had been one of Rockefeller Junior's pet
projects. In March 1932, he attempted to persuade local officials to
split the cost of building a new road fifty-fifty, but they insisted that
he pay the total cost himself. He refused and abandoned the project.
Route 117 was not relocated until his son's governorship. One mile of
it runs through Rockefeller lands, but, I have been told, the family has
never transferred the property to the state.

It should be noted that the Rockefellers have made the Pocantico
Hills territory into a family enclave by, among other things, accumu-

The proposed highway, which would be called the Hudson River Expressway, was to be six lanes wide and forty-seven miles long. It was needed, the argument went, to relieve future traffic congestion on Routes 9 and 9A, the old, narrow north-south roads that run through towns and villages in the Hudson River Valley corridor. The idea was not new. A version called I-87, 90 percent federally funded, had been mapped out in 1956. It would have split the Rockefellers' Pocantico Hills lands in twain, running between Laurance's house and John's farm on one side and Nelson's house and David's farm on the other. On February 10, 1961, two years after Nelson had taken office as Governor, the DPW made public a plan for relocating the proposed I-87 five miles east. The proposed Hudson River Expressway also would not cross Rockefeller lands. Instead, it would run through the towns of Tarrytown, North Tarrytown and Ossining. Tarrytown, with a population of 12,000, would lose many homes, a recreation facility, parts of two schools, a firehouse, the state police barracks, Washington Irving and Tarrytown Board Clubs, the village's Losee Park, public and private waterfront property, a commuter parking area, an insurance company and several other business sites. Nearly 10 percent of the residents of North Tarrytown would lose their homes, and over 200 black families in Ossining would be displaced by the road.

Conservationists, both in government and in private life, objected to the Hudson River Expressway proposal. In a letter to the Secretary of Commerce recommending that no Federal funds be appropriated for the expressway's construction, Sec-

lating nearly all of the property in the immediate vicinity of the estates, tearing down commercial structures, and persuading the New York Central Railroad to close down a passenger station, tear down various structures and yards, and move its tracks a mile east.

retary of the Interior Udall wrote: "Such an expressway in the highly scenic and significantly historic corridor along the Hudson River would seriously impair the values we are all trying to preserve." The Interior Department's 1966 report, "Focus on the Hudson," recommended that the expressway "not be constructed." Fishermen contended that dumping landfill in the shallows along the river's shoreline would be detrimental to marine life. The New York State Conservation Department reported later that fish and shellfish beds in the areas would be lost permanently and that siltation from the 9.5 million cubic yards of fill required by the expressway could block spawning runs of shad, striped bass, sturgeon, herring and other fish for two to three years.*

Some local officials favored the expressway's construction. Westchester County's planning commissioner said that it "will result in cleaning up the shoreline of the Hudson"; the county's commissioner of parks, recreation and conservation said the construction would provide an opportunity to "clean up the riverfront and provide a magnificent scenic drive." Early in 1966 the state sweetened the expressway proposal by promising to build a riverfront park along four miles of the proposed route. There would be sand beaches, marinas for 400 boats, bicycle and hiking paths, fishing piers, a golf course, badminton and tennis courts, swimming pools, picnic areas, a restaurant and parking for 2,000 cars. The park would not please conservationists, however: it would be built on landfill in the Hudson.

As criticism of the expressway proposal mounted, one thing

* Fishermen must drive Governor Rockefeller wild. "Don't worry," he commented during a discussion at Binghamton on January 21, 1969, about power plants' using river and lake water for cooling purposes, "we'll find a way to save the fish so you sportsmen can destroy them."

became certain. Assemblyman Lawrence A. Cabot, through whose district the expressway would run, once delivered a load of mail protesting the proposed route to Governor Rockefeller in Albany. Cabot later told William Rodgers, author of *Rockefeller's Follies*, that "the Governor just glanced at the mail and listened to my report. Then he said to me, 'That's odd. I haven't heard a single objection to the expressway.' He kept a straight face, too. He added that he was determined to build the road."

Passage of the bill calling for construction of the expressway was no guarantee that it would be built. In fact, in order to make the proposal politically palatable, the state decided to build only the northernmost stretch, 10.4 miles long. In addition, the Hudson River Valley Commission could recommend disapproval of construction, although this seemed unlikely. Laurance Rockefeller, the commission's first chairman, praised the proposal, asserting that the expressway would provide tourists excellent "visual access" to the river. It turned out, furthermore, that Alexander Aldrich, the second executive director, was only too eager to please Governor Rockefeller. Aldrich wrote to his cousin:

> Judging from past performance, my instinct is that the Commission will want to hold a public hearing on the Expressway. . . . I believe it is extremely unlikely that the Commission will disapprove the road in its final findings. There is ample precedent for this kind of approval following a public hearing. . . . If all goes well, the chances are that the Commission will approve the road (possibly with some minor suggestions) on or about Friday, March eighth. . . . I have discussed the schedule with Bert Hughes [of the State Transportation Department] and he agrees that it sounds reason-

able. . . . Public hearings [by the commission] . . . will not affect the construction schedule at all.

The hearing was held. Forty-three persons spoke on the proposed expressway. Forty-one were opposed to its construction.* Nevertheless, the commissioners gave their unanimous approval to the expressway's construction. Their recommendation said:

> The expressway is vital to the growth and strength of the whole Hudson Valley. . . . The expressway will not have an unreasonably adverse effect upon the scenic, historic, recreational and natural resources of the valley when compared with its profoundly positive commercial, industrial and residential benefits.
>
> Construction of the expressway, coupled with local initiative and intelligent planning, will give the communities involved a greatly needed opportunity for economic growth and expansion.
>
> Present traffic conditions in the area are extremely congested, and projections for 1985 point to an impossible condition.† The proposed improvement of Route 9 and Route 9A as alternatives to the expressway will not provide the needed traffic relief, nor provide the economic advantages which will flow from the expressway's development.
>
> Access to the Hudson is not now possible for the vast major-

---

* The two speakers in favor of construction were John Domzella, Republican Mayor of Ossining, and Will Osborn, president of the Hudson River Conservation Society. At a meeting held a month after the hearing, 97 percent of the Society's 472 members voted against the expressway's construction. Osborn resigned summarily.

† According to Nancy Mathews, assistant to conservationist-lawyer David Sive, traffic counts were taken during the four-to-seven P.M. rush hour. The state used these figures as averages over full twenty-four-hour periods.

ity of the general public. The expressway, the interchange of Route 117 and the proposed state, county and municipal parks in conjunction with the expressway provide the mechanism for the use and enjoyment of the river for large numbers of the general public.

The expressway's impact upon the natural resources of the river will not constitute a significant impairment of these resources.

The Commission's deepest concern is with the valley's human resources, present and future. The benefits of the expressway are pervasive: opportunities for an improved employment climate and enhanced tax base, greatly expanded recreational facilities and reduced cost of road transportation. Most important, the expressway will substantially reduce the accident record on Route 9.

The commission recommended that families displaced by the expressway be relocated by the State Department of Transportation; that sizes of interchanges be limited in order to limit destruction of commercial property; and that recreational and tourist facilities be built between the expressway and the riverbank.

The notion of "compatible development" of a natural resource was expressed beautifully in the report. But conservationists believed that the commission had brushed aside the question of the proposed expressway's ecological impact. It was at this point that they lost any respect they might have had for the commission. They had learned that it was nothing but Governor Rockefeller's rubber stamp.

After Congressman Ottinger's legislation gave the Secretary of the Interior the right to review the expressway proposal, and given the Interior Department's announced opposition, expressway construction still was not guaranteed. Governor Rockefeller had to apply pressure. He summoned Secretary Udall and several department staff members to a conference in New York in January, 1968. The conference was a success. On May 3, Udall met with the director of the Bureau of Outdoor Recreation to inform him that the department was reversing its position; the expressway would be backed. At the time, several reviews of the proposal were underway. An Interior Department task force, which had been appointed in February, was studying the proposal's recreation aspects. (The report was not filed until May 31.) The Corps of Engineers had requested a report on the application for dumping landfill in the Hudson from the Fish and Wildlife Service on April 22. (This report was not filed until December.) Udall did not discuss these studies-in-process during the May 3 meeting. Moreover, he did not take into account the results of two hearings that had been held by the New York State Department of Transportation in February. At the first hearing, thirty persons had spoken, and only two, the Republican Mayor of Ossining and a spokesman for the Ossining Taxpayers Association, had been in favor of the expressway proposal. At the second hearing, only one out of forty-three speakers had been in favor of the proposal.

The Interior Department did not make its new position on the expressway public for several months. In the meantime, the Bureau of Outdoor Recreation prepared a memorandum called "Benefits to the Rockefeller Estate from the Expressway." It mentioned that the Rockefeller family had announced the donation for park purposes of 165 acres of riverfront property valued at about $6 to $8 million. The memorandum went on to say:

on the other hand about 75 acres of the southwestern portion of this property adjacent to highways 9 and 117 would be developed commercially. The specific types of development have not been made known; however . . . they would possibly be research and office buildings. Undoubtedly the Rockefellers could receive substantial sums from the sale of the 75 acres for commercial purposes or from developing the area and leasing it if they elect to do so. However, the expressway is not needed in order for this area to be developed. New Route 117 is already under construction which would end at the southwestern corner of this property at Highway 9.

Probably the greatest financial benefit to the Rockefeller family would accrue from the fact that the expressway together with the extension of Route 117 from the expressway to U.S. Highway 9 will open up the Rockefeller holdings to people from as far away as New York City. Presently U.S. Highway 9 and 9A would have to be used to reach this area from New York City. The high-speed expressway, even though only about six miles are involved, would undoubtedly be an influencing factor to commuters or to industry.

As the months went by without any signal from the Interior Department, Nelson and Laurance Rockefeller became a bit impatient and edgy. Laurance put in a telephone call to the Bureau of Outdoor Recreation on August 20. A subordinate in the department wrote a memorandum on the call:

Mr. Rockefeller said that he was with his brother, Governor Nelson Rockefeller, and he was calling to find out the status of Interior's review under the Hudson River legislation. . . . They wanted to be sure that Interior had not lost track of the application. He said that he understood the Corps [of Engineers] was ready to move but could not do so until receiving Interior's comments. He added that he understood Congressman Ottinger was putting great pressure on Secretary Udall to oppose the Expressway and implied that Governor Rockefeller was prepared to exert counter pressure if necessary. I told Mr. Rockefeller that the Expressway matter had not fallen between the cracks at Interior. . . . Mr. Rockefeller said he was glad to hear that the matter had not been sidetracked and would convey the foregoing information to his brother. I told Mr. Rockefeller I would inform the Secretary of his call.

Some time later, Udall told a journalist that he had "never felt such pressure" as he had felt from the Rockefellers on the expressway issue, although he was at a loss to explain their insistence. "The whole thing was a matter of Laurance laying all his influence on the line," Udall said. He finally decided to make his non-opposition to the expressway proposal public in November. The instructions pertaining to publication of his reversed position were, in part:

> The letter to the Corps is to give the rationale for Udall's non-opposition. It is to state something to the effect that while he initially had reservations about the expressway, he is influenced by the findings of the two groups that made on site reviews of the Hudson and, accordingly, will not oppose. Udall's feelings are that his decision is a very limited one in view of the fact that the State and Governor Rockefeller have prime responsibility. . . . A press release should be prepared at the time the letter goes to the Corps of Engineers. The press release should indicate that the Secretary's decision is based on Bureau of Outdoor Recreation's recommendations or on the results of two studies performed by Interior officials.

(Testimony at Congressional hearings revealed that the two Interior studies—by the task force appointed in February and by another task force appointed in July—were based on a New York State report that had been completed in one month, without original field work, but relying on earlier studies, some of them from the 1930s.)

In the face of the recommendations by the Hudson River Valley Commission and the Interior Department, conservationists persisted in their opposition to the expressway proposal, taking the battle into the courts. There the issue was resolved. In 1969 the Federal District Court enjoined the Corps of Engineers and the State Department of Transportation from building dikes (to shore up the expressway) in the Hudson River. The injunction was based on an 1899 statute which forbids the erection of dikes in navigable waters without Congressional consent. The Federal Circuit Court of Appeals upheld this ruling, and in December 1970, the United States Supreme Court refused to hear an appeal.

Six months after the Supreme Court had refused to hear an appeal, the State Department of Transportation offered some five proposals for alternate routes for the Hudson River Expressway, all of them *close* to the east bank of the river. Four of the proposals were for six-lane highways; one called for a four-lane highway with parallel service roads. The department estimated the costs of the proposed expressways at anywhere from $70 million to $310 million. Engineers in the department conceded that between 200 and 450 residential and commercial buildings would be destroyed no matter which route was selected. The department later revised this estimate upward: 490 buildings would be torn down and 740 families displaced by a version of the expressway that would run parallel to the east side of the Penn Central railbed.

No one expected Governor Rockefeller to abandon the

project. But late in November 1971, a couple of weeks after a $2.5-billion state transportation bond issue—which would have financed expressway construction except for between $35 million and $155 million in matching Federal funds—had been roundly defeated at the polls, the Governor announced to a weekend workshop of conservationists at Tarrytown that the expressway was a "dead issue." He called the tactics of the expressway's opponents "political opportunism," but also managed to observe that "people's priorities are changing."

So people's priorities were changing. Were Governor Rockefeller's priorities changing? I want to go back for a moment to March 1967, when the Governor announced a proposal for construction of two bridges across Long Island Sound. He characterized his recommendations for immediate legislative approval of the construction as one of his "unpleasant" duties necessitated by the anticipated growth of highway use in the New York City metropolitan area. One bridge would span the 6.5-mile gap between the town of Rye in Westchester County and the town of Oyster Bay on Long Island. According to the Governor, this bridge would cost $130 million. (He included in this figure neither interest charges on construction bonds nor costs for building connections between the bridge and expressways, however; the bridge's actual cost would be twice his figure.) The second bridge would be a 14.6-mile link between the city of Bridgeport, Connecticut, and the town of Port Jefferson, further out on Long Island. According to the Governor, this bridge would cost $225 million.

Rye Assemblyman Joseph R. Pisani was "unalterably opposed" to Governor Rockefeller's Rye-Oyster Bay bridge proposal. Pisani charged that the bridge would be "obsolete before it is completed." He wrote to William J. Ronan, the Governor's chief transportation adviser, saying, "We must be constantly vigilant to maintain and preserve our suburban communities and to prevent increased destruction of residential communities by ill-conceived roads and bridges that will not answer the transportation needs of tomorrow."

The State Legislature did not respond favorably to Assemblyman Pisani's arguments (perhaps because he did not object to construction of the second bridge further out on Long Island), and Rye-Oyster Bay bridge construction was authorized. Nevertheless, a number of legislators began to introduce bills calling for repeal of the authorization. Year after year these legislators were unsuccessful, as their bills died in committees. These legislators did manage to delay the start of construction, however.

During the 1970 gubernatorial campaign, Governor Rockefeller initiated a study on the Rye-Oyster Bay bridge proposal. The study, done for the State Department of Transportation by eight technical and financial consulting firms at a cost of $162,500, concluded that the bridge was vital to the growth of the metropolitan area, would ease traffic congestion on the eleven major highways in the area such that there would be reductions in air and noise pollution, and would exert relatively minor adverse effects on the local environment. Assemblyman Pisani was "not surprised by the results of the study." He said, "This was something that was predetermined by the powers that be that wanted the bridge. Its conclusion was decided before the study was started."*

* Governor Rockefeller's Rye-Oyster Bay bridge proposal has been widely interpreted as part of a sweet deal with Robert Moses, who had

A lengthy editorial on the Rye-Oyster Bay bridge study was published in the March 1, 1972, edition of *Newsday*, Long Island's major newspaper. *Newsday* recognized that something had to be done about the traffic snarl that plagues Long Island. The editorial was accompanied by a cartoon which showed two men in a prison cell. The caption read, "Like an idiot, I tried to make my getaway on the Long Island Expressway." But *Newsday* asked whether the state had "seriously considered mass transit alternatives" to the bridge. *Newsday* contended that the state had "never fully justified the Bayville [i.e., Oyster Bay] site . . . never fully examined the environmental impact or explored the effect of the bridge on land-use and recreation. . . . Bayville . . . was selected despite traffic studies that showed a bridge further west [i.e., closer to New York City] . . . would lessen metropolitan congestion more effectively. The state cited vague difficulties with access roads further west. But it did not come close to an adequate examination of this alternative." *Newsday* warned that the bridge would create pressure to build more roads and widen existing roads in its vicinity. "Long Islanders," *Newsday* remarked, "can't evaluate the bridge unless the State Transportation Department is frank with them about all the implications."

Newsday was sharply critical of the study in several respects:

> The state's study of the environmental impact of the bridge doesn't lack candor; but it does lack facts. In its most recent

originated the idea. According to this interpretation, the Governor's sponsorship of the bridge was the price for Moses' backing the Governor's master transportation plan for the New York City metropolitan area.

report, the state used wetlands data compiled in 1952. Considering this absence of first-hand information, the conclusions reached in the report are understandably vague. The report skirts critical consideration by pleading lack of knowledge. . . .

Nor has the state addressed itself to the probable effects of the bridge on land-use patterns. Northern Oyster Bay Town is Nassau [County's] last open space preserve. Bridgeheads tend to stimulate development in their vicinity. The Nassau-Suffolk Regional Planning Board has recommended that the shoreline areas be protected from intensive development. Will the bridge make it more difficult to realize that goal? That state has never considered that.

"We recognize the need for another link with the mainland," *Newsday* said in its concluding remarks. "But Long Islanders want to know: Why specifically a Bayville bridge? And what specifically will that bridge do to Long Island?"

In April 1971, while the Rye-Oyster Bay bridge study had been in process, overwhelming majorities in both houses of the State Legislature had passed a bill calling for repeal of authorizations for the bridge's construction. Governor Rockefeller had vetoed the bill on the grounds that the study had not been completed. Attempts to override the veto—rare in the Legislature, which was controlled by the Governor's fellow Republicans—had been unsuccessful. The following year—the study having been completed—the Legislature again voted for repeal and the Governor again used his veto power successfully.

The Metropolitan Transportation Authority (MTA), which has the power to issue construction bonds, was ready. An MTA spokesman said, "All we need is marching orders from the Governor." But the start of construction was delayed. Early in 1973 the Department of the Interior refused to grant an easement for any part of the proposed project which would be over, under, through or on the Oyster Bay National Wildlife Refuge. Habitats of waterfowl, shorebirds and shellfish would be affected by the bridge's construction, Interior Department studies had indicated. In addition, the state faced a legal problem. The town of Oyster Bay had deeded 3,117 acres to the wildlife refuge on condition that they be kept "forever wild." If the state were to attempt to use this acreage for a bridge route, ownership would revert to the town.

State officials began studying ways to challenge the Interior Department's ruling and solve the legal problem. The *New York Times* wrote that Governor Rockefeller was "expected to continue pressing" for the bridge. This did not come as a surprise. Everyone knew that the Governor's priorities had not changed. He was backing Con Ed in the Storm King controversy; he had fought for the Hudson River Expressway until the end; and he had vetoed the Legislature's repeals of authorizations for the Rye-Oyster Bay bridge. In addition, he had been seen working on new ways to gain advantages in troublesome battles with conservationists and their legislative and bureaucratic allies. The establishment of a power plant siting board was one illustration of his determination to get his own way. The Stewart jetport effort was another.

During Governor Rockefeller's first decade in office, an intensive search had been conducted for a site for a fourth major New York City metropolitan area jetport, which the Governor strongly believed was necessary. The New York-New Jersey Port Authority had tried to sell the public on two sites in New Jersey—the first in the Great Swamp area twenty-five miles west of Manhattan, the second twenty miles further west—but public outrage at expected levels of noise and air pollution had persuaded New Jersey officials to oppose these sites. In the latter 1960s Governor Rockefeller had recommended takeover of a Navy-owned field at Calverton, Long Island, but the Port Authority, which the Governor did not control singlehandedly, refused to approve this site.

The search came to an end in 1970, when the Metropolitan Transportation Authority, which Governor Rockefeller *did* control singlehandedly, acquired Stewart Air Force Base—near Newburgh, some sixty-five miles northeast of New York City —and began to operate it as a facility for air cargo and light planes. This was a crucial step in the effort to develop a fourth jetport. To be sure, the New York State Legislature would have to approve the conversion of Stewart to a major jetport. But if Stewart had been owned by the Port Authority, instead of by the MTA, approval by both the New York and New Jersey State Legislatures would have been required. It would have been more difficult to obtain. No doubt the New Jersey Legislature would have been influenced by the Port Authority's calling Stewart an unworkable site, and by the fact that the Authority was building new facilities at the existing Newark, New Jersey, jetport at a cost of $400 million.

In April 1971, Governor Rockefeller announced that he would ask the New York State Legislature to authorize expansion of the Stewart airport so it could handle a large volume of commercial airline traffic. The Governor attempted to forestall conservationists' opposition to his plan as well. "I am determined," he said, "to see to it that we have a great new airport at Stewart, and that we do so with minimum disruption to the Newburgh area. Through sound planning, we can protect the environment, enhance—not destroy—community values. . . . By starting to acquire land now . . . we can develop this facility in an orderly manner." Accordingly, the MTA was to buy up 8,000 acres adjacent to Stewart in order to develop a huge new forest as a noise buffer between the jetport and nearby communities.

It was hoped that conservationists would be satisfied by this. They were not, of course. In midsummer a conservationists' group, the Hudson River Valley Council, initiated a lawsuit in conjunction with seven municipalities and other citizens' groups to stop the MTA from acquiring land for expansion prior to studies and hearings on the proposed jetport. A Federal judge refused, however, to grant a preliminary injunction against the MTA.

Conservationists learned nothing specific about the MTA's long-term expansion plans for the Sewart airfield until September 1972, when Angelo DeSapio, an architect at Transplan, a New York consulting firm engaged in developing a master plan for Stewart, was quoted by a Rome newspaper, *Il Messaggero,* as saying that Stewart would be capable of handling 60 million passengers a year—three times the volume handled at Kennedy International Airport. The plan called for five runways, parking for 88,000 cars, and a high-speed rail connection to Manhattan (which none of the three existing New York City metropolitan jetports enjoyed as yet). It was an ambitious plan to keep secret.

In order to lay the groundwork for building a jetport at Stewart, Governor Rockefeller had used whatever legislative and fiscal leverage he could command. Now he was using secrecy. The Stewart plan had become a battle in the war the Governor and conservationists were waging. Here, on one side of the battlefield, was the Governor, using his considerable public and private sources of power to promote plans for the Storm King pumped-storage hydroelectric plant, the Hudson River Expressway, the Rye-Oyster Bay bridge and the Stewart jetport. There, on the other side, were conservationists, trying to stop the plans from going forward, suspicious of any proposal dealing with the environment that was sponsored by any of the Rockefeller brothers.

In past years the Rockefellers have been able to build and beautify as they have seen fit. They have used their reputations as philanthropists to assume the roles of benevolent paternalists whose projects have carried a seal of *pro bono publico*, and what they have envisioned and executed, even in the name of profit, is seen by many people to be primarily of public benefit. "Thank God for the Rockefellers," these people say when they encounter a Rockefeller project. But in recent years, as we have seen, there has been some decline in public support. Something has gone wrong with the Rockefellers' image. To some people, the Rockefellers have become predatory villains again.

Included in this group are people who are concerned about San Francisco Bay, whose water area has shrunk from 680 to 400 square miles after decades of plugging and filling by developers. In response to widespread public concern that additional filling of tide and submerged lands would result in aggravation of local smog conditions, greater seasonal temperature fluctuations, and danger to fish and wildlife, the California Legislature formed the Bay Conservation and Development Commission (BCDC), which spent three years studying the landfill problem and how the bay might be developed without harm to environmental values. In January 1969, BCDC reported that "any filling is harmful to the bay." It should be treated as a national resource, not as "ordinary real estate," BCDC asserted. Nevertheless, Westbay Community Associates—a group of investors, including David Rockefeller and Lazard Frères & Company of New York; Ideal Basic Industries, Inc., of Denver; and the Crocker Land Company of San Francisco—titleholder of 10,179 acres of the bay floor, intended to proceed with a plan to fill 4,800 acres for a $3-billion real estate project, to be completed within thirty years.

When Westbay ran into opposition at BCDC hearings, a Westbay spokesman, Warren T. Lindquist, complained that they were "all packed with articulate and rabid conservationists" and that "a few rabid conservationists" were depicting David Rockefeller as "a villain." Lindquist counterattacked with the assertion that the project was in the same spirit of *pro bono publico* that characterizes other Rockefeller projects. "We wanted to do something that would be significant, creative and at the same time be profitable," he said. Westbay contended that the project would help the bay realize its full potential. "Our position is that you can have your cake and eat it too," was how Lindquist put it.

Such a notion has seduced some of the people, but not all of the people. One veteran writer on environmental issues remarked recently, "I don't know a working environmentalist who has respect for what the Rockefellers are doing. They are the enemy."

Still, there is a great reservoir of goodwill that can be tapped. Nelson Rockefeller has called his family the "caretaker," not the "possessor" of the vast Rockefeller lands at Pocantico Hills. He has said, "We care very much—my brothers and I, and our children—that this land's beauty of color and contour, its historical significance going back in time to the beginnings of our country, and its real potential for recreation, should not be chipped away—and thus destroyed forever—by haphazard development, by consideration of personal profit, or by aiming at short-range goals." According to the Governor, the family has undertaken "a long-range study of the complicated procedures to be initiated, while we're still alive, to insure that the unique qualities of the land can be preserved and dedicated to the public interest." There is much wealth that the Rockefellers can disburse in an effort to redeem their reputation among conservationists. That reputation can be rebuilt. But the danger will remain that the Rockefellers will use this goodwill, in combination with their considerable power, to pursue their basic interest, which is development.

vi   Philanthropy and Politics: U.S. Military Preparedness

John D. Rockefeller, with perhaps the most hated name in America in the early 1900s, wisely stood back from the operations of his philanthropic institutions. He supplied funds for work to be carried out by professional staffs, and placed authority over the operations in the hands of Gates, Rockefeller Junior and, most important, distinguished boards of trustees who were considered independent of the Rockefeller family and its interests. By the fourth Rockefeller period, when the Rockefeller brothers, inspired by their familial philanthropic responsibility, established their own philanthropic institutions, the good works accomplished by their grandfather's institutions had long since paved over the dirt associated with the Rockefeller name and had been milestones on the road the family had traveled to a high level of public esteem.* Armed with an enviable reputation, the brothers

* It should be noted that the nature of public regard for the Rockefeller name had become such that when Nelson Rockefeller entered elective politics, he could use his fortune on his own behalf without restraint. In fact, he changed the rules for campaign financing. "It wasn't until the first election of Nelson Rockefeller as Governor,"

could become personally involved in the operation of their philanthropic institutions, and this, rather than donations of money, became the cornerstone of their philanthropic effort. They could take a radical step, furthermore. They could expand the work of these institutions beyond such traditional concerns as the promotion of research and education, eradication of disease, support of the arts and preservation of the landscape. The brothers could use their philanthropic institutions to exert political influence. And they would do so in the areas of military and foreign policy.

The brothers did this openly, by using their collective philanthropic fund, the Rockefeller Brothers Fund, to publish their views and recommendations on important political issues in the latter 1950s. Given the nature of public regard for the family by that time, it is hardly remarkable that the use of a Rockefeller philanthropic fund for political purposes was generally accepted. But looking back at what the Rockefeller Brothers Fund actually published, acceptance *was* remarkable. For as a result of this involvement in politics, Rockefeller philanthropy became involved not only in the enrichment of life —philanthropy's traditional goal—but also with weapons of death and destruction.

The road down which the Rockefeller brothers traveled in the fourth period was marked by violence—violence which in no small part the brothers helped bring about themselves. For the Rockefellers had become so influential in public affairs by the 1950s that U.S. military and foreign policy became synonymous with the policies they advocated. And Nelson Rocke-

---

former Congressman Max McCarthy wrote in his book *Elections for Sale*, " . . . that a very wealthy individual was bold enough to pay virtually all his own bills."

feller played the pivotal role in the violent ending to the Attica Prison rebellion, the most dramatic episode in his tenure as Governor of New York. The journey began in the latter 1930s on a peaceful note, however, when Nelson Rockefeller, the most ambitious brother, became involved in improving relations between U.S. corporations (such as the members of the Standard Oil family) and the Latin American nations where the corporations did business. With the onset of World War II, Rockefeller's experience became useful to President Roosevelt. On his recommendation, Rockefeller prepared a memorandum, entitled "Hemispheric Economic Policy," which he delivered to the White House on June 14, 1940. The memorandum urged the adoption by the United States of broad trade, private investment and diplomatic programs toward Latin America. In addition, the memorandum called for a vigorous program for improving cultural, scientific and educational relations between the Americas through "an organization which would not be hampered by the limitations of traditional diplomacy in the promotion of goodwill among the Latin American Republics." This was the memorandum's most innovative recommendation, for such an effort would constitute the United States' first use of culture and education as instruments of foreign policy.*

President Roosevelt had been interested in the preparation of the memorandum. Latin America was considered ripe for Nazi propaganda, which, it was feared, would lead eventually to the establishment of German military bases there. As the memorandum recommended, he created a new agency, the

---

* The organization proposed in the memorandum was the forerunner of such agencies as the Office of War Information, the United States Information Agency and the Voice of America, which would carry out propaganda activities worldwide.

Office of Coordinator of Commercial and Cultural Relations between the American Republics, which later became the Office of Inter-American Affairs. The Coordinator, who was responsible directly to the President, was charged with "maintain[ing] liaison between the Advisory Commission of the Council of National Defense [and] the several departments . . . of the Government . . . to insure proper coordination of . . . the activities of the Government with respect to Hemisphere defense, with particular reference to the commercial and cultural aspects of the problem." The Coordinator's mandate called for his making "effective use of governmental and private facilities in such fields as the arts and sciences, education and travel, radio, the press and cinema" in order to "further national defense and strengthen the bonds between the nations of the Western Hemisphere."

Nelson Rockefeller eventually was appointed Coordinator, and the agency became known popularly as the Rockefeller Office. With a staff of around 1,500 people, the office spent some $140 million on weeding out Nazi influence in Latin American political, business and financial circles, on financial and technical assistance, on cooperative efforts in health, nutrition and education, and on propaganda.

In the post of Coordinator, Nelson Rockefeller also promoted the development of an alliance between the United States and all of Latin America that, as he wrote later in his book *Unity, Freedom and Peace*, would provide "for nothing less than a mutual guarantee of all boundaries of all Latin American republics against aggression from any source." For a while, he got nowhere with his promotion. The idea of including *all* Latin American nations in a mutual security pact with the United States was rejected by Secretary of State Cordell Hull, who branded Argentina's Farrell-Peron regime pro-Fascist. Rockefeller could do little in open opposition to this policy. As Coordinator, he had no direct part in formulating political policy toward Latin America; he had been instructed to cooperate with the State Department, furthermore. Late in 1944, however, President Roosevelt replaced Hull with Edward Stettinius, Jr., reorganized the State Department, and made Rockefeller Assistant Secretary with specific jurisdiction over Latin American affairs. Prospects for the all-nation mutual security pact improved. Stettinius was willing to depart from Hull's policy of ostracizing Argentina. The regime would be tolerated if it promised to rid itself of Axis influences.

In 1945, with the new policy in effect, the pact was joined at a meeting of foreign ministers in Mexico City. Argentina signed the pact in exchange for United States support for Argentine admission to membership in the United Nations, which was being formed. Nelson Rockefeller's work on behalf of the pact was not over, however. As he saw it, the United Nations Charter, which was being written at a conference in San Francisco, could compromise the pact's intent by limiting United States freedom to act in the event of trouble in the Americas. He worked hard for the adoption of Article 51 of the Charter, which permits the formation of "regional groupings" within the United Nations family and states that no provision of the Charter "shall impair the inherent right of individual or collective self-defense if an armed attack occurs against a member of the United Nations."*

* Article 51 permitted the United States to maintain United Nations membership while entering into mutual security pacts, such as the North Atlantic Treaty Organization (NATO) and the Southeast Asia Treaty Organization (SEATO), and engaging in armed conflicts, such as the Vietnam War, on the basis of such pacts.

By this time, the enemy no longer was Fascism. The United States, Laurance Rockefeller wrote later, was faced with the "Communist challenge . . . a challenge organized to exploit every human hope and disappointment for its own ends . . . ruthless and total . . . a challenge not merely to the power and structure of free nations but to the very values and principles from which free civilization draws its meaning and vitality. Since America finds itself both guardian and protagonist of this free civilization, it is America, above all, that is challenged."

The Rockefeller brothers believed that it was a function of their philanthropic responsibility to respond to this challenge. Accordingly, in 1956 over a hundred distinguished American citizens were gathered together by the Rockefeller Brothers Fund in order to study and report on "specific areas of national life," including American military preparedness and foreign policy.* Laurance Rockefeller wrote that those engaged in the project sought to "define the major problems and opportunities [that would] challenge the United States over the next ten to fifteen years [i.e., until the early 1970s], clarify the national purposes and objectives that must inspire and direct the meeting of such great challenges, and develop a framework of concepts and principles on which national policies and decisions can be soundly based."

"The project really sprang from the brothers' and particularly Nelson Rockefeller's general sense of crisis about the

---

* All four Rockefeller brothers living in New York participated. Among the other signatories of the reports were Adolph A. Berle, Jr., Chester Bowles, Arthur F. Burns, John Cowles, John W. Gardner, Roswell L. Gilpatrick, Theodore M. Hesburgh, James R. Killian, Jr., Henry R. Luce, Jacob S. Potofsky, David Riesman, Dean Rusk, David Sarnoff and Edward Teller.

state of the nation and the drift of the world," John Emmet
Hughes, a speechwriter for President Eisenhower and subsequently public affairs adviser to the Rockefeller brothers, said
some years later. "It was conceived as a way for citizens not
in government to lend their talents to the making of national
decisions." Nelson Rockefeller headed the project until May
26, 1958, when he became an active candidate for Governor
of New York State. Laurance Rockefeller presided thereafter.

Of the six reports produced by the Rockefeller Brothers
Fund project, the most important was "International Security: The Military Aspect," which was prepared under the direction of Henry A. Kissinger, then Associate Director of the
Center for International Affairs. The report was written during a dramatic period. America was marching in a bomb shelter crusade. In January 1957, a bill was introduced in the
House of Representatives calling for the establishment of a
nuclear bomb shelter program designed to protect 170 million
people and a Civil Defense Department to be headed by a Secretary of Cabinet rank. The bill was discussed at a four-day
conference sponsored by the Rockefeller Brothers Fund and
organized by Henry Kissinger, and a description of the urban
and suburban shelter programs was published in the March 18
edition of *Life*.* Later in the year, Americans were shocked

* The National Academy of Sciences estimated the programs' cost at
$24 billion, or 10 percent of the total defense budget for the next six-
year period.

According to *Life*, the urban shelter, which would cost $300 per
person protected, was designed to withstand direct nuclear attack. A
network of concrete tubes 20 feet in diameter—built in 500-foot-
long sections with enough space in each section for 1,000 people—
would be sunk deep enough underground so that occupants would be
shielded from atomic blasts. Each section would have its own com-

by two events. In August the Russians successfully tested the first intercontinental ballistic missile (ICBM). In October they placed the first man-made satellite in orbit around the earth. In addition, the missile gap debate was heating up. In the period from 1957 to 1961, during the second Eisenhower Administration, it was assumed that the Soviet Union was producing missiles at the rate that the most pessimistic American intelligence estimates held possible. The commonly accepted belief in the United States was that the Soviet Union would have between 1,000 and 1,500 ICBMs by 1961-62, and since the United States would have only 130 or so, the Russian lead would be between eight to fourteen ICBMs to one.

"International Security: The Military Aspect" was published in December, during a time, the Rockefeller Brothers Fund panel responsible for the report asserted, when technology was developing at an explosive rate, and in such times military advantage could shift quickly from one adversary to another. Indeed, the balance of terror already was shifting in

---

missary, medical facilities, air-conditioning machinery, emergency supply of electric power and water storage tanks. Sub-basements of office buildings adjacent to the tubes and subway tunnels would be used as auxiliary shelters. The tubes would extend to the outer edge of a city in order to provide underground evacuation routes.

Suburban shelters were designed to protect people against radioactive fallout, fires and minor shock waves resulting from direct hits on central cities. Each underground suburban shelter would cost $6,000 and would accommodate 100 people who would have to remain until the immediate vicinity had been washed down thoroughly and scraped of radioactive dust by decontaminating crews. Afterwards, survivors would not be allowed to move outside the decontaminated areas. Tents and food would be brought up from storage. People would live in the tents for two months after their homes had been cleaned and washed down, or until radiation had decreased to safe levels.

favor of the enemy. "By sacrificing the civilian sector of its economy . . . the Soviet Union has caught up with the United States in major fields of technology. In certain areas assigned high priority by the Kremlin, the Soviet Union has surpassed us qualitatively as well as quantitatively." The Rockefeller panel warned Americans that "ever since World War II, the United States has suffered from a tendency to underestimate the military technology of the U.S.S.R. . . . Today Soviet Science is at least the equal to our own in many strategically significant categories. In the military field, the technological capability of the U.S.S.R. is increasing at a pace obviously faster than that of the United States. If not reversed, this trend alone will place the free world in dire jeopardy." The panel asserted that the Russians were reorganizing and re-equipping their ground forces, which were "far larger numerically than our own," for atomic and conventional warfare; were building up ship and submarine fleets; had the capacity to equip submarines with missiles capable of reaching forty-three of our fifty largest cities and 85 percent of our industrial capacity; had operational air warning and defense systems; were modernizing an air force which had "the largest number of planes in the world"; already had a medium-range ballistic missile capability; and an intercontinental ballistic missile capability, which had been tested successfully, would "soon follow."

For the present, the Rockefeller panel asserted soothingly, the United States had military superiority. Our industrial base and production know-how were superior, we had more operational experience in the use of long-range manned bombers, we lay siege to the Soviet Union with our overseas air bases, we had superiority and greater flexibility on the high seas and we had the advantage in the number and variety of atomic weapons. But, the panel warned, Soviet nuclear missiles threatened our air bases and aircraft carriers, and we were vulnerable to surprise attack at home, for our air defense and warning systems were out of date and our civil defense program was "completely inadequate."

The Rockefeller panel warned that "it appears that the United States is rapidly losing its lead over the U.S.S.R. in the military race. For perhaps the next two years, we still possess a superiority in strategic striking power, and any Soviet attack on us would meet a crushing reply. But our position a year or two hence depends on decisions that must be taken immediately. Unless present trends are reversed, the world balance of power will shift in favor of the Soviet bloc. If that should happen, we are not likely to be given another chance to remedy our failings. It is emphatically not too late, however, if we are prepared to make the big effort now and in the years ahead."

The first requirement of the "big effort," the Rockefeller panel asserted, "is a retaliatory force so well protected and numerous that it can overcome any defense. . . . The second requirement is an active and passive defense system capable of protecting the bulk of our striking force, no matter what the scale of foreseeable surprise attack." (Some definitions: by active defense, one means systems for providing warnings of attacks and weapons for shooting down attack vehicles; by passive defense, one means "civil defense"—building shelters, stockpiling supplies and dispersing industrial plants and air bases.) "Deterrence, in short, depends on a combination of power and will. The factor of power requires a retaliatory capability sufficient to overcome any enemy defense and as invulnerable as possible to surprise attack. The factor of will may hinge importantly on a reasonable combination of active and passive defense measures." The panel recommended construction of fallout shelters, a pervasive public information program, and developing and training "cadres charged with supervising civil defense activities, both in possible pre-attack and post-attack phases." We had to be able to "respond with discipline and effectiveness to a surprise attack [in order to] discourage such a move because an aggressor would no longer be able to gamble that a sudden attack might disorganize our society."

In addition to calling for all-out-war preparations, the Rockefeller panel concerned itself with America's willingness and ability to wage "a kind of war new to the twentieth century and highly developed by the Communists—the disguised or obscure war concealed as internal subversion or takeover by *coup d'état* or civil war." The panel called the new kind of war "concealed" or "non-overt" aggression and stated that "we must . . . realize that non-overt aggressions present issues that are deliberately and intrinsically unclear. To ask for certainty in these situations is a prescription for inaction." Instead of inaction, the panel advocated a "willingness to support friendly governments in situations that fit neither the soldier's classic concept of war nor the diplomat's traditional concept of aggression." In order to pursue this active foreign policy, we had to reorganize our armed forces. "It is . . . imperative," the panel asserted, "that in addition to our retaliatory force we develop units that can intervene rapidly and that are able to make their power felt with discrimination and versatility." In summary, "the effectiveness of our power depends on our unmistakable ability and willingness to oppose force with force at whatever level of intensity may be required."

The Rockefeller panel asserted that "in resisting aggression we cannot in advance forgo weapons that technology makes available to all who seek them, including those who might attack. . . . The willingness to engage in nuclear war, when necessary, is part of the price of our freedom." The panel assured us that "morality does not depend on the type of explosive but on the use to which it is put." In any event, *"Very powerful nuclear weapons can be used in such a manner that they have negligible effects on civilian populations*—as high-altitude explosions over purely military objectives, for example." (Italics added.)

As for disarmament negotiations, the Rockefeller panel asserted that "we will make [them] more realistic if we face their inherent difficulty frankly and if we are not seduced by Soviet slogans, which in the past have used these negotiations as a means to disarm their intended victims." The panel warned that "in a dynamic situation, we must continually strive to improve our technological position lest an accumulation of advances by an aggressor ultimately confront us with overwhelming strength. . . . However dangerous the multiplying armaments, the illusion of security brought about by a spurious agreement to disarm would be a poor substitute for vigilance based on strength."

The Rockefeller panel concluded that "programs of great importance to U.S. security now suffer from insufficient funds. . . . When the Korean War ended, it was natural that an effort be made to reduce military expenditures. . . . The budgetary squeeze affected not only force levels, it also slowed down our research in many fields, causing us to lose ground to the U.S.S.R." The panel asserted that our defense budget "will require successive additions on the order of $3 billion each year for the next several fiscal years. The figure does not cover the necessary increases in mutual assistance programs and in civilian defense." The panel recommended continuance of these increases until 1965. "The price of survival, then, is not low. This panel is convinced, however, that the increases in defense expenditures are essential and fully justified. . . . We can afford to survive."

"The main thing," Nelson Rockefeller remarked when "International Security: The Military Aspect" was published,

by far the main thing is to stimulate the public interest and to focus attention strongly on the fact that our country faces a problem that might affect our survival.

If we Americans want to achieve all the other objectives in life which interest us, we must keep our security first. This report represents the thinking of a group of Americans with experience in many fields, and we hope it will be a contribution in the debates that lie ahead. In no sense are we a pressure group and we don't àct like one. I don't mean that having made our recommendations we now lose all interest in them. But there won't be anything like lobbying from us. Our conclusions are available in the report and we hope they'll be useful.

The Rockefeller panel and Nelson Rockefeller reportedly were "delighted" with the report's reception in newspapers and on radio and television. According to the *New York Herald Tribune* of January 6, 1958, he had found interest in the

"Rockefeller report on the United States defense crisis in this time of 'great peril' so great" that 10,000 copies were ordered as a first printing for wide distribution. And that was only the beginning. After Dave Garroway discussed the report on television, 197,800 viewers wrote requesting copies. Through December 1, 1960, more than 160,000 copies of the six Rockefeller Brothers Fund reports—which cost the fund more than $800,000—were sold at retail at fifty and seventy-five cents a copy, and 430,744 more copies were either sold at cost or purchased wholesale for free distribution.

The continuing missile gap debate helped make "International Security: The Military Aspect" a best seller. Although in 1959 American intelligence for the first time revised downward projected Russian missile strength, it was reported that Secretary of Defense Neil McElroy testified in secret Congressional hearings—while transcripts of his testimony were never published, he never denied the reports of what he had said—that the Soviet Union still would have 500 ICBMs and intermediate range ballistic missiles (IRBMs) by the early 1960s. And this, we were told by some experts, would be more than enough to enable the Soviet Union to destroy the 100 or so nuclear weapon launching installations we would have by then. In a January 1960 speech, General Thomas S. Power, head of the Strategic Air Command, asserted that "it would take an average of three missiles in the current state of development to give an aggressor a mathematical probability of 95 percent that he can destroy one given soft target some 5,000 miles away. This means that, with only 300 ballistic missiles, the Soviet Union could virtually wipe out our entire nuclear strike capability within a span of thirty minutes."

After Nelson Rockefeller was elected Governor of New York, he was promoted in some quarters as a candidate for the

1960 Republican Presidential nomination. In a book derived from a series of articles on the Rockefeller family that had appeared in *Holiday* in the fall of 1958, William Manchester wrote that Nelson Rockefeller would be a tonic that would wake America from the somnolence induced by the Eisenhower Administration. A Rockefeller Administration in Washington "would be marked by much . . . not conspicuous there now." It "would effervesce with new ideas, for Nelson himself is a man of quicksilver imagination, who likes imaginative advisers around him. And it would fairly sing with enthusiasm." Rockefeller would preside over "young, candid, burbling men." Manchester called Rockefeller "the greatest advocate of the strenuous life" since Theodore Roosevelt. And Rockefeller's Republicanism would be just as "stridently bully."

Nelson Rockefeller's "quicksilver imagination" was not focused on "the strenuous life," however. "Our country faces a problem that might affect our survival . . . we must keep our security first," he had said. He could not wait to become President before mounting a bully pulpit to expound on the themes of "International Security: The Military Aspect," and he had to speak first not about the outdoors, but about the possibility of having to go underground. In February 1960, he proposed that a $4-million bomb shelter be built underneath the state office building complex located three miles from downtown Albany. The shelter, which would be designed to protect against both nuclear blast and radioactive fallout, would be a working and living space for an underground government, with offices, communications and medical facilities, and accommodations for 640 key state government employees. The Governor also announced plans to convert the basement of the state capitol into a shelter and to build one for himself, his family and his staff at the Executive Mansion.*

In May Governor Rockefeller demanded that annual Federal civil defense expenditures be increased by $500 million. The following month, at the fifty-second annual Governors' Conference, he expounded on more of the themes of "International Security: The Military Aspect." He asserted that "in the years 1961 to 1964, the Soviet Union will have more long-range missiles than America . . . the number of [U.S.] retaliatory missiles will be inadequate," and while the U.S. will "continue to hold a superiority in long-range bombers . . . some of these, such as the B-47, are rapidly becoming obsolete; all of these bombers stand concentrated on less than sixty bases; and every base is completely vulnerable to missile attack. . . . For protection against the ultimate disaster of nuclear attack, we possess no anti-missile defense whatever, nor any effective program to protect our civilian population. . . . The Communist tactical land, air and missile forces are superior both in size and equipment to those of the free nations."

* In the early 1960s Peter K. Ogden, a Greenwich, Connecticut, architect, designed bomb shelters for several of Nelson Rockefeller's residences. At the Albany Executive Mansion, a thirty-foot-square former coal bunker under a brick garage connected to the house by a 150-foot-long tunnel was used; at the Pocantico Hills home, a seven-by-fourteen-foot basement storeroom was converted; at Rockefeller's Manhattan cooperative building, housing thirteen families, a basement area was used for a twenty-five-by-forty-foot shelter; at the Northwest Washington, D.C., home, a fifteen-foot-square shelter was built under the main entrance hall. The tenants of the cooperative agreed to finance the purchase of a generator and a ventilating fan. Other Rockefeller shelters were provided with containers of water, manually operated fans, candles and flashlights, portable sanitary facilities using disposable plastic containers and two-decker cots. "The theory," Ogden said of the shelters, "was to hold them to as unfancy, simple and minimum requirements as possible."

He then proposed numerous long-range goals (which could not be achieved until 1963-64): speed development of mobile missile launching systems such as Minuteman and Polaris; speed research in anti-missile and anti-submarine defense systems; improve satellite warning and reconnaissance capabilities; launch a fallout shelter program; place a substantial portion of the Strategic Air Command on airborne alert and quickly increase its nuclear missile strength; increase the strength of the Army and improve its readiness to engage in battle; increase the strengths of the Marine Corps and supporting naval units; modernize the weaponry and doctrine of all tactical land, sea and air forces; and increase the capacity for airlift operations. Such sweeping proposals would prompt I. F. Stone to write that "no major figure in American politics has worked harder than [Nelson] Rockefeller to push ever higher the billions we allocate to the Pentagon."

The Rockefeller thesis received a less than enthusiastic response from President Eisenhower. In *Waging Peace*, his account of his second term, he wrote that "several features of [Nelson] Rockefeller's published opinions seemed to be based on flimsy evidence." At a meeting of legislative leaders, Eisenhower "called attention to [the Rockefeller] recommendation for an increase in civil and military defense spending of $3½ billion" and said, " 'I suspect that Nelson has been listening too closely to half-baked advisors.' " Eisenhower did not propose that Rockefeller be shunned, however, and said, " 'I think he has a right to express his opinions—he is a prominent Republican. In fact, the National Committee might well invite him to deliver a major address before the Convention.' " Six weeks later, Vice-President Nixon flew to New York to reach an accommodation with Rockefeller on the proposed wording of several planks in the Republican platform on which Nixon soon would run for President. Eisenhower was surprised by the results of the meeting. "On defense," he wrote, "[the Rockefeller-Nixon pact] declared that 'the United States can afford and must provide the increased expenditures to implement fully this necessary program for strengthening our defense posture. There must be no price ceiling on America's security.' That section seems somewhat astonishing, coming as it did from two people who had long been in administration councils and who had never voiced any doubt—at least in my presence—of the adequacies of America's defenses." Nixon explained to Eisenhower, " 'What I'm trying to do is to find some ground on which Nelson can be with us and not against us.' " Eisenhower would not be bullied. He rewrote the platform, saying, "There *is* no price ceiling on America's security. The United States can and must provide whatever is necessary to insure its own security and that of the Free World, to provide any necessary increased expenditures to meet new situations. . . . *To provide more would be wasteful.* [Italics added.] To provide less would be catastrophic." He was satisfied that in raising the defense budget—which had been less than $12 billion before the Korean War—to more than $41 billion in 1960 he was spending enough on national defense. He was satisfied with the fact that lined up on the American side of the balance-of-terror equation were 600 B-52s, 1,000 B-47s (with in-flight refueling) over 200 aircraft on fourteen carriers, plus an unknown number of fighter bombers stationed on bases around the world. General Power had been obliged to call this nuclear capability "the most powerful retaliatory force in the world."

Eisenhower's platform statement did not lay the missile gap issue to rest. John F. Kennedy used it effectively during his successful Presidential campaign that fall. Soon, however, Kennedy was obliged to concede that in fact the balance of terror was not weighted in favor of the Soviet Union. Some months later, Democratic Senator Stuart Symington, a former Secretary of the Air Force who had been a spokesman for the missile gap thesis when Eisenhower was in the White House, explained how the assumed gap had disappeared: by September 1961, American intelligence credited the Soviet Union with having produced only 3 ½ percent of the number of missiles that, according to the estimates of the late 1950s, could have been produced. So instead of having between 1,000 and 1,500 ICBMs, the Soviet Union had between 35 and 52.

As a result, the balance of terror still was weighted on the side of the United States. By the following year—when the United States had more than 50 ICBMs; 80 Polaris missiles on roving submarines; 90 IRBMs in Great Britain, Italy and Turkey; and 1,700 long-range bombers, 300 fighter bombers on carriers and 1,000 land-based supersonic fighters, all with nuclear capacity—the Soviet Union had fewer than 100 ICBMs and fewer than 200 long-range bombers capable of reaching the United States. Indeed, our retaliatory force was so powerful and well dispersed that, even with a much larger striking force, the Soviet Union could not have attacked without the certainty of massive retaliation.

During this period, when the balance-of-terror equation was being reconstructed, Nelson Rockefeller continued to plug for the demands of "International Security: The Military Aspect." He got the New York State Legislature to enact a bill granting real estate tax exemptions for any increase in a home's assessed valuation resulting from shelter construction (up to $100 times the number of persons for whom the shelter was designed). At the Governors' Conference in July 1961, he headed a committee that urged legislative and executive action on stockpiling food, medicine and supplies at strategic locations in each state, on providing alternate, protected seats for state and local governments, and on seeking necessary changes in building codes to facilitate shelter construction. In November he called a special session of the State Legislature and won approval of a hastily drawn bill (there were no public hearings or debate) calling for $100 million in state aid for shelters, with most of the money available as matching funds to meet half the costs expended by schools and colleges that decided to build shelters.

President Kennedy, for his part, appeared to adopt the policy advocated in those passages of "International Security: The Military Aspect" dealing with what the report called "concealed" or "non-overt" aggression. And as the United States became embroiled in what was a civil war in Vietnam, some observers contended that the report was, as I. F. Stone put it, "a blueprint for a U.S. role as world policeman in the nuclear age."* But Kennedy did not appear to be in agreement

---

* It could also be called the blueprint for the increase in military expenditures during the period from 1958 to 1970. As the following table shows, their annual level rose during those missile gap-Vietnam War years by $40 billion, with the average rate of rise matching the $3 billion-a-year rate demanded by the Rockefeller Brothers Fund report:

FISCAL YEAR	U.S. DEFENSE EXPENDITURES
1958	$39 billion
1959-61	$43.7-$45.7 billion
1962-65	$48.2-$49.2 billion
1966	$55.7 billion
1967	$69 billion
1968-70	$78.7-79.5 billion

with the report on such issues as the use of nuclear weapons in limited wars and the dangers of nuclear treaties with the Communists. The 1963 partial test ban treaty prohibiting nuclear tests in the atmosphere, underwater and in outer space, plus all underground tests permitting nuclear debris to escape beyond the borders of the responsible country—which was signed by the United States, the Soviet Union, Great Britain and other countries—worried Nelson Rockefeller. He urged Senate ratification, but with qualifications. "Because the treaty is so identified with the hopes and yearnings for peace," he said,

and because the prestige of the United States has already been so solemnly committed to the treaty, I believe that the United States Senate should consent to its ratification. At the same time, I think the Senate should so advise the President about its concern regarding the treaty itself and the measures it considers necessary to maintain the defense of freedom. . . . The Senate should make clear that the treaty is ratified with the understanding that certain ambiguous language in Article 1 does not prohibit the use of nuclear weapons to repel aggression anywhere. . . . The Administration should take every feasible step to preserve the ability of our military establishment to deter and defeat Communist aggression against free peoples everywhere. Specifically, there should be a national commitment that . . . we must at all times be prepared, able and willing to use nuclear weapons to repel aggression, alone or together with our allies. . . .

The words are those of a man willing to use any means whatever to defeat his enemies.

vii The Shape of
Rockefeller Foreign Policy:
Latin America

The original Rockefeller philanthropic institutions were organized to conduct medical research and to promote public education and health programs. The Rockefeller brothers continued and extended this work, both with the existing institutions and with new ones. In July 1946, for example, the brothers established the American International Association for Economic and Social Development (AIA), a nonprofit organization working jointly with Latin American governmental and private groups on programs in education, health improvement, farm training, road building and financial aid. The following January, the brothers established the International Basic Economy Corporation (IBEC), "a private sector, profit-making development company, which initiates and operates corporate ventures responsive to basic human needs and the economies of developing nations." Initially, IBEC was capitalized at $2 million; this soon was raised to $10,824,000.*

---

* IBEC has grown enormously. In 1969 its total revenue was $256 million; working capital was $34.5 million; and total assets were $176.5 million. According to its 1969 annual report, IBEC has a Supermarket

236

Fourteen years later, the Kennedy Administration founded the Alliance for Progress, a Rockefeller-style economic development program on a much larger scale. Over a ten-year period, $100 billion was to be pumped into the Latin American economy, with United States taxpayers putting up $1.1 billion a year, United States companies and other outside investors putting up $900 million, and the Latins putting up the rest themselves. In order to encourage support for the Alliance in the United States, a dual role was proclaimed for the program: not only would it strengthen Latin America economically, it also would help align the Latin nations against communism. This dual role won Rockefeller support for the Alliance. In April 1962, David Rockefeller told the Economic Club of Chicago that "we have made a firm commitment to Latin America for economic aid and for assistance in containing imperialism. I think the situation warrants substantial expenditures on both fronts on the scale proposed by President Kennedy."

Division with forty-seven outlets in Venezuela, Argentina and Peru; a Poultry Group which develops and supplies breeding stock to the poultry industry in twenty-four countries on five continents; an Industrial Group which designs and manufactures power and control systems, industrial fasteners and cold-formed metal specialties for the chemical-processing and food industries; a Financial Services Group which manages local-currency mutual funds in developing countries (including Argentina, Chile, Thailand and Spain in 1969) and is involved in insurance brokerages; a Textile Division which manufactures and distributes women's apparel woven from silk and cotton in Thailand; and a Food and Housing Group which produces, pasteurizes and distributes foods in the Americas, and has built housing in Puerto Rico, the U.S. Virgin Islands, Jamaica, Eastern Oklahoma and the Great Smoky Mountains in North Carolina. The chairman of IBEC's board is Nelson Rockefeller's oldest son, Rodman.

But David Rockefeller's support for the Alliance was based on certain conditions. In the following year, when the Commerce Committee for the Alliance for Progress, a group of twenty-five businessmen recruited by the Administration from companies active in Latin America, reported that the Alliance was on the brink of collapse, a minority group within the Committee, headed by Rockefeller, complained that the situation was due to the United States' not demanding that Latin American nations institute economic and social development policies favorable to business investment. The Rockefeller group set forth two main requirements for improving the situation. "The first requirement," the group said,

> is that the governments—and, as far as possible, the people—of Latin America know that the U.S. has changed its policy to put primary stress on improvement in the general business climate as a prerequisite for social development and reform. . . . A second requirement concerns a change in the criteria for granting aid. . . . The U.S. should concentrate its economic-aid program in countries that show the greatest inclination to adopt measures to improve the investment climate, and withhold aid from others until satisfactory performance has been demonstrated.

Richard Barnet has written in his book *Roots of War* that "the essence of power is the ability to make things happen." Several years after the Rockefeller group issued its complaint and demands, things happened in Latin America, and the performance of United States business investment improved there. David Rockefeller appeared to be taking some credit for the improvement when he wrote in the April 1966 issue of *Foreign Affairs* that in my view, a primary reason for this relatively good performance, which is of recent date, is a change in the policy which prevailed in the early years of the Alliance of placing too much emphasis on rapid and revolutionary social change and on strictly government-to-government assistance. This approach, while it took account of the fact there is a genuine and urgent need to do away with social inequities, did not encourage the conditions which are essential to stimulating private investment and economic growth. Revolutionary change which shakes confidence in the fair treatment of private property is incompatible with rapid economic expansion. Now that the vital role of private enterprise is being recognized more fully in a number of Latin American nations, we see the development of a more favorable business climate. I am confident that companies and individuals alike, both United States and local, will respond to the increasing opportunity in those countries where this attitude prevails, and that the rate of investment will grow more rapidly as a result. This should make possible more meaningful social reform since it will be accompanied by a rising standard of living. Progress along these lines will not be possible, however, if misunderstandings are allowed to hamper investment and frustrate honest efforts to stimulate a widely shared economic advance.

The seeds of "misunderstandings" were being sown by Communists, according to David Rockefeller. "I have reflected a great deal," he had said in a 1964 speech entitled "The U.S. Business Image in Latin America,"

upon the mounting Communist pressures on our southern neighbors. I have been especially concerned about what seems to me a relentless campaign—in schools and universities, in fields and factories, in political units and professional groups—

to mobilize public opinion against so-called "Yankee imperialism" and in favor of Communist policies. . . . Communist propaganda stridently blames the United States and U.S. business for all the Latin Americans' readily visible ills. Soviet, Castro and now Chinese Communist agents move through city and village cleverly spreading half-truths and whole falsehoods. North American capitalists, they say, are out to exploit resources and markets to the detriment of the host nations; the capitalists want to keep the people in poverty so they can take over their minerals and metals; they are obsessed with excessive profits and have no concern for the land or its inhabitants.

In the speech, David Rockefeller spoke of a Capitalist missionary effort to counter the Communist missionary effort in Latin America. "Every Marxist is a dedicated salesman at heart," Rockefeller said.

What we need today are salesmen for free-enterprise—men who can go abroad not only with an order book but with an ideal; who understand that the most potent force in human emotions is hope; who realize that responsible free-enterprise holds out hope for a better life for people everywhere.

Rockefeller urged U.S. businessmen to take prompt action to "convince Latin Americans that their best interests lie in providing an environment in which both domestic and foreign enterprise can thrive." Three things had to be done. First, Latin Americans had to be convinced that private enterprise could help them achieve economic growth and political stability, "two goals that the majority . . . dearly want." Second, this message had to be delivered to businessmen, national govern-

ments and opinion leaders—educators, intellectuals, profession-
als, labor leaders and the clergy. Third, the validity of the
message had to be demonstrated by U.S. companies' performance in Latin America. "Through our actions," Rockefeller
said,

> we must demonstrate that the exploitive capitalism that the
> Communist propaganda machine constantly inveighs against is
> a thing of the past. We must demonstrate that there has
> evolved a new brand of capitalism, based on the concept of a
> fair profit for free enterprise combined with social responsi-
> bility to the community as a whole.

Five years later, in May 1969, Nelson Rockefeller undertook a mission to Latin America on behalf of the Nixon Administration. The announced purpose of the Governor's visit
was to collect suggestions on how the United States could aid
Latin America's economic development. Rockefeller, who
took along a technical staff of more than twenty advisers,
asked for and was given a free hand in organizing the mission,
which was to be carried out in four separate visits.

The first stage of the mission was a whirlwind visit to seven
Latin American countries in eight days. (The stopover in one
capital lasted four hours.) The mission's reception was described as relatively cordial, despite anti-American demonstrations along the way. After a student had been killed in
Tegucigalpa, Honduras (police claimed a patrolman's gun
went off when he fell with his finger on the trigger), a smiling
Rockefeller braved the streets to shake hands with crowds of
students and other citizens. "I'm trying to get understanding
going both ways," he said.

The second visit occurred two weeks later. When Rocke-feller arrived in Ecuador, he said, "I bring no new programs, no easy remedies or simple slogans. From this mission may re-sult new U.S. policies, but this mission does not bring them with it. Let us talk frankly about what is bad and what is good, of hard realities, not only of pleasant things." In Quito, the capital city, the hard reality was that banks, stores and schools were shut down, traffic was paralyzed, and students fought police with bricks and stones. Rockefeller was driven through the city's back streets, a helicopter hovering over his car. Since students had seized the streets behind the Presiden-tial palace, the mission had to meet with the President and a dozen groups of politicians and businessmen in a hotel. More than 1,000 soldiers and policemen guarded the talks.

When the United States announced a suspension of arms sales after U.S. tuna boats charged with violating Peru's self-declared 200-mile offshore limit had been seized and fined, Peru canceled Rockefeller's visit. The mission went on to Bolivia, but fear of student demonstrations limited the visit to a three-hour meeting at a heavily guarded airport. Then, in re-sponse to threats of unrest, the Venezuelan and Chilean gov-ernments barred the mission.

The third stage of the tour included Brazil, Uruguay, Ar-gentina and Paraguay. In order to insure against disruptions, Brazil's military government warned the press not to print anything unfavorable about the mission, including news of dis-turbances in other countries. Some 2,500 militant students and dissidents were rounded up and placed under preventive de-tention. In Paraguay, the military dictatorship brought out a carefully selected crowd of 3,000 to welcome the mission. But Rockefeller had to hold over an extra day because Montevideo,

Uruguay, his next scheduled stop, was being hit with rioting and fire-bombing. (Fire damage in a General Motors plant was estimated at $1 million.) Montevideo remained so unsafe that officials held meetings with the mission at the resort town of Punta del Este. And there was trouble in Argentina, even with the country under military rule. Two weeks before the mission's scheduled visit in Buenos Aires, thirteen IBEC supermarkets had been fire-bombed, and on the day Rockefeller met with Argentina's President (for two hours), a labor leader who had opposed a general strike to protest the visit was assassinated. The government had to declare a nationwide state of siege in order to put down intense anti-government terrorism and labor unrest.

On the final visit, four people were killed by trigger-happy soldiers in Santo Domingo. Dominican terrorists, threatening the mission's departure from the city, sent a warning message, "They shall not pass." The departure was not very dignified. Mission bus windows were kept closed despite the stifling heat, and riders held their briefcases against the windows as protection against shattered glass. Truckloads of troops armed with rifles and submachine guns accompanied the buses as they sped to the airport. Armed forces personnel were stationed fifteen feet apart all along the route out of the city. Frogmen patrolled the waters underneath a bridge.

At last there was Haiti, where François (Papa Doc) Duvalier, "President for Life," was in control. A crowd of 10,000 cheered Rockefeller's motorcade from the airport, and 35,000 more subjects were assembled at Independence Plaza in front of the Presidential palace in Port-au-Prince. Rockefeller and Duvalier conferred for little more than an hour, then appeared arm in arm on a balcony to wave at the crowd.

On the final flight back to the United States, Rockefeller remarked,

> The disillusionment is very real. Blame must be equally accepted throughout the Western Hemisphere. We can't cover it up. You have no idea how much we are telling these people what to do and how to do it. But there are also forces at work that do not want to see us closer together. It is very important that there be an understanding that these forces do exist and that all is not well in the hemisphere.

In September *The Rockefeller Report on the Americas* was delivered to President Nixon. It was written by Nelson Rockefeller and chief aides James M. Cannon, Hugh Morrow and William Butler, a vice-president of the Chase Manhattan Bank. George Woods, former president of the World Bank and trustee of the Rockefeller Foundation, was sent copies for his comments. No other members of the Rockefeller mission to Latin America saw the report in draft or final form before it was released to the public, according to Jerome Levinson and Juan de Onis in their book *The Alliance That Lost Its Way*.

The report suggested that the United States urge other industrial nations to grant trade preferences to the Latin American nations (which constituted the only block of developing countries without trade preferences anywhere); that punitive measures such as the Hickenlooper Amendment (which required the United States to cut off aid funds to any government that expropriates property of U.S. companies and does not take "appropriate steps" toward compensation within six months) be voided when they "interfere with the process of development or impugn the sovereignty of other countries";

that the restriction that all aid loan money be spent in the United States be relaxed, and that Latin American countries be allowed to spend it anywhere in the hemisphere; that the requirement that half the goods purchased with aid money be transported in U.S. ships (which were expensive) be repealed; that the Assistant Secretary of State for Inter-American Affairs be promoted to Undersecretary of State, and that the new position have full Cabinet rank.

To be sure, these economic recommendations could have been written without Nelson Rockefeller's having set foot in Latin America. The report did take the four visits into account, however. In addressing itself to the events that had engulfed the Rockefeller mission, the report declared, "Forces of anarchy, terror and subversion are loose in the Americas. . . . Clearly, the opinion in the United States that communism is no longer a serious factor in the Western Hemisphere is thoroughly wrong." Such groups as youth, labor and the clergy were "vulnerable to subversive penetration and to exploitation as a revolutionary means for the destruction of the existing order." Even the "new military," which was "often becoming a major force for constructive social change in the hemisphere," might be infiltrated. "Special mention should be made," the report said,

> of the appeal to the new military, on a theoretical level, of Marxism: (1) it justifies, through its elitist-vanguard theories, government by a relatively small group or institution (such as the Army) and, at the same time, (2) produces a rationale for state-enforced sacrifices to further economic development.

There were ways to deal with the latter problem, according to the *Rockefeller Report*:

One major influence counteracting this simplistic Marxist approach is the exposure to the fundamental achievements of the U.S. way of life that many of the military from the other American countries have received through the military training programs which the U.S. conducts in Panama and the United States.

In addition, the report, lamenting the decrease in Latin American military assistance from a level of $80.7 million in the last year of the Eisenhower Administration to $21.4 million for fiscal 1970, urged the United States to increase the level of military assistance earmarked both for training security forces and for providing military assistance to existing governments. The report also urged Latin-Americanization of the fight against Communist subversion, saying that the U.S. military missions south of the border were too large and conspicuous and should be reduced in size.

On the one hand, the *Rockefeller Report's* recommendations were, as Levinson and de Onis put it in their book, "a highly perceptive, intelligent, and imaginative response on the part of U.S. business leadership having interests in Latin America to the problem of potential revolutionary social change in Latin America." On the other hand, as these authors point out, Nelson Rockefeller set forth the belief in the report that "the government of the United States has the ultimate responsibility of maintaining order in the hemisphere." This, the report said, was fundamental to our security:

The United States [the report declared] has allowed a special relationship it has historically maintained with the other nations of the Western Hemisphere to deteriorate badly.

Failure to maintain that special relationship would imply failure of our capacity and responsibility as a great power. If we cannot maintain a constructive relationship in the Western

Hemisphere, we will hardly be able to achieve a successful order elsewhere in the world. Moreover, failure to maintain this special relationship would create a vacuum in this hemisphere and facilitate the import in the region of hostile foreign powers.

In *The Rockefeller Report on the Americas*, Nelson Rockefeller set forth a solution to the problem of Communist penetration into Latin America that complemented his brother David's. While both of them expressed philanthropic concern for alleviating human misery in Latin America, they sought primarily to preserve U.S. dominance in the Western Hemisphere. David promoted a missionary effort on behalf of the free-enterprise system and socioeconomic development policies emphasizing the guarantee of a favorable climate for U.S. business investment; Nelson promoted increased military assistance to existing governments willing to maintain at atmosphere in which the free-enterprise system and U.S. business investment could thrive.

In another sense, Nelson Rockefeller's 1969 mission to Latin America was a signal event in his long battle against his country's enemies. For while the threat of nuclear annihilation might have seemed real to him as he went about urging increased military expenditures and building bomb shelters, it could not have been as intimately threatening as the violence that had marked the mission, when he had come closer to being harmed by the enemy than ever before. To be sure, he had come through the mission untouched. But he would have to face the enemy again. And when he did, he would act as if the violence in 1969 had affected him profoundly, as if it had convinced him beyond a doubt that the established order could be brought down unless maximum force was used to smash the enemy.

viii   Attica

On Thursday, September 9, 1971, in Nelson Rockefeller's thirteenth year as Governor of the State of New York, a rebellion broke out at the correctional facility under his authority at the village of Attica. The rebellion was triggered by a misunderstanding that had occurred on Wednesday afternoon in a prison yard. A guard had mistaken a white prisoner's demonstration of football moves to a black prisoner as the beginning of a fight. When the guard attempted to take hold of the black prisoner from behind, the prisoner spun around and hit him. Several guards then ordered the black prisoner to leave the yard, but he managed to move into a protective crowd of prisoners. The white prisoner vehemently protested the guards' order. At that point the guards decided not to press the issue.

After a night of rumors that guards had beaten the two prisoners, neighbors of the white prisoner rebelled while on their way to breakfast. They overpowered five guards in the vestibule of their cellblock, beating one of them fiercely, according to a prisoner who looked on. The rebels then ran

248

down to the intersection of the four prison yards, where a manually operated gate was always left open during the breakfast hour. They fractured the skull of the guard in charge of the gate. They then had easy access to three other cellblocks.

The rebels captured thirty-eight guards and brought them to the prison's "D" yard, where 1,300 prisoners, most of them black and Puerto Rican (the prison's population was 75 to 85 percent black and Puerto Rican), were massed. (Not all of the prisoners had come there by choice. At one location, some thirty inmates who had not wished to be liberated by the rebels had got a set of keys and locked themselves in their cells. The rebels had found another set, however, and had brought out everyone from cells they could unlock, except for seven inmates who had managed to hide under their bunks.) Scores were settled with certain guards. Some of them were beaten severely; one guard's arm was fractured. Then the rebels selected security guards from among their ranks to protect the hostages, who were stripped, bound and blindfolded. The rebels issued a manifesto demanding that they be given "complete amnesty, meaning freedom from any physical, mental and legal reprisal" and "speedy and safe transportation out of confinement to a nonimperialistic country"; that they be placed under Federal jurisdiction; that Attica prison be reconstructed under supervision of the inmates; and that "immediate negotiations" be conducted through a panel of civilian observers composed of men the prisoners knew they could trust.

Russell G. Oswald, the recently appointed State Commissioner of Correction, believed initially that he could secure the release of the hostages through negotiations. In July a group of prisoners calling itself the Attica Liberation Faction had sent him a manifesto containing twenty-seven demands dealing with medical care, work conditions, diet, parole procedures and religious expression. Oswald had responded by spending two days at Attica talking to prisoners and pleading for time to usher in reforms he promised for prisons statewide. When the September rebellion broke out he returned confident that his reputation as a reformer was good enough to enable him to reason with the rebels. After allowing Herman Schwartz, a Buffalo law professor who had dealt with prisoners' rights suits, and Arthur O. Eve, a black State Assemblyman from Buffalo, to go into the prison yard to talk to the rebels, Oswald consented to the rebels' demand that he confront them himself.

Commissioner Oswald went into the prison yard on three occasions, but made little progress toward ending the rebellion. For one thing, he and the prisoners simply did not communicate. At the first meeting Oswald noticed that the prisoners were not paying close attention to his remarks, although he was responding favorably to their demands. At the second meeting, which was held before newsmen and television cameras, the prisoners appeared to be directing their demands and rhetoric as much to the cameras as to Oswald. Dr. Warren Hanson, a surgeon from the nearby town of Warsaw who worked in the prison yard for three days while the prisoners held control, said later that the prisoners "saw themselves as important. People used to having no voice suddenly started role-playing, with leaders developing a kind of megalomania." Oswald contributed to the theatrical air himself: he obliged television crews by performing a speech twice because of a bad angle on the first take.

More important, the question of whether reprisals would be carried out against the prisoners became the principal issue in any settlement that could end the rebellion. This was a sensitive issue; it would not be resolved easily, for prison officials in similar situations in the past had not lived up to their ends of agreements. Prisoners who had been transferred to Attica from the prison at Auburn, where there had been a one-day uprising in November 1970, reminded Commissioner Oswald that the Auburn authorities had reneged on a promise that there would be "no reprisals" after hostages had been released. The Attica rebels forcefully rejected his assertion that many prisoners had expressed "confidence in my sincerity." As one of the rebels said, "There ain't going to be no fast negotiations. We know you can play games, but you are not going to play games and find any hostages alive. Mind you, we are ready to die."

No progress toward ending the rebellion was made on Thursday night and Friday morning. One of the rebel leaders went to the office of the prison superintendent to work with Commissioner Oswald and Professor Schwartz on the wording of a Federal Court injunction barring reprisals against the prisoners. But when Schwartz brought the signed injunction to the prisoners on Friday morning, jailhouse lawyers called it inadequate, and it was torn up. Subsequently, at Oswald's final meeting with the prisoners, he was threatened. He then decided not to meet with them any more, but to fulfill their request that a group of observers be brought to Attica.

When the observers arrived on Friday they found a huge armed force laying siege to the prison. Inside, according to New York Times Associate Editor Tom Wicker, one of the observers, there was "remarkable unity" among the prisoners. They were well organized. Their security arrangements were "excellent." No racial discord was apparent to Wicker. "The prisoners referred to themselves constantly as brothers and stressed again and again their determination to stand together."

But there was tension among the prisoners. Two white prisoners who were talking to a white television reporter were suddenly pulled away. They were tried by the rebel leadership for treason, pronounced guilty, stripped, blindfolded and led away to cells. Doctor Hanson saw what he interpreted as a pattern of "psychological deterioration" among the prisoners. Two suffered fits, two more collapsed from nervous pressure, another went rigid. An elderly prisoner walked around holding a crucifix and moaning "they're going to kill me." Another prisoner attempted to stab himself. A makeshift mental hospital was set up, and stolen sedatives were administered.

Tension among guards, state troopers and prison and state officials ran high. "The emphasis on guns and clubs during the crisis was incredible," Wicker wrote. "Once, standing alone and unarmed at the steel gate [a rebel leader] refused to negotiate any further because the room beyond was packed with so many men bearing clubs, rifles, pistols, shotguns and tear gas launchers. Three or four blocks from the prison, tourists were stopped at roadblocks by as many as four armed men, each carrying a club, a pistol, a rifle. . . . These guns, moreover, were in the hands of men who left no doubt they wanted to use them. Correction Commissioner Oswald's long delay of the assault and his efforts to negotiate were met with impatience and anger by the prison staff; the observers who were trying to prevent bloodshed saw hostility at every turn. A guard, bringing them a box of food said as he put it down, 'If I'd known it was for you people, I wouldn't have brought it.' "

When Wicker tried to give a progress report to police, guards and relatives of the hostages, he was called a "nigger-lover," a "son-of-a-bitch," and a "dirty doublecrossing bastard" who ought to be "strung up." When Bobby Seale, chairman of the Black Panther party, arrived at Attica, a law officer said, "It's a goddamn shame that that black bastard is so close that I can almost touch him. I'd like to take this rifle and blow his brains out." Another said, "Look at those nigger-loving white sons-of-bitches lapping over him, like he's something good to eat. Lord knows I'd like to blow his guts out—sure'd like to kill him."

Rumors of atrocities spread. According to one rumor, a guard had been castrated. Robert Douglass, Governor Rockefeller's chief of staff and personal representative on the scene, and Walter Dunbar, Commissioner Oswald's deputy, told Doctor Hanson that rebels had thrown two hostages and a pile of wood into a bathroom and set it on fire. Hanson told them that the story was "nonsense," which it was, as were the other rumors.

The observers' task was to draft a contract for reforming the prison and dealing with the rebellion that would be acceptable to both the state and the prisoners. On Friday night the panel of observers went into the prison yard and compiled a list of the prisoners' demands. A three-man committee then conferred with the local district attorney on the key question of criminal amnesty. On Saturday morning they managed to reach an agreement that there would be no "indiscriminate mass prosecutions." The full panel then spent the afternoon and part of the evening fashioning a contract containing twenty-eight proposals in language the state was willing to accept. They included an end to censorship of reading matter, the right to be politically active, a more nutritious diet, and expanded rehabilitation and education programs. The most important proposal, which dealt with the rebellion, called for administrative, not criminal, amnesty, whereby the state agreed that prisoners would neither suffer any kind of harassment nor be charged with any crimes against property. Commissioner Oswald said he could accept these proposals and signed them. Together with the local district attorney's agreement, these proposals became the state's offer for a settlement to end the rebellion.

Unbeknownst to the observers, a black prisoner had escaped from the rebel stronghold. Officials then began to indicate to the observers that they had independent sources of information about battle preparations in the prison yard. The pressure for an assault on the yard increased. At four-thirty on Saturday afternoon the guard whose skull had been fractured died. The problem of amnesty for the prisoners became more difficult.

Before the observers presented the state's offer on Saturday night, Bobby Seale was permitted to address the prisoners. He did not attempt to convince them to accept a settlement based on the state's offer, as some observers had hoped he would; he said only that he was leaving to consult with fellow Black Panther party leader Huey Newton. After Seale left, spokesmen for the observers presented the proposals they had worked out with the Wyoming County District Attorney and Commissioner Oswald as the best they could do. The prisoners, massed in a threatening crowd in the dark, angrily denounced the proposals. They told the observers to "go back and do better" in a second round of negotiations. But there would be no second round. Negotiations had reached an impasse.

Seale returned to the prison on Sunday morning. He intended to speak not about the set of proposals the observers had worked out, but about demands that rebels be given safe conduct to a "nonimperialistic country," that prisoners be given the right to supervise the reconstruction of Attica prison, and that prisoners be put under Federal jurisdiction. Commissioner Oswald refused to let Seale into the prison yard unless he spoke about the set of proposals the state had agreed to. Seale was affronted and left.

The observers could see preparations being made for an assault to retake the prison yard. They pleaded with Commissioner Oswald to postpone the attack. He issued an ultimatum calling on the prisoners to release the hostages and accept the proposals he had worked out with the observers, but he would not delay much longer.

As preparations for the attack were in the final stages, the observers appealed to Governor Rockefeller to come to Attica to confer with them. Tom Wicker later testified, "I thought that if he [Rockefeller] came to Attica, two things would transpire. First, it would be a symbolic gesture to the inmates of his concern. Second, if he would come, we could maintain the status quo for one or two or three days and thus break the impasse in negotiations. Someone might give." There was no thought to have Rockefeller speak to the rebels, but he might have seen the makings of a massacre and halted it. But Rockefeller refused the observers' appeal. "In view of the fact that the key issue is total amnesty, I do not feel that my physical presence on the site can contribute to a settlement," he said. "I do not have the constitutional authority to grant such a demand and I would not even if I had the authority because to do so would undermine the very essence of our free society—the fair and impartial application of the law."

The observers managed to delay the attack on the prison

yard on Sunday. They were allowed to visit the yard one more time, late in the afternoon. But they did not manage to convince the prisoners how desperate the situation was.

On Monday morning State Senator John Dunne, the head of the State Legislature's Penal Codes Committee and the chairman of the observers, appealed for one last chance for the prisoners. Commissioner Oswald issued his ultimatum a second time. It gave no hint of the nature of the impending attack, however. Many prisoners believed that as long as they held hostages, only gas, clubs, fire hoses and rubber bullets would be used by the assault force. In order to show their only source of strength, the prisoners positioned eight bound and blindfolded hostages on a catwalk at the center of the prison; prisoners stood behind the hostages and held knives to their throats.

State officials in charge of the siege were convinced that the thirty-eight hostages had no more than a slim chance of survival. Commissioner Oswald, according to Wicker, "was obviously suffering." He told the observers that he was "going through the tortures of hell." He said he liked to think that he was "partisan in favor of life," but the prisoners' "intransigence" and "innumerable butchery threats" left him no choice but to "go in."

Command of the assault passed from Commissioner Oswald to the state police when a helicopter dropped choking gas into the prison yard. As soon as the gas began to take effect, troopers on the roofs of cellblocks opened rifle fire on the catwalk where the eight hostages were being held. Troopers firing shotguns assaulted the catwalk and invaded the yard. Their weapons were loaded with 0-0 buckshot, each shell containing nine to twelve pellets the size of a .38-caliber slug, which spread out in a widening pattern. State troopers fired more than 300 rounds; according to testimony received by a commission investigating the assault, prison guards also fired weapons. Thirty-eight men were killed, including nine hostages and twenty-nine prisoners. Two hostages and eleven or twelve prisoners were killed on the catwalk; the rest were killed in the yard.

"There's always a time to die," Congressman Herman Badillo, one of the observers, said as he looked out at the helmeted troopers. "I don't know what the rush was." After the assault, prisoners were stripped and run through a gauntlet of club-wielding troopers. Then the prisoners were made to crawl into the cellblocks on their hands and knees, with their faces in the dirt. According to an inmate listening from a cell near the entrance to the cellblock, the beatings intensified when the rumor of castration of one of the hostages was repeated among the guards and troopers.

After the assault, the two white inmates who had been tried and convicted of treason by the rebel leadership and a convicted murderer who had been hitting his fellow prisoners and threatening the hostages were found in cells with their throats slashed and multiple stab wounds. These three, plus the guard who had died in hospital from a fractured skull and the thirty-eight men who had been killed during the assault, brought the total death count during the Attica rebellion to forty-two.

On Monday morning, immediately after the assault, state officials asserted that prisoners had slashed the throats of the nine hostages who had died on the catwalk and in the prison yard. The prisoners could not have shot their hostages, state officials pointed out. Commissioner Oswald's inventory of the hundreds of homemade weapons recovered after the assault turned up Molotov cocktails, shears, table knives, steel and metal pipes, spears, tear-gas guns and projectiles, wire bolos, a half-dozen razors, swords, and bats with extended spikes, but no guns.

Governor Rockefeller was not personally available for comment on Monday. Instead, he issued a statement:

> Our hearts go out to the families of the hostages who died at Attica.
>
> The tragedy was brought on by the highly organized, revolutionary tactics of militants who rejected all efforts at a peaceful settlement, forced a confrontation and carried out cold-blooded killings they had threatened from the outset.
>
> We can be grateful that the skill and courage of the state police and correction officers, supported by the National Guard and Sheriff's deputies, saved the lives of twenty-nine hostages—and that their restraint held down casualties among prisoners as well.
>
> It was only after four days and nights of patient 'round-the-clock-negotiations with the prisoners by Commissioner Oswald and the citizens' committee, exploring all possible means of securing the release of the hostages, that the state police went in to rescue the hostages and restored order.
>
> I have ordered a full investigation of all the factors leading to this uprising, including the role that outside forces would appear to have played.

There was not one word of sympathy for the thirty-two dead prisoners and their families in the Governor's statement. The state was slow in identifying the dead prisoners. Identification tags tied around their toes by prison officials were labeled only "P-1" to "P-32," the "P" standing for "prisoner." The medical examiner performing autopsies on the dead prisoners had to take fingerprints and wait for them to be identified before he could identify the dead men. On the day after the assault on the prison yard some forty black residents of Rochester, relatives of Attica prisoners, stood in a drizzle outside the medical examiner's office waiting for word about the identities of the dead men inside and for information about prisoners injured during the assault. They said they had been unable to get state correction officials to tell them anything about the condition or whereabouts of their relatives.

On Tuesday, as newspapers carried a UPI dispatch that began *Following is a list of five guards and four civilian employees killed by rebelling prisoners at the Attica State Prison,* the medical examiner who performed autopsies on eight of the hostages murdered during the assault on the prison yard announced that "all eight cases died of gunshot wounds. There was no evidence of slashed throats." An autopsy performed on the ninth hostage, forty-four-year-old Carl Valone, who had been taken to a hospital in nearby Batavia because of inadequate medical facilities at Attica, revealed that he had died of gunshot wounds in his side. The hostages had not been killed by the prisoners, as state officials had claimed. A relative of the Valone family, who asked to remain anonymous because he had a government job to protect, was blunt in assigning responsibility for Valone's death. "We feel," he said, "that Carl was killed not by the prisoners but by a bullet with the name Rockefeller written on it."

Nelson Rockefeller did not meet with the press until Wednesday, the day after the announcement that the nine hostages who had died during the Attica assault had been killed by state troopers, not by the rebellious prisoners. At a conference held at the request of newsmen, Rockefeller said that he still disagreed with the position that he should have gone to the prison in order to buy time to obtain a peaceful settlement of the rebellion. The prisoners' demands for complete amnesty from criminal prosecution and "free passage— as they described it—to a nonimperialistic country," he said, "had political implications beyond the reform of the prison, which it was not possible for us to conform to and at the same time preserve a free society in which people have any sense of security." The prisoners' stand had "hardened not softened, so I then said no, I would not come, I didn't think a useful purpose would be served. I think this whole thing raises a very serious question as to whether someone who has been condemned under the law and sent to jail can use innocent hostages to force the release of the criminal. If the Governor has to be the one who negotiates, and if the Governor does, and this can be true all over the country, we may find ourselves in a position where the next time they say, 'We won't negotiate with anyone but the President'—and I think we get into an intolerable situation."

The decision to storm the prison yard was made, Rockefeller said, at the point when the prisoners "just lined up eight of the hostages, bound, blindfolded, with an executioner with a knife at his throat. . . . There was no alternative but to go in." "Did you come out better than you thought you might have?" he was asked. "Frankly, yes," he replied. Asked about the statement concerning the "bullet that had the name Rockefeller written on it," he replied, "I can understand—with the tremendous emotional situation that exists, the tremendous pressures that are in existence as a result of this—the emotional reactions are going to be very sharp." Asked if he thought the troopers had had an "emotional reaction" when they assaulted the prison, he replied: "No, I don't. I think they did a superb job."

Rockefeller also described the feelings of relief he had experienced while Robert Douglass told him over the telephone that the first twenty-one hostages were being brought safely out of the prison yard: "I want to tell you I was absolutely overwhelmed. I just don't see how it was possible, with 1,200 men in there armed, with electrified barricades, with trenches, with a pledge that they would go down fighting to the last man, how it was going to be possible." When asked "What does this tell you about the prisoners, Governor, the fact that so many men emerged unharmed?" he replied, "What it tells is that the use of this gas is a fantastic instrument in a situation of this kind."

On September 13, 1972, the first anniversary of the assault on the Attica Correctional Facility, the New York State Special Commission on Attica, a group of nine persons who had been selected by a panel of the state's ranking judges and charged by Governor Rockefeller with conducting "a full and impartial investigation" of events surrounding the Attica rebellion, issued a 518-page report. The Commission and its staff had interviewed more than 3,000 prisoners, prison employees, state troopers, National Guard troops and the townspeople of Attica. The Commission concluded that, contrary to Rockefeller's assertion, the rebellion had not been planned, but had broken out spontaneously; the assault could not have saved the lives of hostages if prisoners had intended to kill them; weaponry used in the assault made inevitable the death and injury of innocent people; reprisals were carried out against the prisoners. Special attention focused on the Commission's conclusion that Rockefeller should have gone to the prison before ordering an armed assault. The Commission acknowledged that he had been faced with a difficult decision and agreed with his view that he could not and should not guarantee amnesty for major criminal acts. But while conceding that there had been virtually no probability of a settlement without a guarantee of amnesty and that Rockefeller would have faced great problems had he gone to the prison, the Commission said it believed "that the presence of the Governor would have had a stabilizing effect on troopers and correction officers taking part in the assault and rehousing of the inmates . . . that the Governor should have gone to Attica . . . because his responsibilities as the state's chief executive made it appropriate that he be present at the scene of the critical decisions involving great loss of life. . . ."

The explanation for Nelson Rockefeller's refusal to go to Attica during the rebellion—whether to consult with the panel of civilian observers, negotiate with the rebelling prisoners, or observe for himself the makings of the massacre—can be found in the statement he issued after the assault to retake the prison yard was over. "The tragedy," his statement said, in what would be in contradistinction to the report published by the State Commission on Attica, "was brought on by the highly organized, revolutionary tactics of militants. . . ." The statement concluded with the Governor's assertion that he had "ordered a full investigation of all the factors leading to this uprising, *including the role that outside forces would appear to have played.*" (Italics added.) Governor Rockefeller believed that he had been confronted by a revolutionary vanguard, not by men caught up in a spontaneous rebellion. He believed that his responsibility had been to take a tough line.

As he told Commissioner Oswald eleven days after the assault, "Of course, there was more at stake than saving lives. There was the whole rule of law to consider. The whole fabric of our society, in fact." In light of the threat revolutionary forces posed, the lives of the hostages were of secondary importance. It was justifiable that the assault force had been armed with weapons that indiscriminately killed hostages, prisoners who threatened the hostages and prisoners who could not escape from the prison yard themselves. With the whole fabric of society at stake, is it any wonder that at the press conference, held two days after the assault *at the request of newsmen* (perhaps Governor Rockefeller believed he did not owe the public an explanation for his actions during the rebellion), Governor Rockefeller's answers to questions about the massacre were so glib? In his view, the killings had been preventive homicide, not a massacre.

Commissioner Oswald's view of what had been at stake during the Attica rebellion became the same as Governor Rockefeller's: "The disinherited and the villainous, the alienated and the pawns, the flotsam and jetsam of society, and a new generation of revolutionary leaders focused on the prisons as the point of leverage. Here was where the Establishment could be made to buckle," he wrote in *Attica—My Story*, his book about the rebellion. Why, then, did Oswald himself telephone Governor Rockefeller and ask him to come to Attica, as if to say that he too believed that revolutionary forces could demand the Governor negotiate with them? In his testimony before the State Commission on Attica, Oswald said: "I suggested [during the telephone call to the Governor on Sunday evening] that it might be appropriate for someone as warm and understanding as Governor Rockefeller to walk that last

mile and come, although I went on to express the view that I
didn't feel that it was going to be productive." He had extended the invitation not because he believed the Governor
could resolve the impasse in the negotiations with the prisoners
—which Oswald considered an impossibility—but for an entirely different reason: Oswald had had a "deep concern for
his [Rockefeller's] public image. . . . I was concerned about
the Governor's reputation as a humanitarian." Oswald saw
that his responsibility was not only to put down revolution
but also to defend the reputation of the ultimate product of
our society: Nelson Rockefeller, who carries the reputation
of a humanitarian, a reputation earned by his family's having
made a great fortune and having disbursed vast sums to philanthropic causes for the whole of the twentieth century.

ix   Summing Up

All is forgiven the philanthropist. No matter what else the Rockefellers do, and no matter how they do it, the public's high regard for them, earned by their philanthropy, does not diminish. Philanthropy is the essential element in the making of Rockefeller power. It gives the Rockefellers a priceless reputation as public benefactors which the public values so highly that power over public affairs is placed in the Rockefellers' hands. Philanthropy generates more power than wealth alone can provide.

The Rockefellers use this power, as they have proclaimed with their symbolic decoration of the Union Church at Pocantico Hills, to discharge a deeply felt philanthropic responsibility. But in doing so, they operate as if, with their long involvement in private philanthropy and successful commercial enterprise, they have special competence for promoting the public interest. They operate as if this gives them special license to ignore and override any opposition, to use their power to influence public officials, and to reject valid and popular alternatives to their own plans—as they have done in support of

265

development projects in New York State. They operate as if they believe that because their inspiration to discharge a philanthropic responsibility led them to establish private philanthropic institutions that have accomplished good works, the public interest is served when other Rockefeller needs and desires are satisfied. They operate as if they believe that by satisfying their egos as philanthropists and builders—as they have done with Lincoln Center, the Albany Mall, the World Trade Center, Battery Park City and the Harlem State Office Building—they serve the public interest. They operate as if they believe that when special interests, including themselves, benefit from such projects as Manhattan Landing, the benefits that trickle down to the public are sufficient justification for those projects. The Rockefellers seem so confused on this point that they will even commit a philanthropic institution to promoting themselves and their interests—as they have done by using the Museum of Modern Art to enhance the profitability of Rockefeller business enterprise, the value of a Rockefeller art collection, and Rockefeller personal and political prestige.

Except for the unarguably good works accomplished by the Rockefeller philanthropic institutions, the Rockefellers have exhibited no special competence for promoting the public interest—not for all their money, all their experience in private philanthropy and all their involvement in public affairs. Even if the Rockefellers could operate without opposition, and satisfy their own needs and desires totally—needs and desires which the Rockefellers identify with the public interest—their version of a new Garden of Eden would not be a total success. Their great construction projects are not serving us well. Lincoln Center's constituents, trapped in that monument, are on the brink of financial ruin. While the realization of the

Rockefeller-style Garden of Eden proceeds, New York City becomes a dollar machine, rather than a place for people to live in. To working environmentalists, the Rockefellers' support of Consolidated Edison's plan to build a pumped-storage hydroelectric plant on Storm King Mountain and their promotion of such projects as the Hudson River Expressway, the Rye-Oyster Bay bridge and the Stewart jetport reflect no special competence for management of natural resources in the public interest. And is it in the public interest to finance terror campaigns demanding huge increases in U.S. military spending, when the United States already maintains military superiority and will continue to retain it in the foreseeable future?

The Rockefellers do have a special competence: to organize private and public power and combine power with their philanthropic inspiration for the purpose of making profit. Whether the Rockefellers are pursuing their philanthropic responsibility by promoting the building of entirely new cities and towns throughout the United States or by aiding the social and economic development of Latin America, profits are made.

But it would belittle the Rockefellers to say that they intend profit to be the ultimate result of their activities. They are after something else. Allan Nevins talked about it in the trial balance he made at the end of his sympathetic biography of John D. Rockefeller. What he and the other industrial giants of his time, including Carnegie and Westinghouse, "were really interested in," Nevins wrote, "was competitive achievement, self-expression, and the imposition of their wills on a given environment." Rockefeller's fortune was accumulated as a by-product of his enterprise. He was motivated primarily by an interest in achieving and using power.

The Rockefellers use power not only for financial gain, but also to promote the well-being of mankind, and this twofold use is a hallmark of their power—but not the only hallmark. So deeply do the Rockefellers feel a need to discharge their philanthropic responsibility that they have become paternalists whose use of power is not benign. The Rockefeller brothers—the dominant generation now—have been corrupted by power. Anyone standing in the way of a program or project they believe to be in the public interest they damn as a frivolous obstructionist who must be shoved aside. Paternalism and contempt repeatedly mark the brothers' defense of their commitments to favored projects. Some time after the New York State Legislature and the United States Department of the Interior had voiced opposition to construction of the Rye-Oyster Bay bridge proposed by Governor Nelson Rockefeller, he was asked by reporters if he still intended to proceed with the construction. "Yep," he replied. Asked how he could in view of the Interior Department's opposition, he declared: "That's up to me. You'll find out as the scenario unfolds." It is as if the Rockefellers decorated the Union Church with Biblical scenes depicting visions and the handing down of scrolls in order to indicate that they are the Chosen People of the twentieth century, sitting on a board with God as Chairman and they as trustees of His Word, and to reject their programs and projects is to reject His Will.

Ultimately, it does not matter why the Rockefellers are driven to wield power—whether to discharge a philanthropic responsibility, to make profits, or to control their environment. What does matter is that excessive power—which can be, and is, used in ways not entirely benign—is concentrated in their hands, and it is up to society to protect itself against such concentrations of power. One way to do so is to limit inheritances. Another way is to battle the Rockefellers in the courts, as conservationists are doing. But we must also deal with ourselves. We must make our society more philanthropic, make our institutions serve the public interest, so that the private philanthropist is no longer anyone special, no longer anyone who is rewarded for his giving with power.

POSTSCRIPT

On December 11, 1973, with a little more than a year left of his fourth term, and despite a campaign pledge to finish the term, Nelson Rockefeller announced that he would resign as governor of New York State on the following Tuesday. The move has been widely interpreted as the start of a campaign for the 1976 Republican presidential nomination.

What of the prospects of a Rockefeller presidency? One of the major problems with the presidency is that over the past several decades presidents have accumulated too much power. If Nelson Rockefeller were to become president, the power of the presidency would greatly and dangerously increase. And so would Rockefeller power. This would happen because of the Rockefeller family's deep penetration into so many important public and private areas of American life. Rockefeller would have the means to expand presidential and Rockefeller power to unprecedented and undreamed-of proportions. He and his brothers would not only be kingpins of the philanthropic establishment, of new-cities construction, of the modern art establishment, of the conservation and development of our natural resources, and of banking and finance; in addition

...One year later

Nelson Rockefeller has been confirmed through the procedure spelled out in the Twenty-fifth Amendment to the Constitution as Vice President of the United States. While the congressional hearings on the nomination touched on the extent of the Rockefeller family's vast financial interests, nothing was done to insulate the nation from the conflict-of-interest potential inherent in Rockefeller power. And now the threat of Rockefeller power to our checks-and-balances system of government is more real than ever.

New York City
December 19, 1974

Rockefeller Family Tree

Rockefeller Family Tree

THE ROCKEFELLERS

FIRST GENERATION

John D.
(1839-1937)
m. Laura Spelman, 1864

SECOND GENERATION

John D., Jr.
(1874-1960)
m. Abby Aldrich, 1901
    Martha Baird, 1951

THIRD GENERATION

Abby (1903-)	John D. 3rd (1906-)	Nelson (1908-)

FOURTH GENERATION

Abby M. O'Neill	Sandra	Rodman
Marilyn M. Simpson	John D. IV (Jay)	Ann R. Coste
	Hope R. Spenser	Steven
	Alida	Michael (*d.*)
		Mary Strawbridge, Jr.
		Nelson
		Mark
		(*from a second marriage*)

Laurance S.	Winthrop	David
(1910-)	(1912-1973)	(1915-)
Laura M. Case III	Winthrop Paul	David, Jr.
Marion Weber		Abby A.
Lucy R. Waletzky		Neva R. Kaiser
Laurance (Larry)		Margaret D.
		Richard G.

Appendix:
Rockefeller Philanthropic Funds

Of the three famous philanthropies founded by John D. Rockefeller and Frederick T. Gates, two remain in existence: the Rockefeller Institute for Medical Research, which began to admit graduate students in the mid-1950s (there are no undergraduates) and is now called the Rockefeller University, and the Rockefeller Foundation. The third, the General Education Board, was incorporated into the Foundation in 1960, after having disbursed $324 million over six decades.

The Rockefeller University, which has an endowment of around $200 million and a budget of around $19 million a year, occupies a crowded fifteen-acre campus in Manhattan, on the edge of the East River, to the north of the Queensborough Bridge. Included in its population of more than 1,500 are 85 senior faculty members, 120 junior faculty members and 250 researchers-in-training, about 100 of whom are students. Among the principal fields of research are animal behavior, cell biology and mathematics. There also is a small research hospital on campus, involved in treating obesity, and in weight-control and methadone-maintenance programs. The university plans to bring in more faculty and staff to handle increasingly complex research; endow ten new chairs in such fields as neurophysiology, biochemistry and mathematical physics; provide more fellowships; finance new work in environmental sciences, reproductive biology and biomedical sciences; provide more laboratories and new library and computer centers.

The Rockefeller Foundation, which has assets of more than $800 million and disburses about $50 million a year, occupies two floors of the Time & Life Building at Rockefeller Center and maintains offices in Berkeley; Lincoln, Nebraska; Boston; New Haven; Charlottesville, Virginia; Brazil, Ceylon, Chile, Colombia, India, Italy, Mexico, Nigeria, the Philippines, St. Lucia, Tanzania, Thailand, Trinidad, Tunisia and Uganda. There are about 200 employees in New York and about 100 in the field staff.

The Foundation concentrated its efforts primarily on public health and medical education during its early years. Later, it broadened its activities—supporting fellowship programs, largely for foreign scientists and scholars pursuing research and advanced training in the United States; providing grants to institutions and individuals engaged in research in such fields as the medical and natural sciences, languages and foreign relations; and participating in agricultural assistance programs, in Mexico in the early 1940s, and in Asia since the 1950s. In addition to food production, the Foundation's current foreign interests include population stabilization (with grants made entirely to universities and other organizations in the United States) and development of university centers. Domestic interests include support for the performing arts, enhancement of educational opportunities for minority groups, alleviation of racial discrimination and poverty, and improvement of the quality of the environment. New departures are indicated by the Foundation's current president, Dr. John H. Knowles, who told the Council of Foundations' annual meeting, in May 1971, that private foundations will have "a crucial role to play" in a forthcoming "renewal of effective private and public action" geared toward finding "new ways of harnessing our incredible energy to solve our monumental domestic problems."

Data on current Rockefeller philanthropic funds follow:

ROCKEFELLER FOUNDATION. Established in 1913 by John D. Rockefeller. Contributor: John D. Rockefeller ($183 million, securities priced at market value on date of gift). Assets as of December 31, 1971: $831 million. Contributions by the end of 1971: $1.13 billion. Trustees (1971): W. Michael Blumenthal, John S. Dickey, C. Douglas Dillon, Robert H. Ebert, Robert F. Goheen, J. George Harrar, Theodore M. Hesburgh, Arthur A. Houghton, Jr., Vernon E. Jordan, Jr., Clark Kerr, Mathilde Krim, Alberto Lleras Camargo, Bill Moyers, John D. Rockefeller IV, Robert V. Roosa, Nevin S. Scrimshaw, Frederick Seitz, Frank Stanton, Maurice F. Strong, Cyrus R. Vance, Clifton R. Wharton, Jr.

SEALANTIC FUND. Established in 1938 by John D. Rockefeller, Jr. Substantial contributors: John D. Rockefeller, Jr. ($33 million by December 31, 1959), and the Rockefeller Brothers Fund. Assets as of December 31, 1970: $4.7 million. The fund mainly has supported training, building and endowment programs at schools of theology throughout the United States; it was also active in local philanthropy at Seal Harbor, Maine, and Pocantico Hills, New York, until 1968, when this work was taken over by the Rockefeller Family Fund. Contributions by the end of 1970: $31.2 million. Trustees (1970): Dana S. Creel, Director of the Fund; Lindsley F. Kimball; David Rockefeller, President of the Fund; Laurance S. Rockefeller, Vice-President of the Fund; John E. Lockwood, Counsel; Steven C. Rockefeller; Marilyn M. Simpson; Hope R. Spenser.

JACKSON HOLE PRESERVE, INC. Established in 1940 by John D. Rockefeller, Jr. Substantial contributors: John D. Rockefeller, Jr. ($19.4 million by December 31, 1959), Laurance S. Rockefeller, Nelson Rockefeller, the Rockefeller Brothers Fund. Assets as of December 31, 1970: $25.7 million, including ownership of Grand Teton Lodge Co. ($11.8 million) and Caneel Bay Plantation, Inc. ($10.2 million). The corporation's purposes are "to restore, protect and preserve, for the benefit of the public, the primitive grandeur and natural beauties of the landscape in areas noted for picturesque scenery. To maintain and develop historic landmarks and other features of historic or scientific interest in such areas, and to provide facilities for the public use, appreciation and enjoyment of the scenic, biological, scientific and historic features of such areas." Contributions by the end of 1970, mainly for budgets of conservation groups and acquisition of land: $9 million. Trustees (1970): Horace M. Albright; Allston M. Boyer (deceased); Kenneth Chorley; Harold P. Fabian; Mrs. Lyndon B. Johnson; Melville B. Grosvenor; Samuel H. Ordway, Jr. (deceased); Laurance S. Rockefeller, President of the Association; Steven C. Rockefeller; Gene W. Setzer, Executive Vice-President; Fred Smith; Conrad L. Wirth.

ROCKEFELLER BROTHERS FUND. Established in 1940 by the Rockefeller brothers. Substantial contributors: John D. Rockefeller, Jr. ($134 million), and Martha Baird Rockefeller ($13.4 million from her trusts). Among the members of the third Rockefeller generation, only Winthrop has provided more than 2 percent of the total contributions to the fund. Assets as of December 31, 1971: $238 million. In the New York area the fund has contributed to civic improvement and cultural projects (especially conservation and theater projects) and to educational, health, religious and welfare groups. Generally grants have gone to groups with citywide and statewide scope, but in recent years projects of local or neighborhood character have been supported. Outside New York State, grants usually have gone to groups with programs of national or international scope. The fund has also supported and published studies dealing with such subjects as military aspects of international security and the state of the performing arts. Contributions by the end of 1971: $111 million. Trustees (1971): Detlev W. Bronk, former President of the Rockefeller University; Dana S. Creel, President of the Fund; John W. Gardner, former Secretary of Health, Education and Welfare and head of Common Cause; William McChesney Martin, former Chairman of the Federal Reserve Board; Abbey R. Mauzé; Abby M. O'Neill; the Rockefeller brothers; Hope R. Spenser. Principal Officers: Laurance S. Rockefeller, Chairman; David Rockefeller, Vice-Chairman; Dana S. Creel, President; William M. Dietel, Executive Vice-President; Robert C. Bates, Vice-President and Secretary; Gene W. Setzer, Vice-President; David G. Fernald, Treasurer; John E. Lockwood, Counsel.

AMERICAN INTERNATIONAL ASSOCIATION FOR ECONOMIC AND SOCIAL DEVELOPMENT (AIA). Established in 1946 by the Rockefeller brothers. Substantial contributors: members of the Rockefeller family, the Rockefeller Brothers Fund, the International Basic Economy Corporation, Price Waterhouse & Co., Creole Petroleum Corp. (subsidiary of Standard Oil of New Jersey), Shell Caribbean Petroleum Corp., Mene Grande Oil Co. (subsidiary of Gulf), International Petroleum Co. (subsidiary of Standard Oil of New Jersey), Socony-Vacuum Oil Co. Assets as of December 31, 1970: $12,300. The association has supported agricultural, educational, youth and credit programs in rural areas in Latin America, mainly in Venezuela and Brazil. Contributions by the end of 1970: $12 million. Directors (1970): Nelson Rockefeller, John E. Lockwood.

AGRICULTURAL DEVELOPMENT COUNCIL. Established in 1953 by John D. Rockefeller 3rd as the Council on Economic and Cultural Affairs; name changed in 1963. Substantial Contributors: John D. Rockefeller 3rd, the Rockefeller Brothers Fund; the Ford Foundation and the Agency for International Development support specific projects. Assets as of December 31, 1971: $4.7 million. "The council supports teaching and research related to the economic and human problems of agricultural development, primarily in Asia." Contributions by the end of 1971: $7.7 million. Trustees (1971): John D. Rockefeller 3rd; Charles S. Denison, international consultant; J. Norman Efferson, Dean, College of Agriculture, Louisiana State University; Walter P. Falcon, Deputy Director, Development Advisory Service, Harvard; Nicolaas Luycx, Director, The Food Institute, East-West Center, Honolulu; Donald H. McLean, Jr., President, Lahey Clinic Foundation; Arthur T. Mosher, President of the Council; William I. Myers, Professor of Farm Finance Emeritus, Cornell; M. B. Russell, Chief of Party, University of Illinois Team, Jawaharlal Nehru Agricultural University; Vernon W. Ruttan, Director, Economic Development Center, University of Minnesota; William H. Sewell, Vilas Research Professor, Department of Sociology, University of Wisconsin; Gilbert F. White, Director, Department of Behavioral Science, University of Colorado.

ROCKWIN FUND. Established in 1956 by Winthrop Rockefeller. The fund "obtains most of its income in the form of contributions of marketable securities and other items of value, such as antique automobiles and books, which are usually sold as soon as possible by the fund." Assets as of December 31, 1970: $14,400. The fund contributes to hospitals, public health programs, community funds, public schools, libraries, scholarship and student-loan programs, conservation and cultural-relations programs in Arkansas. Contributions by the end of 1970: $1.8 million. Directors (1970): Bruce Bartley; Thomas E. Downey; Robert Shults; Winthrop Rockefeller (deceased); Craig Smith, President of the Fund; Herman Shirley.

AMERICAN CONSERVATION ASSOCIATION. Established in 1958 by Laurance S. Rockefeller. Substantial contributors: Laurance S. Rockefeller, Nelson Rockefeller, the Rockefeller Brothers Fund, Jackson Hole Preserve. Assets as of December 31, 1970: $530,000. The association contributes to budgets of conservation groups and to educational, research and publishing programs in conservation. Contributions by the end of 1970: $1.8 million. Trustees (1970):

Horace M. Albright; Allston Boyer (deceased); Kenneth Chorley; Dana S. Creel; Melville B. Grosvenor; Samuel H. Ordway, Jr. (deceased); Laurance S. Rockefeller, President of the Association; Steven C. Rockefeller; Mrs. Lyndon B. Johnson; William H. Whyte, Jr.; Conrad L. Wirth; Gene W. Setzer, Executive Vice-President; George R. Lamb, Assistant Secretary; John V. Duncan, Secretary; Daniel M. Brosnan, Assistant Treasurer.

MARTHA BAIRD ROCKEFELLER FUND FOR MUSIC, INC. Established in 1962 by Martha Baird Rockefeller. The fund received a bequest of $5 million from the founder in 1971. The fund has assisted young musicians, musical scholars and other specialists and musical organizations and training centers (other than colleges and universities). Contributions by the end of 1969: $3.4 million. Trustees (1969): Martha Baird Rockefeller (deceased); Dana S. Creel; Robert C. Bates; Donald L. Engle; Mrs. Helen Thompson; Carlos D. Moseley.

JDR 3RD FUND. Established in 1963 by John D. Rockefeller 3rd. Assets as of August 31, 1971: $4.6 million. The fund has supported exchange programs in the visual and performing arts between Asian countries and the United States, encouraged and helped establish arts programs in public schools throughout the United States, and sponsored and published surveys on attitudes of college students. Contributions by the end of 1970: $4 million. Trustees (1971): Samuel B. Gould, Chancellor Emeritus, the State University of New York and Vice-President, Educational Testing Service; George F. Kennan, Permanent Professor, The Institute for Advanced Study, Princeton; Sherman E. Lee, Director, Cleveland Museum of Art; Donald H. McClean, Jr., President, Lahey Clinic Foundation; John D. Rockefeller 3rd, President of the Fund; Datus C. Smith, Jr., Vice-President; Hope R. Spenser; Phillips Talbot, President, Asia Society; Kenneth T. Young, Jr., Former Senior Visiting Fellow, Council on Foreign Relations and Visiting Lecturer, The Fletcher School.

ROCKEFELLER FAMILY FUND. Established in 1967. Substantial contributors: Martha Baird Rockefeller, John D. Rockefeller 3rd, Laurance S. Rockefeller, David Rockefeller, the Sealantic Fund, the Rockefeller Brothers Fund. Assets as of December 31, 1971: $400,000. Program: "In its grant-making program, the Fund has reflected . . . many of the varied interests of its trustees. Broadly, these concerns have touched on education, fair housing, population control, day care centers, conservation and environmental matters, and educational experiences for the inner-city child. After the election of younger members of the family to the principal offices of the Fund in 1971, an effort was made to narrow the Fund's field of interest. Thus, in June 1971, the Trustees set forth the following five general areas: Education (alternative community elementary schools in Boston and New York, 'open classroom' or 'integrated day' approaches to education and early childhood education), Arts (education of teachers interested in developing skills in environmental education; bringing together graduate students in urban planning, new town developers and municipal officials engaged in urban renewal), Equal Opportunity (women), Conservation (protection of open spaces and natural lands) and Institutional Responsiveness (information on social responsibilities of corporations, Ombudsman programs, obtaining accessibility to key communications media)." Contributions by the end of 1971: $1.1 million. Trustees: Ann R. Coste, Neva R. Kaiser, David Rockefeller, David Rockefeller, Jr., John D. Rockefeller 3rd, John D. Rockefeller IV, Laurance Rockefeller, Laurance S. Rockefeller, Peggy Rockefeller, Sandra Rockefeller, Winthrop P. Rockefeller, William K. Simpson, William J. Strawbridge, Jr., Lucy R. Waletzky. Honorary Trustees: Abby R. Mauzé, Nelson Rockefeller, Winthrop Rockefeller (deceased). Officers: David Rockefeller, Jr., President; Ann R. Coste, First Vice-President; William J. Strawbridge, Jr., Second Vice-President; Dana S. Creel, Director; Robert W. Scrivner, Secretary; David G. Fernald, Treasurer; Donal C. O'Brien, Counsel.

GREENACRE FOUNDATION. Established in 1968 by Abby Rockefeller Mauzé. Assets as of December 31, 1971: $2.5 million, including a $1-million vest-pocket park which was opened in December 1971 on a sixty-foot-wide site at 217 East Fifty-first Street in Manhattan. The foundation's principal purpose is "establishing, equipping and maintaining one or more parks in the city of New York for the benefit of the general public." Trustees (1970): Mrs. Mauzé, President of the Foundation; Laurance S. Rockefeller; Allston M. Boyer (deceased); Mrs. Abby M. O'Neill; Mrs. Marilyn M. Simpson; Donal C. O'Brien, Jr.

Selected Bibliography

JOHN D. ROCKEFELLER AND STANDARD OIL:

John D. Rockefeller: Robber Baron or Industrial Statesman?
Edited by Earl Latham (Boston: D. C. Heath, 1949)
Study in Power: John D. Rockefeller, Industrialist and Philanthropist by Allan Nevins (New York: Charles Scribner's Sons, 1953)
The Oil Barons by Richard O'Connor (Boston: Little, Brown, 1971)

ROCKEFELLER FINANCIAL POWER:
The Rich and the Super-Rich: A Study in the Power of Money Today by Ferdinand Lundberg (New York: Lyle Stuart, 1968)
Millionaires and Managers by S. Menshikov (Moscow: Progress Publishers, 1969)

ROCKEFELLER JUNIOR:
John D. Rockefeller, Jr.; A Portrait by Raymond B. Fosdick (New York: Harper, 1956)

ABBY ALDRICH ROCKEFELLER:
Abby Aldrich Rockefeller by Mary Ellen Chase (New York: Macmillan, 1950)

The Rockefeller Brothers:

Those Rockefeller Brothers: An Informal Biography of Five Extraordinary Young Men by Joe Alex Morris (New York: Harper, 1953)

A Rockefeller Family Portrait, from John D. to Nelson by William R. Manchester (Boston: Little, Brown, 1959)

Nelson Rockefeller, A Biography by Joe Alex Morris (New York: Harper, 1960)

Profile on David Rockefeller by E. J. Kahn, Jr. (*The New Yorker*, January 9 & 16, 1965)

Rockefeller's Follies: An Unauthorized View of Nelson A. Rockefeller by William A. Rodgers (New York: Stein and Day, 1966)

David by William Hoffman (New York: Lyle Stuart, 1971)

Profile on John D. Rockefeller 3rd by Geoffrey T. Hellman (*The New Yorker*, November 4, 1972)

Philanthropies:

The Story of the Rockefeller Foundation by Raymond B. Fosdick (New York: Harper, 1952)

The Memoirs of Frederick T. Gates (*American Heritage*, April, 1955)

The Rockefeller Foundation: How It Operates by Greer Williams (*Atlantic*, April, 1964)

The Money Givers: An Examination of the Myths and Realities of Foundation Philanthropy in America by Joseph C. Goulden (New York: Random House, 1971)

Construction Projects:

Radio City: Cultural Center? by Frederick Lewis Allen (*Harper's*, April, 1932)

Look at Rockefeller Center by Frederick Lewis Allen (*Harper's*, October, 1938)

A Rockefeller Enters 'Show Biz' by Seymour Peck (*New York Times Magazine*, November 18, 1956)

Fifty Years on Fifth (New York: International Press, 1957)

Athens on the Subway by Frederick Gutheim (*Harper's*, October, 1958)

Second Report of the Downtown-Lower Manhattan Association (1963)

Lincoln Center, Tomb of the Future by Benjamin Boretz (*The Nation*, March 22, 1965)

Music Hall: Still the No. 1 hit; Last of the Motion Picture Palaces (*Business Week*, December 25, 1965)

The Metropolitan Opera, 1883-1966; A Candid History by Irving Kolodin (New York: Knopf, 1966. 4th ed.)

The City Within a City; the Romance of Rockefeller Center by David G. Loth (New York: Morrow, 1966)

AIA Guide to New York City Edited by Norvall White and Elliot Willensky (New York: Macmillan, 1968)

Third Report of the Downtown-Lower Manhattan Association (1969)

New Communities for New York (A report prepared by the New York State Urban Development Corporation and the New York State Office of Planning Coordination, 1970)

Public Works: A Dangerous Trade by Robert Moses (New York: McGraw Hill, 1970)

Zeckendorf The autobiography of William Zeckendorf with Edward McCreary (New York: Holt, Rinehart and Winston, 1970)

Lincoln Center for the Performing Arts by Ralph G. Martin (Englewood Cliffs, New Jersey: Prentice Hall, 1971)

High prices and slow progress plague government complex (*Engineering News Record*, June 24, 1971)

What Price Glory on the Albany Mall? by Eleanor Carruth and Jo Degener (*Fortune*, June, 1971)

A Tale of One City by Jack Rosenthal (*New York Times Magazine*, December 26, 1971)

Corporation Towns (*Ramparts*, January, 1972)

Two Car Manufacturers Test Another Type of Profit Vehicle (*Engineering News Record*, March 2, 1972)

New Towns, Urban Rehabilitation: The Predevelopment Costs by David Rockefeller (*Vital Speeches of the Day*, April 1, 1972)

CONSERVATION:

A Contribution to the Heritage of Every American; the Conservation Activities of John D. Rockefeller, Jr. by Nancy Wynne Newhall (New York: Knopf, 1957)

Hearings before Subcommittee on Fisheries and Wildlife Conservation of the Committee on Merchant Marine and Fisheries, House of Representatives, Ninety-first Congress, First Session, on the Impact of the Hudson River Expressway Proposal on Fish and Wildlife Resources of the Hudson River and Atlantic Coast Fisheries, June 24, 25, 1969, Serial No. 91-10 (Washington, D.C.: U.S. Government Printing Office, 1969)

The Hudson River: A Natural and Unnatural History by Robert Boyle (New York: W. W. Norton, 1969)

Road to Ruin by A. Q. Mowbray (New York: Lippincott, 1969)

Our Environment Can be Saved by Nelson A. Rockefeller (Garden City, New York: Doubleday, 1970)

Superhighway—Superhoax by Helen Leavitt (New York: Ballantine Books, 1970)

Rocky's Road by Joseph L. Sax (*American Heritage*, February, 1971)

ART:

Modern Architects by Alfred H. Barr, Jr., Henry-Russell Hitchcock, Philip Johnson and Lewis Mumford (New York: The Museum of Modern Art, 1932)

Organic Design in Home Furnishings by Eliot F. Noyes (MOMA, 1941)

Painting and Sculpture in the Museum of Modern Art Edited by Alfred H. Barr, Jr. (MOMA, 1948)

Modern Art in Your Life by Robert Goldwater in collaboration with Rene d'Harnoncourt (MOMA, 1953)

Profile on Alfred H. Barr, Jr., by Dwight Macdonald (*The New Yorker*, December 12 & 19, 1953)

The Tastemakers by Russell Lynes (New York: The Universal Library, Grosset & Dunlap)

The Proud Possessors by Aline B. Saarinen (New York: Random House, 1958)

The Fabulous Life of Diego Rivera by Bertram D. Wolfe (New York: Stein and Day, 1963)

Twentieth Century Art from the Nelson Aldrich Rockefeller Collection by William S. Lieberman (MOMA, 1969)

Art of Oceania, Africa and the Americas from the Museum of Primitive Art by Robert Goldwater, et al. (New York: The Metropolitan Museum of Art, 1969)

Rocky as a Collector by James R. Mellow (*New York Times Magazine*, May 18, 1969)

New York Painting and Sculpture: 1940-1970 by Henry Geldzahler (New York: E. P. Dutton, 1969)

Merchants and Masterpieces: The Story of the Metropolitan Museum of Art by Calvin Tomkins (New York: E. P. Dutton, 1970)

The John D. Rockefeller 3rd Oriental Collections by Gordon B. Washburn; *Rockefeller Bronzes: The Indian Tradition* by Pratapaditya Pal; *Rockefeller Ceramics: China and Japan* by Peter C. Swann (*ARTnews*, September, 1970)

U.S. MILITARY AND FOREIGN POLICIES:

Prospect for Tomorrow: The Rockefeller Panel Reports (Garden City, New York: Doubleday, 1961)

Unity, Freedom & Peace A Blueprint for Tomorrow by Nelson A. Rockefeller (Garden City, New York: Doubleday, 1968)

Polemics and Prophecies 1967-1970 by I. F. Stone (New York: Random House, 1970)

The Balance of Terror, A Guide to the Arms Race by Edgar M. Bottome (Boston: Beacon Press, 1971)

Roots of War by Richard J. Barnet (New York: Atheneum, 1972)

LATIN AMERICA:

An Alliance that is Making Little Progress (*U.S. News and World Report,* February 25, 1963)

The U.S. Business Image in Latin America: Economic Growth with Freedom by David Rockefeller (*Vital Speeches of the Day,* October 15, 1964)

What Private Enterprise Means to Latin America by David Rockefeller (*Foreign Affairs,* April, 1966)

The Rockefeller Report on the Americas (Chicago: Quadrangle Books, 1969)

Rockefeller Reports Half Right on Latin America by Richard O'Mara (*The Nation,* December 1, 1969)

The Alliance That Lost Its Way: A Critical Report on the Alliance for Progress by Jerome Levinson & Juan de Onis (Chicago: Quadrangle Books, 1972)

ATTICA:

Attica: The Official Report of the New York State Commission on Attica (New York: Praeger, 1972)

Attica—My Story by Russell G. Oswald, edited by Rodney Campbell (Garden City, New York: Doubleday, 1972)

Index

THE MOST POPULAR AND BESTSELLING NON-FICTION FROM PINNACLE BOOKS

BURN AFTER READING, by Ladislas Farago. Here are the spymasters, the heroes, the traitors, and all the cryptic subtlety and horrific violence that marked their grim activities. The more gripping because it really happened—it's all fascinating, particularly if you bear in mind that the same sort of thing is going on right this minute, as clandestinely and just as ruthlessly. By the author of GAME OF THE FOXES and PATTON. Fast-moving, smoothly written, yet fully documented.

P090—95¢

THE CANARIS CONSPIRACY, by Roger Manvell and Heinrich Fraenkel. An astounding chronicle of the plot to kill Hitler. This is the documented story of the work of Admiral Wilhelm Canaris' Department Z, pieced together from the accounts of survivors and told in full for the first time. This group attempted to liquidate Hitler in order to make peace with the allies, but before the plotters could achieve their goal, the conspiracy was discovered and broken by arrests, executions and suicides. One of the most incredible stories to come out of World War II.

P093-$1.25

DIVINE THUNDER, by Bernard Millot. This is the story of the kamikazes, the suicide pilots of Japan during World War II, and of why, when the need arose, they were ready to die without hesitation. In both soldiers and civilians, a mystical reverence for the homeland was almost second nature. The author describes their devastating assaults and the American reaction to them and he reveals what made the kamikazes men of such strange grandeur and heroism. With original drawings.

P108-$1.25

THE KENNEDY WOMEN, by Pearl S. Buck. Here are the fascinating and extraordinary women of the Kennedy family. With the skill of a journalist, the artistry of a gifted storyteller, and the seasoned eye of a biographer, Pearl S. Buck paints a portrait in words of the women who bear one of the most famous family names in history. From Rose, the durable and dynamic matriarch, to JFK's young Caroline—and including Kathleen, Rosemary, Patricia, Jean, Eunice, Ethel, Joan and Jacqueline—these are the ladies of our times.

P113-$1.50

STAND BY TO DIE, by A. V. Sellwood. The heroic story of a lone, embattled WW II ship. It was a small Yangtse river steamer, manned by a makeshift crew of fugitives. She sailed from war-torn Singapore to do battle with the armed might of a Japanese fleet. It was an epic naval action. Heroism was the order of the day. There were no lean British cruisers to divert the Japanese guns, there were no RAF planes to provide air cover. Just one bullet-riddled tub that wouldn't say die! The story could have been lost forever, as it has been for many years, had not A. V. Sellwood pieced together the almost unbelievable story of "the most decorated small ship in the navy."

P171--95¢

SIEGE AND SURVIVAL: THE ODYSSEY OF A LENINGRADER, by Elena Skrjabina. A diary of one of the most devastating sieges in history. During the siege of Leningrad which began on September 8, 1941, nearly one-and-one-half million people died—of hunger, of cold, of disease, from German bullets and bombs. Elena Skrjabina survived. She endured. This book is a record of that experience, and it has been acclaimed by critics everywhere. *Publishers Weekly* said that it is "written in unadorned but eloquent prose that is remarkably effecting." *Bestsellers* said "It is human."

P199--95¢

VIZZINI!, by Sal Vizzini, with Oscar Fraley and Marshall Smith. The secret lives of our most successful narc! Sal Vizzini may die because he wrote this book. He was formerly an undercover agent for the Federal Bureau of Narcotics—an assignment which took him to Naples, where he became a "friend" of exiled Mafia chieftain Charles "Lucky" Luciano; to Burma, where he blew up a heroin factory; to Lebanon, where he outwitted a Communist gun-running ring; and to Atlanta, Georgia, where he posed as a con in the Federal pen. He was shot three times, knifed twice, beaten nearly to death, and had several contracts put out by the Mafia to kill him. Many of the men now in jail will learn for the first time who put them there.

P226-$1.25

WALKING TALL, by Doug Warren. The true story of Buford Pusser a sheriff who has become a living legend. Buford is an honest man, a good man, he has tried to clean out the criminal element of his community. In doing so he has been shot eight times, stabbed five, rammed by a speeding car, had his home fire bombed, and was trapped in an ambush that killed his wife. But, Buford still lives. He raided the prostitution houses, the gambling dens and illicit moonshine stills and almost single handedly ousted crooked officials. His story has been made into a major motion picture by Cinerama.

P478-$1.25

BUGSY, by George Carpozi, Jr. The wild but true story of Benjamin "Bugsy" Siegel. By the time he was twenty-one, this handsome hoodlum had done almost everything a professional mobster could do. It was Bugsy Siegel who transformed a sandy wasteland into Las Vegas. The same Bugsy Siegel who hob-nobbed with Hollywood's royalty and was treated almost as a king himself. He traveled widely, ate in the finest restaurants, and owned an estate in Beverly Hills. His women were legion. But never far beneath the surface was a hard-eyed killer—a killer who died as violently as he lived.   **P244–$1.25**

MICKEY COHEN: MOBSTER, by Ed Reid. Finally—the brutal truth about a well-known gangster! This is a story that Mickey Cohen would rather *not* have told, but a story that can no longer be kept secret. Mickey Cohen is a man who has always been larger than life, who is part of the social history of our time. He's a member of the Jewish Mafia, who has lived hard and lived flamboyantly; who brags about deeds most would want hidden; whose friends have been jet-setters, criminals, evangelists, film stars, politicians, and members of the Holly-wood social scene. Right now, he's down but not out, and don't ever count him *out*! Not until the end.   **P257–$1.25**

SUSAN HAYWARD: THE DIVINE BITCH, by Doug McClelland. The triumphs and tragedies of a fiery and talented screen star. Susan Hayward has lived a life to pale even her most vivid screen roles. There were two marriages, twin sons, and con-stant strife that persists to this day. She was a feminist before the fashion—with femininity plus and a drive to achieve that led her far from the Brooklyn tenement where she began her life. This is the first book ever on one of the First Ladies of the movies' Golden Age: Susan Hayward.   **P276–$1.25**

INSIDE ADOLF HITLER, by Roger Manvell and Heinrich Fraenkel. This is *not* a book about politics. It is *not* a book about warfare. What is it then? It is a book about the mind of a man, a probing portrait into the personality development of the most hated man of the 20th century. **INSIDE ADOLF HIT-LER** is by two of the most renowned Third Reich historians. Their most recent books, *The Canaris Conspiracy* and *The Men Who Tried To Kill Hitler*, have sold millions. Here, for the first time, is an in-depth analysis of the public and private personal-ities of Adolf Hitler.   **P277–$1.50**

This is your Order Form . . .
Just clip and mail.

_____	P090	BURN AFTER READING, Ladislas Farago	.95
_____	P093	THE CANARIS CONSPIRACY, Manvell & Fraenkel	1.25
_____	P108	DIVINE THUNDER, Bernard Millot	1.25
_____	P113	THE KENNEDY WOMEN, Pearl S. Buck	1.50
_____	P171	STAND BY TO DIE, A. V. Sellwood	.95
_____	P199	SIEGE & SURVIVAL, Elena Skrjabina	.95
_____	P226	VIZZINI, Sal Vizzini, with Fraley & Smith	1.25
_____	P478	WALKING TALL, Doug Warren	$1.25
_____	P244	BUGSY, George Carpozi, Jr.	1.25
_____	P257	MICKEY COHEN: MOBSTER, Ed Reid	1.25
_____	P276	SUSAN HAYWARD: THE DIVINE BITCH, Doug McClelland	1.25
_____	P277	INSIDE ADOLF HITLER, Manvell & Fraenkel	1.50

TO ORDER

Please check the space next to the book/s you want, send this order form together with your check or money order, include the price of the book/s and 25¢ for handling and mailing, to:

PINNACLE BOOKS, INC. / P.O. Box 4347,
Grand Central Station / New York, N.Y. 10017

☐ CHECK HERE IF YOU WANT A FREE CATALOG.

I have enclosed $_____check_____or money order_____
as payment in full. No C.O.D.'s.

Name_____

Address_____

City_____State_____Zip_____
(Please allow time for delivery.)